FUNNIER

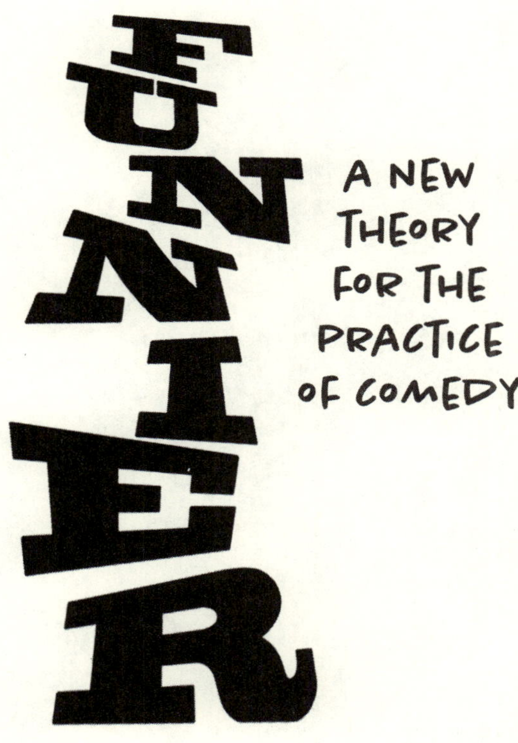

ANNE LIBERA

FOREWORD BY
ASHLEY NICOLE BLACK, CHELSEA DEVANTEZ,
ARIEL DUMAS, AND JENNY HAGEL

NORTHWESTERN UNIVERSITY PRESS
EVANSTON, ILLINOIS

Northwestern University Press
www.nupress.northwestern.edu

Printed in the United States of America

10 9 8 7 6 5 4 3 2 1

Library of Congress Cataloging-in-Publication Data

Names: Libera, Anne, author | Black, Ashley Nicole, 1985– writer of foreword | Devantez, Chelsea, writer of foreword | Dumas, Ariel, writer of foreword | Hagel, Jenny, writer of foreword
Title: Funnier : a new theory for the practice of comedy / Anne Libera ; foreword by Ashley Nicole Black, Chelsea Devantez, Ariel Dumas, and Jenny Hagel.
Description: Evanston : Northwestern University Press, 2026.
Identifiers: LCCN 2025031387 | ISBN 9780810149366 paperback | ISBN 9780810149373 ebook
Subjects: LCSH: Comedy | Comedy—Technique
Classification: LCC PN1922 .L53 2026 | DDC 809.917—dc23/eng/20250715
LC record available at https://lccn.loc.gov/2025031387

All my students past and present:

You are the reason this book exists.

CONTENTS

PART 2
Making It Funny

PART 3
Making It Funnier and Better

FOREWORD

ASHLEY NICOLE BLACK, CHELSEA DEVANTEZ, ARIEL DUMAS, AND JENNY HAGEL

Oh hello dear reader,

We are four of Anne's former students who all went on to majestic comedy careers, head writing television shows for icons like Amber Ruffin, Jon Stewart, and Stephen Colbert, working with comedy masterminds like Bill Lawrence and Samantha Bee, and writing lines for the likes of Harrison Ford and Bugs Bunny. Comedy can take you a lot of interesting places. One of us has even seen Mike Myers's bare feet up close while writing a script. It's fun to be a lady in comedy. Perhaps Anne will cover that in a later chapter! Anne taught us all so much, but one of the main components of improv and ensemble comedy is the art of collaboration, therefore we will be writing this foreword while holding hands, which may make typing difficult, but the metaphor seems worth it. Good luck to us, and to you if you choose to keep reading.

Chelsea here. I was Jon Stewart's head writer. (I've also held many other wonderful jobs and written a book, which you won't find as impressive, but trust me, those things were cool, too!) I was nineteen years old when I first encountered this wild art form called "improv." I'd stumbled inside an improv theater that night simply because the show was free, and, well, that was enough for me. During the show I had an out-of-body epiphany that I wanted to devote my life to comedy, but at that moment I felt wildly behind my peers in this realization. I raced to my dorm and began searching for how I could learn as much as I could about comedy, and that's how I found Anne Libera. Miraculously, I came across a small article in a college theater magazine announcing a program called Comedy Studies run by Anne through Columbia College, where all they taught, 24/7, was different subjects within comedy. It was a revolutionary program in academia that never existed before. I was one of Anne's students in the third semester of that Comedy Studies program, which is where Anne taught us the tools we needed to pursue our dream career.

In this fantastic book you will hear Anne talk about how she can't make you funny, but she can make you *funnier*. Let me further elucidate her premise with a little anecdote. After graduating from Comedy Studies, I took as many other classes as I could and performed and wrote as many shows as possible around the city until finally, I felt like I was ready to audition for one of the paying jobs at The Second City. The big day came and . . . I didn't get the job. Neither did my friend and classmate, Ashley. We auditioned again and again and again and never got the gig. After trying everything we could think of, we eventually confided in our former teacher, Anne, begging her for some wisdom. Seeing our desperation (and hopefully our budding talent!), Anne told us that if we could get six other people willing to take a weekend class, she would teach an audition workshop. At that point it had never occurred to me that you could even teach tools for an audition, I just assumed a great audition had to happen magically, as if a good audition was a baby that the stork drops off if it's in the mood. But over the course of three hours that Saturday, Anne taught us the tools of crafting a good intro line, how to pivot when our scene partner threw out a scene-ruining line, and how to highlight the skills they actually look for most at the auditions. After taking Anne's workshop, I auditioned for the theater one more time and finally, I was hired to work for The Second City. On a cruise ship. Oh, I'm sorry, were you expecting me to say I booked a movie, or starred on the Mainstage the next day??? No, no—cruise ship, baby! (I hope "how to survive as a comedian aboard a cruise ship when bottles of wine are $1" is taught in this book, because that's gonna be important.) Not only was I hired, but almost every single person who took that workshop was later hired. That's right, I said *almost* every person in that workshop got hired. Because like Anne says, she can't make you funny if you're not. She can't give you talent, nor can she make sure you have a great audition, if you don't innately have one in you. But she can give you the tools to make you better, the tools to teach you how to craft the ideas and creativity swirling around inside you, and if you study them and harness them, you too can drink really terrible wine on a cruise ship! Well, I'm now passing the baton to a bestie you just read about in my anecdote.

It's me, Ashley! I also got hired to work on a cruise ship, and the way you survive when wine is only $1 is you have the wine with Diet Coke. Yes, that's in the same glass. It's called a "ship sangria," and I'm sorry I've now burdened you with the knowledge that this is a thing that people who live on cruise ships do. But that's just a peek behind the curtain of a glamorous career in comedy!

Okay, let's flash forward to a couple of years after my ship days. I am at the Republican National Convention standing across from a voter, or a local politician who has never been on a comedy show before, interviewing them for *Full Frontal with Samantha Bee*, or I'm standing across from a fabulous celebrity who has never done sketch comedy on the set of *A Black Lady Sketch Show*, and they are nervous because they don't think they're funny. I always said the same thing: "Don't worry. You don't have to be funny. I will make you funny." I know that sounds egotistical, and that confidence is ugly on women, but when people are nervous and you need to get some comedy out of them fast, it's important to sound very confident in your shared success no matter your actual thoughts about the likely outcome. And it has the added benefit of being true. Anyone can be funnier if given the right tools, and it doesn't take that long to impart them. Maybe the desperation of being on camera *right now* helps, I don't know. I'm not the one writing the book, okay? But almost every time, if I can get you to say what you mean with conviction and intention—and almost always with fewer words. I don't know why, but a lot of people think their joke will get funnier if they add more words to the middle of it. It will not! That's not part of the foreword, just something I wanted to share while I had you here: If you say something like you believe it is both true and important, you've just created a character with a comedic point of view, and we are halfway to improvising a comedic scene together. Now all I have to do is take the opposite point of view, or enthusiastically agree, or comment on how what you said made me feel, or even just stare at you for a beat and let out a deadpan "Oh-kaaaay" and there you have it: Setup, punch line, we're in a comedy scene.

This took me years to learn at The Second City from teachers like Anne Libera who had a lot of great tools and techniques but mostly, at the core, were teaching us how to get out of our own way, stop trying to be funny, and say what we, or our characters, really thought and felt. If you can figure that part out, you're funny. Then the tools will make you funnier. And then, maybe you too will be lucky enough to drink wine and Diet Coke out of the same glass on a cruise ship after making a room full of people laugh. It's the best feeling in the world. The making people laugh part, I mean—the cheap wine and Diet Coke will make you feel sick, and don't you dare say I didn't warn you.

Okay, goodbye, turning this over to my much funnier friend, Ariel!

Thank you, Ashley—I love you, despite how wrong you are about me being funnier. Ariel Dumas here. I'd like to congratulate you on purchasing, borrowing, or shoplifting this book. Within these pages, Anne has taken comedy—one of the most mysterious, ephemeral experiences in the human condition—and broken it down to show you its fascinating innards. It's hefty, practical stuff. It's exactly the kind of book you can leave out on your janky coffee table to prove to your visiting parents, "Look: I am taking my comedy career seriously. I am working hard to turn this hobby into something lucrative. One day, it will earn me enough money to put you in one of the nicer senior homes. Or at least buy myself an actual bathmat."

I wish I'd had such a book when I started studying comedy. At age twenty-six, fresh from having spectacularly failed at auditioning for MFA acting programs, I moved to Chicago to enroll in the Second City Training Center's improv program. Quite simply, it changed my life. The highlight was the very last level of the program, when Anne Libera herself directs the final sketch show. I had written myself a scene where I played a wealthy, horny old woman (typecast!) who'd sublet her spare room to a handsome young man from Craigslist. I mostly wrote it to show off the wig I'd inherited from my dead great-grandmother, but on the first performance, I was thrilled to find that the audience actually thought it was funny. The second night, I hammed it up more. They laughed more. Third night, I went totally nuts, sloshing my fake martini all over the stage. And from the audience: crickets. Zip. I was dumbfounded. Afterward I asked Anne what happened. She explained that yes, you can write the jokes, you can say the jokes, but none of that matters if you don't feel the feelings. In that particular scene, it was the relationship that mattered, not the bits.

It was such a brilliant insight, and the whole experience reflects what I took away from my experience at Second City: that success in comedy isn't just about who's funniest. It's about who's willing to do the hard work of showing up, listening carefully, asking questions, being willing to change, and, farther down that list, yes, it's about who has the best wig.

If you have this book in your hands, you're already miles ahead of the pack. Because Anne has given you the tools you need to understand how comedy works, and in turn, create the best comedy you possibly can. It might change your life. For me, it transformed what was supposed to be a one-year grad school substitute into five years of classes, auditions, shows, tours, and friendships, then a full-time career and, at long last, a bathmat to call my own.

Throwing it back to Chelsea, who's steering this foreword ship as heroically as the captain of a Norwegian Cruise Line. Thanks, Chels.

We would pass this part of the foreword to Jenny Hagel, but Jenny is currently on her 80,000th word for the book she is working on right now. Which kind of speaks for itself—this stuff works! Jenny writes for Seth Meyers and Amber Ruffin and *still* had the time to write an entire hilarious book. That's the kind of skill set Anne is going to teach you—how to find and wield an entire shed of creative tools, so that you too can multitask a plethora of writing projects across the finish line. Because yes, when you work in comedy there are magical moments, muses, and embers of divine creativity that'll feel like a little angel with a fat booty delivered them just for you, but that's only like 5 percent of the time. The other 95 percent of the time, that fat-bootied angel muse is on vacation. She does not work a lot. So most of the time you are on your own, which requires a refined skill set so that even in your more tired and uninspired moments, you can reach into the abyss and find the funny.

You're going to do great, because you now have something special that we were all lucky enough to receive in our careers: the wisdom of Anne Libera.

FUNNIER

INTRODUCTION

I'd like to start by getting one thing out of the way.

I am not funny.

If you polled anyone who went to grade school, high school, or college with me, I would be among the last people that any of them would have pegged for a career in making people laugh. In fact, a college teacher of mine once gave me the direction "You know how when you make a joke at a party and everyone just stops and looks at you blankly? You should play the character like that."

I started working at The Second City in their box office shortly after I graduated from college and fell in love with improvisation, which led to me creating and performing sketch comedy written through improvisation. Because I am not a "naturally funny" person, I had to figure out how comedy worked for me specifically. I discovered that my own best comedy often came out of starting with recognizable behaviors rather than "funny ideas." Even better for my brain, I realized that jokes and premises had an underlying logic that pleased my puzzle-solving brain. These insights turned out to be particularly useful when I started directing and teaching. I had a toolbox of useful techniques I had discovered in my own work that I could share.

Flash forward: I have now spent over thirty years working at The Second City in Chicago as a performer, teacher, and director. My former students and colleagues have careers all across the comedy industry.

I have three offices where I do my work.

My first office is on the third-ish floor of Piper's Alley, the complicated building that houses The Second City's theaters, classrooms, and offices at the corner of Wells and North Avenue in the Old Town neighborhood of Chicago. If you come visit me here, you have to text me when you get to the building so I can come get you. Otherwise you'll definitely get lost trying to find me—the "building" is actually five or six buildings that were all combined into something like a mall in the late 1980s, and the layout resembles a drawing by M. C. Escher. My Second City office has no windows, but lots of shelves packed with books, along with photos of casts I have been in and directed. There are a lot of recognizable faces in these pictures—young versions of people who are now famous (like Stephen Colbert or Tina Fey or Steven Yeun—yes, he did comedy before he did *The Walking Dead*, and he's very funny as well as being a great actor), but also young versions of people whose names or faces you might not know but who have gone on to do significant work in comedy over the years. One wall of my office is all bulletin board, with production calendars, and index cards with sketch names on them like PROTAGONIST GENE, SPACE OPERA, UNITED CENTER, BLACK MOLLIES.

In this office, I have meetings with my stage manager about rehearsal schedules and what kinds of costumes we need for the Elf on the Shelf boy band song—the white felt mittens she created were pure comedy gold, by the way. I talk to performers about sketch ideas and give advice to former students about what's next in their careers. I have Zoom meetings about creative strategy. And I spend a lot of time staring at those cards and moving them around into various arrangements, thinking about how certain sketches, in a certain order, will affect an audience.

My second office is at Columbia College Chicago, where I am an associate professor and coordinate the BA degree in Comedy Writing and Performance that I created in 2011. This is in the Theater Department building in the south Loop. If you come to visit me there, you'll get off on the fourth floor and go down a hallway. This office has windows, a lot of books, and framed comedy albums from the '50s and '60s on the walls. I do a lot of talking to students in this office, helping them figure out how to graduate or whether they want to try stand-up instead of improv or why the premise of the sketch they're writing isn't working.

As a college professor, I frequently refer to myself as someone who backed into academia. I do not have a terminal degree. It's simply that the more I directed and taught, the more I recognized a need for useful ways of categorizing, theorizing, and thinking about comedy that matched the ways comedy is actually made. The people I admire most in comedy, and the most influential, are usually some combination of writer/director/performer/producers, and they translate their work across mediums. I wanted to train comedians to think and practice across roles, mediums, and contexts. Programs like that didn't exist, so I had to create them. I developed new ways of thinking and talking about comedy with collaborators who shared my perspective and taught with me in those programs.

I did research but found that much of the information was in two categories: academic work defined by the discipline and medium of the academic involved, or popular books written by practitioners drawing from their own specific area of expertise. There was little available that addressed what had become obvious to me and my collaborators: that we need to stop thinking of comedy as a genre of a particular medium. It isn't only a style of film or theater or television. It doesn't come last after you have learned the "serious stuff." It is in a class by itself. The comic manifests itself across mediums in ways that are connected, and it has its own theory, impulses, and processes.

My third office is the attic of my house on the north side of Chicago. It has a view of the El, but it's on the ground here, like one of those trains that circles an amusement park. This office has a desk but also an exercise bike, and since it used to be the "playroom" for my two kids, there are games, Legos, stuffed animals, and American Girl doll furniture underneath and behind the desk and the table where I taught Zoom comedy classes during the pandemic. I wrote and rewrote a lot of this book in this office, you'll recognize details from it in the examples I use when I discuss comedy creation.

Here's the second thing I'd like to get out of the way.

Are women funny?

Yes.

Third thing.

We have to address the frog in the room.

In 1941, the novelist E. B. White and his wife, the great *New Yorker* editor Katherine White, wrote in a foreword to an anthology of humor that "analyzing humor is like dissecting a frog. No one is very interested, and the frog dies of it."[1] Since then, it seems that every writer who addresses theory of comedy and humor has felt the need to somehow apologize for what they are doing by referencing the Whites' frog. Mike Sacks's excellent book of interviews with comedy writers is called *Poking a Dead Frog.*

Here's what I have to say about the frog. There is no question that analyzing a joke or a comic moment can and often does make the joke less funny to those involved in the analysis. Who cares? Detailed analysis of any work of art will ruin the immediate response to it: Once you have taken a novel apart and discovered its components, you will appreciate it all the more, but you won't have the same swept-up feeling you had the first time you read it. Same thing with a joke or a sketch or a show.

The point of analyzing comedy is to understand the mechanisms not because you want to laugh at the joke again but because you want to learn how to make another joke that is just as good or better. You learn why the joke worked and how it tricked you. And you understand how to use the tools of that particular joke and apply it to your own thoughts and ideas. Every artist and artisan takes apart the thing they love to understand the inner workings. A disassembled clock doesn't tell the time. But sometimes you have to take a clock apart in order to discover how it works. Then you put the pieces back together so that the clock will run again. It's what we do when we want to understand things.

It may mean that we will never laugh quite as hard at a bit once we have taken it apart. But the good comedy, the really excellent comedy, will still be great. And we will still appreciate what makes it great.

So, what do you need to know about the rest of this book? We're going to analyze comedy. We're going to think about how it works and why.

We'll start with an overall theory of comedy. Not a theory of humor. For the purposes of this book, I'm defining comedy as a created piece intentionally designed to elicit laughter or humor in an audience. Lots of times we laugh at something that isn't comedy—you can laugh at your friend tripping over their own feet, you can find humor in a Bernese mountain dog puppy playing with a lemon, but it isn't necessarily comedy. The choice to put the lemon in front of the puppy and film it, though, might be.

We will then look at what I have identified as the five components of comedy: jokes, physical comedy, narrative, character, and point of view. Of these, jokes are perhaps the only one that is unique to comedy, but I would argue that in comedic works, all five play a unique part. We will examine these components separately, but in modern comedy we rarely see just one at a time. Traditional sitcoms have a simple repetitive narrative and include jokes and physical comedy that are sourced out of comic characters. Even the most joke-based format of stand-up will use three or four of the components. The stand-up comedian Taylor Tomlinson tells stories that include multiple jokes, and her specific point of view on the world and persona are at the center of her appeal. We have a habit as a culture of seeing jokes as comedy. But comedy is larger than jokes.

Because I am an academic, however backward, I'll take some time to go over some of the most prominent theories of humor and laughter and make the case for the distinct differences between comedy theory and humor theory. I will provide an overview of the current neuroscience and social science on laughter as well as insights about humor and laughter to be derived from behavioral science. But because I am mostly a practitioner and teacher, I'll also look at how those theories contain tools and practices that can be leveraged in comedy creation.

The second part of the book is focused on comedy creation. As I said earlier, I am not a naturally funny person, but I have spent decades working in the field of comedy. In this section, I'll share the tools and knowledge that worked for me, for the performers and writers I collaborate with, and for my students. I will do a deep dive into how to use my theory of comedy to generate comic ideas and then how to build on those initial ideas to create and perform various types of comedy.

In the third part of the book, I'll look at methods for revising original comedy. Most comedy is performed in front of audiences and then revised based on their feedback. We will break down how the elements and components of comedy work together to generate laughter in a specific audience and how you can use that knowledge to revise comedic work in order to get the responses you are looking for from your chosen audience.

In the last section, I'll address the concept of comedy ethics and how comedians can evaluate for themselves whether and how to tell a specific joke in front of a specific audience. There are also guidelines here for what I refer to as "good comedy hygiene," suggestions for healthier methods of creation and collaboration.

Throughout, I try to use as many examples as I can of how the comedy point I am making shows up in comedy that has already been made. As part of the college program I oversee, I teach a class called History and Analysis of Modern American Comedy, and I'll refer to a lot of historical comedy examples I use in that class. I also include as many modern examples from as many types of comedians and comedy as I can. If you recognize the references, good for you—you're a probably a comedy nerd like me. Most of you won't, and I have included a bibliography of sorts at the end of the book with some explanations about who is who along with a suggestion of what examples you might want to check out from their work and suggestions on where to find those examples.

I also use examples from my own work as a performer, a writer, and (most often) as a director and teacher of comedy. Most of this took place at The Second City in Chicago, where I have worked my entire adult life. While working there I have been lucky to watch, meet, and collaborate with some of the most amazing comedians of our time—all those people whose faces show up in photos in my office. Some of these comedians have names you'll recognize from film and television, some are less famous but actively working in the comedy industry, and some have chosen for all sort of reasons to bring the skills they honed in comedy and improvisation to other industries like health care, sales, law, and education.

One of the things I value most from my work in improvisation is the concept of ensemble. An ensemble might be a group of people, but even more than that, to me ensemble is a way of behaving. Ensemble behavior means that what you make with your ensemble is intentionally different from what you might make on your own. Most of my adult life, I have approached my work—as a teacher, a director, a leader, a creator—from an ensemble perspective. As a result, it's a particularly odd thing for me to write a book by myself. Comedy and improvisation is very much an oral tradition—it happens in front of an audience, we make discoveries together. Nothing I know about comedy is mine alone, and lots of ideas and exercises have come to me from other people. Check out the endnotes for credit for exercises, concepts, and ideas I have learned from other people and from ensembles I have been a part of. When I reference a premise written by a student or performer I have worked with, I'll do my best to credit them in the endnotes as well.

I will generally default to the pronouns *they* and *their* when I am looking at comedy or comedy creators in situations where gender is not an issue. If I use *he* or *she*, I am doing so intentionally because I believe the gender matters to the comedic. While we live in a society that is much more aware of gender fluidity than ever before, it is also true that gender is frequently associated with a number of recognizable traits used in comedy. Power and status correlate to our cultural associations with gender performance. Gender markers create certain expectations in an audience that can be reversed or exaggerated. As much as possible, I will be using an awareness of whether gender is germane or important to the comedic effect on the audience and choose pronouns where that effect is apparent.

I'm going to be using the terms *comic* and *comedic* interchangeably. More and more the term *comic* is being used to describe story told with images and cartoons. There are, of course, multiple intersections between comedy and cartooning (there's a reason we call them "comics" and distinguish comics from graphic novels). If I am referring to a comic of that sort, I will make sure that it is specifically noted.

The final thing: Can you teach just anyone how to be funny?

This is a question I get all the time. Interviewers ask me this. Parents of potential students ask me this. A member of the Columbia College curriculum committee asked me this when I was first proposing the degree in Comedy Writing and Performance.

And the answer is no. You can't teach just anyone how to be funny. In the same way that no one is ever going to teach me how to do more than a couple of pull-ups. I just don't have the natural arm strength to do it. And this is all completely beside the point. Natural talent and aptitude exist in all arts and fields. Why should comedy be any different?

My guess that the reason this question is so pervasive is that comedy feels like magic. It evokes an automatic response in us that is out of our control: a laugh. Plus, it makes us feel like someone has read our minds: "How did you know I felt that way?" "How did you put this thing into words that I have always known or felt but never been able to speak?"

But the fact of the matter is that comedy isn't magic. It is a series of learned skills and understandings. And with this practice and knowledge, you might not become as funny as one of the greats (in the same way that I will not become an Olympic athlete). But just as training will make me better at a sport, so will training make you better at comedy.

Ultimately, the goal of this book is to give you the tools to think about and make comedy for yourself. It may be professionally on a stage or onscreen, but it may be the intentional use of comedy in all the various places in which you may want to create it. In marketing or a meeting—comedy is a way of getting your message across in a way that is both friendly and sticky. To choose to be funnier is to choose to be smart about how you use the most interesting and potentially dangerous tool at our disposal and one that has been a part of humanity from the beginning, possibly from before we had language as humans. Comedy may be thought of as not worthy of serious study, but it definitely rewards serious study. My hope is that this book will lead you toward a greater appreciation of how that serious study will help to make you funnier.

PART 1

THINKING ABOUT COMEDY

Humor is the sensation of amusement, we feel it. We have, literally, a "sense" of humor.

Laughter is a sound we make when we feel humor or amusement. We also laugh for all sorts of reasons that aren't connected to humor and amusement. We laugh because other people are laughing or because we feel embarrassed. And for what it's worth, we often don't laugh out loud when we are actually amused.

I define comedy as something intentionally created to generate humor or laughter in an audience. There can be good comedy. There can be bad comedy. There is comedy that works and comedy that doesn't work. But the thing that makes it comedy is that it is intentionally created to evoke a response of humor or laughter in its chosen audience.

There are moments when people laugh at created things that were not intended to be comedic. We could call that "unintentional comedy." People laugh or find humor in life for all sorts of reasons. They also find humor in things someone else created that wasn't originally meant to be comic. You might laugh very hard with your friends while watching a terrible movie, but that doesn't make the movie a comedy. On the other hand, a television show or performance piece that is created to showcase "unintentional comedy" (say, a blooper show) would be defined as comedy.

It's probably worthwhile to examine laughter for a moment Looking at the experience of laughter specifically can help to highlight the differences between comedy, laughter, and humor. Think back on a time you laughed hard, really really hard. What was it? Who or what provoked it? But also, what was happening? Where were you and what was the context?

I'll tell you mine. I was driving a car with my friends Jen and Piero. We had just spent some ten hours in a small conference room at the University of Chicago working intensely on an improvisation-based workshop that was going to be rolled out to all of the first-year entering U of C students for their fall orientation. Our bodies were tired, our brains were tired. As I pulled off Lake Shore Drive at Belmont heading west, I looked to my left and commented on a jogger running toward the lakefront. I do not remember what I said—it was just an observation out of my extremely tired brain. Maybe something like "She looks like she puts a lot of effort into being a jogger." There was a pause and then all three of us burst into hysterical laughter. Why? It doesn't seem funny now—in fact, I don't remember my exact words. But at that moment it was sidesplittingly, pee-your-pants funny. It was both true (whatever it was) and, more than that, a perfect expression of where my brain was and what I saw in that moment. Just straight up a mirror image of what I was seeing and the way I was seeing it. This was not comedy. But it was a moment of humor and laughter.

There were so many things happening in this moment. There was a social element. I was with two close friends, and we were in a shared private space. There was a heightened emotional element—we were all deeply tired and a little bit on edge, worried that the work we were in the midst of might not pay off. There was some cruelty to it—as I say, I don't remember what I said, but I'm pretty sure it was not a flattering observation of the woman involved. However, it was obviously true—or at least true to all three of us—in that moment. And there was a fair amount of surprise involved. I am known for being a person who doesn't make intentionally nasty remarks.

But it wouldn't be funny to you, even if I explained it in detail. Because you had to be there. You had to know what we knew and be where we were and feel the way we felt to "get" it.

Laughter is situational, dependent on contexts and information of all kinds. As human beings we laugh for any number of reasons. We laugh when we are tickled. We can generate laughter when we want to be included or a part of a group. We laugh to show those in power that they have power. We laugh to demonstrate our agreement and understanding. We laugh when we learn or discover something; in fact, some research from China suggests that the same part of the brain that processes humor also processes insight.[1]

We laugh because we feel uncomfortable or because we feel shame. We laugh when we are embarrassed. We laugh because we are cold. In fact, many comedy theaters intentionally keep the temperature colder to encourage laughter. David Letterman famously kept the Ed Sullivan Theater at a brisk 55 degrees because it made his jokes land better.

Laughter is social—we laugh more when we are closer to other human beings. The Second City Training Center has a rule for student performances in the final level of our conservatory program. They need to have twenty-five audience members in order to have a show. This is for preview performances where they are developing material. What we know from experience is that in the theater where we hold these performances, we need at least twenty-five people in order for those audience members to respond enough that we can tell (through their laughter) whether the material is working for that particular audience. In a smaller theater, we might need fewer people. It seems that being in closer proximity with a certain number of other humans is required for an audience to feel comfortable laughing. (Not always: Ever been the person sitting on the train reading a book or listening to a podcast and inadvertently letting loose with a guffaw?) But there seems to be some social element to laughter.

We can occasionally point to the interconnecting web of circumstances and information that has created any one instance of we ourselves laughing and explain it. But even in doing so, it is difficult to re-create. And while we can certainly theorize about why others have laughed in the past, we are even more likely to be mistaken.

Mary Beard, in her book *Laughter in Ancient Rome*, maintains that we genuinely don't know what prompted the laughter of the ancient Romans. She warns about "the assumption that if only we worked hard enough at it, the joke would make sense to us too, that it could be translated into terms we understand. Of course, that must sometimes be so. . . . But in any individual case we must not assume that successful translation between the Roman world and our own is possible. There is a danger that the question 'What made the Romans laugh?' might be converted, by an act of spurious empathy, into the question 'What do I think would have made me laugh, if I were a Roman?' "[2]

If the reasons we laugh in any given moment (or throughout time) are so difficult to reconstruct, to build something with the intention of making other people laugh is a useless endeavor. But again, we're not talking about laughter—we're talking about comedy.

The moment in my car is *not* comedy even if I could explain it to you in detail. Ultimately these moments of uncontrollable laughter aren't reproducible, I can't take them from one audience to another. They were discovered, not created.

But that doesn't mean we can't figure out how to make people laugh. And that's what this first part of the book is all about, a theory of comedy that you can use to create things that will make your chosen audiences laugh.

1 A THEORY OF COMEDY

A theory of comedy is fundamentally different from theories of humor and laughter. A theory of comedy is useful to those who want to make an audience laugh, but it doesn't need to explain all situations of laughing. It is useful for those who want to analyze and break apart someone else's comedy and see what makes it tick. If a theory of comedy provides insight into the elemental pieces that are manipulated to create comedy, it should then assist comedians to play with those elements to generate an initial comic idea or framework from which to build a comedic piece. And the same theory that helped us analyze what worked in another comedian's success should also provide a path toward analyzing our own comedy and revising it so that it will fairly reliably make our intended audience laugh.

A theory of comedy should help comedy creators create comedy. It should help them to make what they have created better. As simple as that. Ideally a good theory of comedy will encompass a multitude of tools and allow for many—though not all—of the situations in which humor and laughter occur.

We laugh because of a number of neurological, social, and physical mechanisms. A theory of laughter or humor is connected to those mechanisms. A theory of comedy is about how we intentionally manipulate those mechanisms in pursuit of amusement and laughter from a specific audience.

When I teach, I ask my students to list for me the things that people laugh at. Here are some examples from those lists:

- People falling
- Kids swearing
- Dick jokes
- Puppets
- Shock humor
- Contradictions
- Sex
- Identity
- Metahumor
- People with disabilities talking about their disabilities
- Spot-on stereotypes
- Farts
- Awkward situations
- Things that are relatable
- Angry people
- Teen angst
- Failed murder attempts
- Surprise
- Cringey situations
- Slapstick
- Hyperexaggeration of society
- Stupid white people
- Dogs in clothes

Then, together we look for connections and patterns. Pretty quickly we start to find that all the answers cluster around three elements, and that if you look deeply at any given answer all three elements exist there in some form. I refer to these elements as recognition, pain, and distance. I am arguing here that those are the essential materials we manipulate and adjust when we intentionally make comedy.

Recognition

For comedy to work for us or for an audience, we have to "get" it. It has to either correspond to our lived experience of the world, our intellectual knowledge of how things work, or confirm our reasonable assumptions based on those things. Our internal thought process states, "This corresponds with the stories I believe about the world." Or as film director and improv comedian Mike Nichols put it, "I think a laugh is just a very loud Yes."[1] I refer to this element as recognition. When we are creating or revising comedy it can be helpful to think about this element as including related ideas and words like *understanding, knowledge, schema, relatability, sense, logic, familiarity.*

There is a lot of talk about "truth in comedy." In fact, there is a book about improvisation by that name. When I was first formulating my theory, I called this element "truth" instead of "recognition." I liked the idea of truth as the core element of comedy; it felt poetic and resonant. But the fact of the matter is that whether something is empirically true does not appear to be germane to whether it is funny to us or useful in comedy. It doesn't have to *be* true; we just have to understand it *as* true. You could tell me a very funny story about the sport of cricket that is absolutely based in 100 percent truth and I wouldn't find it at all funny. I have almost zero knowledge of the sport of cricket. I don't have the schema to appreciate the joke whether or not it is true.

It's also possible for something to be absolutely, factually accurate and not "feel true." For example, did you know that one twelve-inch pizza is bigger than two eight-inch pizzas?[2] As our human brains evolved, they developed shortcuts in order to work more efficiently. In this case, most people use a shortcut for one kind of measurement (length) that doesn't work for another kind of measurement (diameter). Psychologists call these shortcuts heuristics. Comedians can make great use of the errors and biases inherent in heuristics, and we'll look into those a little bit later. For now, let's just be clear that it is entirely possible for something to be true but to not be recognizable.

And vice versa. There are many things that are unlikely or implausible if you examine them closely but still feel deeply recognizable. This is the source of a million conspiracy theories discussed ad nauseam on the internet. Stephen Colbert's essential statement of his character in the first episode of *The Colbert Report* was contained in a word he coined: *truthiness*. A quick Google of the word leads to this definition: "the quality of seeming or felt to be true, even if not necessarily true." Stephen was satirizing a trope of right-wing politics and punditry when he said, "I know some of you may not trust your gut, yet. But with my help, you will. The truthiness is, anyone can *read* the news *to* you. I promise to *feel* the news *at* you." "Truth" in comedy, like truthiness, isn't facts. It is felt. It is recognition.

Recognition can easily be manufactured. One way to manipulate an audience into recognition is by using what is called the "rule of three." We set up a pattern. We repeat it. We repeat it again, and the audience "gets" it. They were expecting it. And they reward themselves and us with laughter for that piece of recognition.

The essence of traditional sitcom is establishing a strong character the audience knows so well that they can predict how that character will likely respond in any given situation. It doesn't matter if the behavior itself is realistic or recognizable in the general population. Lucy Ricardo on *I Love Lucy* rarely, if ever, responds to situations in her life like an actual human being in the world, but once we get the essence of this fictional character, we recognize and enjoy her actions.

On a recording I have of the classic one-liner comic Henny Youngman, he ends his set using his catchphrase, "Take my wife, please!," without any of the setup or punch line structure or timing used in his other jokes. If you are unfamiliar with Youngman's work, it doesn't seem funny at all. But the audience laughs. They know the line is famous. They may not even understand the joke, but they laugh because they recognize it and they enjoy knowing that they know it.

Mary Beard references a joke from roughly 200 BCE, but she might just as easily have been referring to Youngman's audience when she says, "Laughter might have been prompted by the sheer familiarity of the quip. As the cliché goes, old jokes are the best—in the sense that they cause us to crack up not through the disruptions of incongruity or the pleasures of derision (as many a modern theory has it) but through the warm recollection of all the other occasions on which just the same joke has worked as intended. Laughter is as much about memory, and about the ways we have learned to laugh at certain cues, as it is about uncontrollable spontaneity."[3]

Improv comedians will often drop a reference to a well-known television show or commercial tagline that was popular during the childhood of the bulk of the audience members to get a laugh. It is something of a cheap trick because the audience will laugh in response to their own knowledge. They pat themselves on the back for recognizing the reference. We use this all the time at Second City when a company goes on tour—we know that mentioning a local politician or a well-known suburb is likely to get the laugh of recognition. In our corporate division, we have what we sometimes refer to as the "Bob from Accounting" effect—just dropping the name of someone familiar from the company offices will elicit a big laugh.

The other primary facets of the element of recognition are logic and insight. The simplest pun is at its base a game of logic. A pun creates an expectation in its audience by using a word that has two different and somewhat opposite meanings or two words that sound the same but are quite different, and then it reveals that the initial expectation was incorrect and there is another interpretation that logically *makes as much or more sense*. That's important. It's funny because it logics out. For example, in the riddle that begins, "Where does the general keep his armies?," the natural expectation is that the word *armies* refers to a military fighting force of some sort. The punch line, "In his sleevies," reverses that assumption and instead substitutes a version of *armies* that is instead a childish way of referring to a body part. It is of course terribly silly but also completely logical.

The audience has jumped to a conclusion. They don't just laugh because they discover that they are wrong. They also laugh because there is a moment of insight, of what feels like truth, they "got" the joke. If your audience is confused, they won't laugh. Conversely, if the joke is too easy to get, you may receive a laugh, but it won't be an insight laugh. It'll be more like the memory laugh that Mary Beard describes above.

However, the logic doesn't have to be that of the tangible world. It can be logical in the way that dreams are. Stand-up comedian Steven Wright has a bit about accidentally trying to fit his car key into the keyhole of his house and then starting up the house and driving it around the block. On its face, this is completely unrecognizable No one has ever driven their house around the block unless they lived in an RV. But it still feels logical. How? This joke contains two pieces of recognition—the first is a common experience of pulling out the wrong key, the second is a recognition of a natural but surprising logic in which a house behaves like a car.

One of my personal favorite kinds of laughs to get in a theater is the just slightly delayed one, where there is a beat or two after the punch line before the laughter begins and then it builds as members of the audience get the punch line in a rolling wave of recognition.

There is a sense of discovery to these laughs. One of the hallmarks of great improvisation is how it re-creates recognizable human behavior. This isn't a joke-based laugh; it is discovered as the audience watches. An audience sees two people interact and, through this behavior, intuits what is going on, and then laughs because they recognize what is happening (even if the characters may not).

Pain

The second major element of all comedy I refer to as "pain." As with the element of recognition, this piece of the comedy puzzle encompasses a number of mechanisms and experiences. Most of the traditional theories of humor are focused on this one aspect. They are describing a form of pain that triggers laughter or humor.

When we create comedy, we play with a variety of types of pain, and often more than one in any given comedic moment. It surfaces in the re-created (and sometimes actual) physical pain of slapstick—people falling down, getting hit with pies, slipping on a banana peel. But there is also mental and emotional pain—embarrassment, awkwardness, insult humor. It might be taboo or vulgarity—the saying of things we shouldn't say. A violation of norms. Tension. Incongruity. Cognitive dissonance. Error. Novelty and surprise on their own can be pleasant or painful, depending on the circumstances. In comedy they provide the same sort of spice as the other items under this umbrella.

All comedy contains at least a frisson of pain. As I noted earlier, most of the humor from simple puns comes from recognition. But there is also a light cognitive dissonance of two different meanings existing simultaneously. And the minor discomfort at the error of having jumped to the wrong conclusion.

A couple of years ago, I gave a keynote talk at a conference, and afterward I was approached by one of the attendees. She wanted to know how comedy created by a beloved character like Gracie Allen could possibly include pain on any level. From her perspective, there was nothing dark about the character.

Gracie Allen worked in vaudeville, radio, and television for over thirty years alongside her husband George Burns. The central conceit of their act was Gracie's "illogical logic." She took things literally, focused on the wrong elements, missed the point. But if you looked at the world through Gracie's eyes, it all makes perfect sense. Think about this exchange from their 1950s-era television show:

> GEORGE: What beautiful flowers!
> GRACIE: Well, I wouldn't have gotten them if it weren't for you.
> GEORGE: How?
> GRACIE: You told me that when I went to visit Clara Bagley in the hospital to take her flowers. So, when she wasn't lookin' I did![4]

Gracie is adorable. She makes sense to herself, but to the rest of the world and her audience, she's wrong. Quite wrong, in fact—in this case she stole a sick woman's flowers. In real life, she could be arrested or at the very least upset her friend. She's darling, but she's also delusional, and if you looked at the show from that perspective, it would be painful indeed.

But it isn't painful. It's funny, and this clip generally gets a laugh from my students when I show it, nearly seventy years after it first aired. What makes it funny instead of a tragic tale of a woman out of sync with society?

Recognition and pain aren't the only things we use in making comedy. Truth and pain are the essence of tragedy. The final piece of the puzzle is a context that allows the audience to see those two elements from a perspective that suggests these elements are inconsequential in the end (which is why theatrical and film comedies have often ended in marriage), or that they are, to use a word from Peter McGraw's theory of humor, "benign." In this way, comedy is connected to horror films or roller-coaster rides in that it contains the thrill of something that would normally scare or terrify us but in a context that renders it safer.

Distance

The quote "Life is a comedy to those who think and a tragedy to those who feel" gets at the essence of this final element.[5] I use the term *distance* to describe a perspective that allows us to look objectively, to evaluate with our minds instead of our feelings. The philosopher Henri Bergson said that "the comic demands something like a momentary anesthesia of the heart."

How do we create distance? It can be temporal—hence the saying "Comedy is tragedy plus time."[6] It can be social distance: According to comedy filmmaker Mel Brooks, "Tragedy is when I cut my finger. Comedy is when you fall into an open sewer and die." It can be psychological: An overabundance of exposure to certain kinds of pain or suffering can create the kind of mental distance from our own trauma that results in black humor like the gallows humor of the condemned or of soldiers in the trenches.

I would also argue that certain comic tropes—such as a funny tone of voice or a comic device like wordplay—create some distance all on their own. An audience recognizes a tone in the delivery of a joke that suggests it is not meant to be believed or taken as real. The kind of razor-sharp precision of language that is true wit is another way to create distance—the choice of the specific words allows for an intellectual appreciation that pre-empts too much emotion. In my personal experience there are certain comedians whose presence and demeanor are just naturally safer than others, such as Nathan Fielder or Quinta Brunson. Because audiences trust them instinctively, they can push boundaries or get away with much edgier material if they choose to do so. Conversely, there are comedians who feel much more dangerous, and their persona can provide a sort of pain that lends piquancy to a more banal comic moment.

It's not quite as simple as just mashing the three elements together and suddenly achieving laughter—although that isn't a bad way to start. Take something recognizable, combine it with something painful, and then exaggerate or minimize it and you'll have an initial kind of comedy that you can play with and revise. But there is also an alchemy to it—a precisely right combination of the three that creates a moment of comedy gold.

2 COMEDY IS RELATIVE

All of these elements are relative for any individual or group. What I find recognizable or true depends on my own personal life experience—what I know, what I understand. You may have a completely different set of personal references, thus your "recognition" will be entirely different from mine. Similarly, different people find different things painful. And what is necessary to create a feeling of safety that allows us to laugh is not only dependent on our personality and preferences—it also changes depending on the context.

One of the primary jobs of a comedian is to manipulate the three elements until they find the sweet spot where recognition, pain, and distance come together in just the right balance and create laughter or amusement in a chosen audience. And chosen audience is an important piece of this puzzle. If I want to get the largest number of people to laugh (as on a network situation comedy), then I need to choose elements that are broadly familiar and generally understood to be painful, then manipulate mechanisms and contexts that provide distance for the most people. This is likely to create comedy that generates laughter for a lot of people but might not necessarily make any one of those people laugh particularly hard.

The comedy that makes us individually laugh the hardest tends to be the comedy that sits at the furthest edge of our own personal levels of recognition and pain. Those are the jokes or moments that feel as if they were written just for us, the moments that make us feel as if we are somehow in communion with the comedian who creates them. We feel that they understand and see the world the way we do. Inside jokes also do this—there is mutually experienced truth.

How to balance elements of the recognition/pain/distance triad depends on a large number of factors. There are multiple contexts outside the comedian's control that affect the reception of any particular piece of comedy. For example, the same joke about getting laid that gets uproarious laughter in a small bar late at night will get profound and uncomfortable silence during the day for a keynote speaker at a business conference. The audience at this bar might be fairly homogeneous—maybe mostly white men in their early twenties—and thus have lots of things in common. To generalize for our imaginary experiment in comedy: These are men who like sports, they are interested in sex and drug culture, and as members of a somewhat privileged class, they aren't really worried about offense. They've been drinking, too, which has both loosened their inhibitions and to a certain extent (depending how much they have been drinking) provided a measure of personal distance, since they are "feeling no pain." Plus the room is dark, so they don't feel as if their laughter puts them on display.

The conference audience, in this example, are more diverse in terms of age, color, ethnicity, and gender. They are awake and caffeinated. They are there with their coworkers, bosses, or maybe potential clients. They feel a little vulnerable. The room is well lit, so there's little anonymity. A joke about having sex with an unattractive woman while on a mind-altering substance is not going to go over well with this group. Even the very same men who laughed uproariously in the club would, sitting next to their female boss, find that joke to be less true, more painful, and significantly less benign.

On the other hand, the conference audience will have a number of areas of commonality and recognition that a good comedian can exploit. They are in a mutual industry, so references to buzzwords or common industry difficulties will be appreciated in a way that the late-night bar audience would be indifferent to.

One of the biggest challenges I've ever faced as a director was being sent to revise a show that was running on a cruise ship with an itinerary around the western Mediterranean. Ship audiences in general are difficult. A major element of cruise culture is the idea that every customer complaint about anything is taken extremely seriously. Many cruise passengers choose this type of vacation because they want to be taken care of and avoid having a bad experience. I'm going to repeat that: They want to avoid having a bad experience. They don't want to be made uncomfortable. And they are willing to sacrifice the possibility of a peak experience to avoid discomfort. So, there is lots of food, not highly spiced or interesting but familiar and abundant. The music is unchallenging and popular. Cruise ship audiences are aware of what makes them uncomfortable and will try to avoid that discomfort at all costs and will complain vociferously if they are made uncomfortable.

Add to that, the audiences in Europe were primarily German or Spanish speakers with English as a second (but not necessarily strong) language. Our initial intuition had been to create a show that included many silent and physical pieces. We had failed to realize that a great deal of Second City's silent material is created in a cabaret environment and frequently makes use of references to sexuality or violence. Those scenes played very well in a show where the audience already knew and trusted the performers (and had gotten to know them through shared language and dialogue) but weren't nearly so successful for a cruise ship audience.

What we discovered on that long trip along the coasts of Italy and France was that our best bet was not to focus on pain elements at all. Since this audience was looking for comfort and safety, the comedy for this group needed to rely on the safest element of the comedy triad: recognition.

Sure enough, the segment we created, a series of short scenic jokes and comedic images reflecting the events our audience had experienced during the cruise (towel animals, soft-serve ice cream, the required safety drill, and especially the show that preceded us in the grand showroom—a cheesy musical revue of '70s disco music) was an enormous hit with our audience. They loved seeing their experience reflected back to them from the stage and in a simple fashion, the idea that everyone seated around them also knew these things intensified the laughter.

To return to the recognition/pain/distance model, let's look at what we did. We brainstormed material that was unique to the experience of traveling on a cruise ship in Europe (I was lucky that my performers had been on the ship for two months and had a wealth of stories and observations about ship life). We picked the most recognizable of these experiences and applied a couple of simple pain points—the mild cognitive dissonance of seeing personal experience on the stage and simple visual jokes whose primary mechanism was surprise.

I want to point out that while we were creating this piece, the actors pitched me a number of funny and quite biting pieces that pointed out the hypocrisies of class and social caste they had become aware of while on the ship. Cruise ships are their own mini–floating kingdoms with a strong class system and a favor-based internal economy among the workers that is not dissimilar to a prison system. Much of what the performers showed me was recognizably true, painful, and absolutely impossible to put on the stage for that audience on that ship. The audience would have had to have enormous levels of safety to contemplate their own participation in this system, let alone to begin to have enough objectivity on it to find it funny in the way my highly educated and cynical American performers did.

The (insert name of whatever ship you happen to be on) Experience became a standard offering in all our cruise ship shows—we added or subtracted bits depending on the ship, its itinerary, and the other entertainment offered.

Just as it did for my work on the cruise ship, the recognition/pain/distance triad can function for the creator of comedy in two important ways.

First, it can assist in the initial creation of a comic idea. When Second City does corporate comedy shows for businesses, one of the first things we do is to survey the people hiring us. We ask for commonalities, jargon, frustrations, well-known stories or events. In other words, we scavenge for the elements of recognition and pain that this audience shares. One of the most successful prompts I use for creating a sketch show or for generating student standup is to make lists of events, obsessions, or minutiae from the writer's own lives. These don't need to be unusual, but the more specific the better. What I find is that the minute we stop beating our heads against a wall trying to come up with "funny" ideas, the better comedy we create. Our own lives are an abundant and organic source of experiences and observations that contain multiple points of recognition and pain we can use to build our comedy.

The triad theory is even more useful in the revision process. It gives us three different ways to interrogate our comedy and find how we can make it work better. If a joke doesn't land, perhaps the audience didn't have the information they needed to recognize it and we need to find ways to provide more specifics in the setup or exposition. Maybe they understood, but the joke doesn't have enough punch—they aren't surprised or affected strongly enough. The next step is to find ways to make the pain aspect stronger. If they were too uncomfortable, we need to provide a context that makes it safer for them to laugh. Perhaps the character who is being humiliated is too sympathetic or nice, so they don't seem to deserve the pain and we just feel bad for them? In the revision we can create a context in which the character is more aware of the potential for humiliation in their circumstances and decides to forge ahead anyway with a certain kind of hubris. This makes the pain that gets inflicted on them more deserved and thus safer to laugh at. Or we can go the complete opposite way and make the character exaggeratedly innocent and undeserving. That adjustment provides a different kind of distance because the character is a little bit dumber or less real.

As a demonstration, let's look at the way I helped to revise a sketch that had a great deal of comedic potential from the outset but also dealt with subject matter that had (and still has) the potential to be very painful or difficult for an audience.

I've been lucky over the years to teach and direct some exceptionally funny people. I was working with a group of former students on an independent show. One of the ensemble members was Jordan Klepper, who went on to work for Comedy Central on *The Daily Show* as well as his own projects. Jordan brought in a sketch premise to be improvised in which he played a political candidate giving a press conference. The character was nearly perfect: He was young, he was charming, he was a doctor who had found a cure for cancer and was now hoping to bring his considerable skill and intelligence to governing the nation as a vice presidential candidate. In the middle of the press conference, he makes a comment about how much he hates Anne Frank and then moves on to talk about world hunger. A member of the press corps interrupts him to ask, "Did you just say you hate Anne Frank?" The candidate confirmed that he did—in fact, he loathes her. "Have you read that diary? Nothing but whine, whine, whine."

For our ensemble in rehearsal, it was clear that the sketch had the potential to be very funny but also that it required care in order to work for an audience outside the relative safety of the rehearsal room.

Let's take a moment to analyze this sketch and talk about how we had to adjust as we continued to iterate it. There's a great deal already in the premise that works.

Recognition. There is a general understanding that politicians are not supposed to offend any potential constituency.

Politics often creates situations in which one flaw can be blown up by the media and sink a campaign. This was especially true during the time we were working on the sketch in the early 2000s, maybe a little bit less true in the era of Donald Trump.

Anne Frank wrote a widely popular and venerated diary.

There is a common experience of disliking someone whom everyone else seems to revere.

Pain. Anne Frank was a Jewish teenager who wrote her diary while hiding from the Nazis and later died in a concentration camp. That's an enormous amount of pain right there.

Also, incredible incongruity. No one hates a dead teenaged martyr who wrote about how she thinks that people are really good at heart.

It's surprising and novel: There are very few people who would admit to hating Anne Frank, least of all a political candidate.

Distance. The initial observation was said quite casually by the character.

Jordan Klepper as a performer has an affability and warmth that creates an immediate level of psychological safety.

To make the sketch work for an audience, we had to make a number of adjustments—mostly in the area of distance. In my experience, two of the biggest pain points for audiences are death and religion. This sketch referenced both.

First, we had to make sure the incongruity was simple. The character had to hate Anne Frank specifically, and not be antisemitic in any way. We needed to ground his "hate" in minor details: It needed to be based in the sort of elements that make us hate annoying teenagers (more recognition). We also needed to heighten all of the character's good aspects (he may not have been a doctor who cured cancer in the initial version), so that this hatred was an aberration. We made him oblivious: Somehow this was the first time he had heard that his annoyance with Anne Frank was in any way unusual. We did this by putting the focus on the reporters. The story of the scene was a group of people who normally would jump on a candidate's flaw but found themselves desperately trying to make it OK and save this man from himself. Finally, we had to put the sketch later in the running order of the show it was featured in—we had to create even more safety by making sure that our audience trusted the cast and their point of view on the world before bringing this level of "edge" into the revue.

We were also adjusting all these elements with a specific audience in mind. We knew that this sketch would be performed later at night for a young, generally upper-middle-class, primarily white audience who were required to study the Holocaust in middle school, were politically liberal, and were not particularly religious. We would have made very different choices if we were adjusting these elements for more economically, culturally, and generationally diverse audiences like those on a cruise ship. And I should be clear, I would never have put this sketch in a cruise ship show. Not unless I was looking to be fired.

As we'll look at more deeply in a minute, one reason comedy resists analysis and taxonomy is that it so often works on multiple levels and uses multiple mechanisms simultaneously to create an effect in its chosen audience. In the Anne Frank sketch, there are many areas of recognition, lots of different pain points, and we used a variety of techniques to create distance for the audience. For the cruise ship audience in my earlier example, we needed to pay attention to levels of context, experience, and expectation that were not under our control to create comedy that reliably produced laughter.

The comedy theory of recognition, pain, and distance not only provides guidance for generation and revision of comedy but also does so by embracing this complexity. It provides an underlying structure that supports clearer analysis of existing comedy and paths to the generation and revision of new comedy.

You'll notice that in my examples above, I don't really mention jokes at all. Which is not to say that there weren't jokes in the sketch or in the cruise ship show—there were, and we spent some time working on them. But our primary focus as comedians in these instances was in revising comedic elements that were not joke based. To really understand how comedy works, we need to think about comedy as more than just jokes.

3 THE FIVE COMPONENTS OF COMEDY

Even though comedy has traditionally not been seen as a discipline worthy (or even capable) of being studied, there is actually a fair amount of lore out there. If you dig into this lore, what you notice is that a lot of it tends to be medium or discipline specific. Masters of their particular craft (theatrical clowning, TV sitcom writing, satiric parody news writing) have developed deep reservoirs of knowledge and theory and have eventually chosen to share it. One of my personal frustrations as a reader of these books was that while this information was interesting and useful to me, it didn't directly reflect my own understanding about comedy and comedians. There are contexts that require a specific set of comedic skills, but comedy itself has principles that cross the boundaries of genre and medium. There is a tendency among those who write about comedy to miss this and instead create theory based in their individual narrower experience, ignoring the elements of comedy that exist outside their specific area of expertise.

If you start with jokes as the essence of comedy, then you are likely to find yourself assuming that *all* comedy is based on the mechanisms of jokes (primarily incongruity and surprise). If you start with clowning as the essential element of comedy, you may choose to believe that all comedy is about play and the relationship between audience and performer. And so on.

In my work and teaching I have identified five areas in which comedy functions differently from drama across a variety of mediums: jokes, physical comedy, character, narrative, and point of view. No single one of these components is the essence of comedy. We rarely see comedy that utilizes only one of these components at any given time. Most often they function in combination, and it is this combination that generates content that is comedic. But for the time being, I'd like to consider them separately and roughly in order of complexity.

Jokes

Jokes are unique to comedy—so unique that they are sometimes misunderstood as being all of comedy. But they are unique to comedy. We can tell because when jokes happen outside comedy, we signal it—we call them "cosmic" jokes or "dark" comedy.

The definition of a joke is simple: A joke is a setup and a punch line.

The setup to a joke sets up an expectation of some kind.

You can think about a setup in a number of different ways. A setup provides the information that will drive the joke. You can also think of a setup as creating a story. Or a setup can frame an initial picture. A setup can be a question that suggests a certain sort of answer.

The punch line reframes the setup in a way that reverses that expectation.

A couple of different ways to think about the punch line: A punch line takes the information from the setup and twists it in some way that is unexpected and surprising. Or it shows you that the story you thought you were being told is a completely different and opposite story. You can also think of the punch line as reframing the picture that the setup created. For example, in a filmed joke, the setup might show us a couple sitting in a car in a rainstorm. In the punch line, we open the frame a bit and discover that the couple is sitting in a car, but the rain is being generated by a car wash. Or the punch line can answer the question posed in a way that reveals there is a completely different way to answer the question than you expected, as in the pun-based riddle "Where does the general keep his armies?" from the previous chapter. A joke is a mathematical equation with multiple possible solutions. It is a question with more than one right answer.

Small children will try to make up their own jokes. The first thing they grasp is that the punch line should be surprising. This is how we end up with jokes like "Why did the monkey eat a banana? Goldfish!" (Actual joke told to me by a four-year-old). But there is more to a joke than a surprising answer. In a strong joke, most likely to get laughter from multiple audiences over time, the punch line must not only be surprising but also satisfy the setup. It must defy our expectations but on further examination be just as correct an answer as the one we originally assumed. Ideally, it should be better. There should be information in the setup of the joke that we have ignored because of an assumption that it wasn't big enough or important enough or because some other earlier information anchored us on a different outcome. A punch line should not just cause us to think "I was wrong" but also "Of course! How could I have missed that?"

Jokes don't have to be fully verbal. A one-panel cartoon is a joke. Depending on the cartoon, the setup can be the picture and the punch line can be the written tag at the bottom of the picture or vice versa. Just like a verbal joke, you are looking to create a kind of equation where each side is roughly equal, so there shouldn't be something in the picture that isn't in some way, shape, or form addressed in the tagline at the bottom.

A headline from the parody newspaper (now online news site) *The Onion* is also a joke. It uses the fact of its parody as part of the setup. In a headline like "World Death Rate Holds Steady at 100 Percent" we jump to an assumption about the topic because we have assumptions associated with headlines in general.[1] The setup doesn't need to be particularly explicit because if a newspaper is reporting on the "World Death Rate," we are already assuming a certain kind of finish to the headline: that it would offer new information on a particular census or report, as opposed to an eternal truth on human mortality.

Comedic films, especially during the silent era, utilize gags—a sort of visual joke where we are set up through our limited vision of what we see, and when the angle of the frame shifts, we discover that we misunderstood the picture. At the end of Buster Keaton's film *One Week,* a couple is attempting to move their house to a new location, and it is stuck halfway across a set of railroad tracks with a train heading straight toward them. Just in time they jump out of the way, covering their eyes, and the train roars by—right past the house, on the track behind the one the house is sitting on. They hug each other with relief, only to have a train appear from the outside the frame in the opposite direction and smash the house to smithereens.

In sketch comedy, there is a kind of scenic joke known as a blackout—because the lights black out quickly after the scene is done to punctuate the joke. In a blackout the audience believes they are watching the beginning of a longer scene, but after a short period of time it is revealed that these assumptions are incorrect, and the sketch is quickly reframed with a joke punch line.

The early television comedian Ernie Kovacs used a kind of blackout in his various television sketch shows—frequently making use of visual or camera tricks (often in a way that was surreal). For example, a dial telephone is seen on camera and as expected, a finger comes in to dial it but surprisingly—and a bit disturbingly—does so by poking through the center of the dial.

Physical Comedy

The term *physical comedy* tends to conjure images of slapstick: someone slipping on a banana peel or having a cream pie hit them in the face. While this is iconic, I want to suggest that we broaden our definition of physical comedy. Think of physical comedy as comedy that is processed not through our cognition and understanding of words but through our senses. This definition of physical comedy allows us to include a number of elements that have always been a part of the comedian's toolbox, but rarely identified in this way.

This is also the place where we begin to recognize (as we will throughout this book) that often our comedy contains multiple components or that there is crossover between two categories. Some of what I discuss next also contains an element of joke, but the essence of the joke requires the physical element to work.

We can have comedy that is purely visual—objects that are out of proportion with their environment. One of my favorite examples of this is the Stay Puft Marshmallow Man in the film *Ghostbusters*, who is not only out of proportion to how we would normally see him as a picture on a package but is also incongruously threatening New York City. In addition, he is a familiar object that is out of place or (in this case) replacing a better-known monster film object: the giant attacking lizard.

There is a significant difference between a traditional setup and punch line joke and this kind of visual comedy. In a verbal or written joke, our experience is linear. The setup creates the expectation, and *then* the punch line reverses that expectation. In the second, we are aware of the expectation and the reversal of the expectation simultaneously.

We experience this simultaneous reversal of expectations when we see adult sunglasses on a baby. Or dachshunds dressed up as actual hot dogs in a bun. It's a baby and it's also a grown-up. It's a dog and it's also a hot dog (in which there is an added layer of a visual pun).

Caricatures are another kind of visual comedy that is based primarily in recognition: A picture reveals something we see when we look at another person while also being distorted. They are funny because they mimic how our brain works. We don't see everything equally. In the same way that small children may recognize their grandmother primarily by the color of her gray hair and thus see Grandma on the street in every woman whose hair is the same color, a caricature reveals that we know an actor more by his nose than by his entire face. And of course, a caricature includes elements of incongruity. There are multiple pain points here, since it is exactly the face and not really the face at all—it plays with our understandings of our own perceptions. Cartoons and puppets both seem to use a version of the same mechanism—they are funny to us because they both resemble and do not resemble the things they are portraying. This confusion is a kind of pain on its own as well as providing a layer of distance. Additionally, bad things can happen to cartoon characters, and we can laugh because they are not "real" to us. Puppets can wallop each other with sticks in ways that simulate human beatings, but their materials are so clearly not flesh that we can take pleasure in the simulated pain.

Returning briefly to the one-panel "gag" comics I mentioned earlier. An interesting aspect of these sorts of comics is that the setup and the punch line are available at the same time. However, unlike the earlier examples, we don't experience them simultaneously. Either the picture or the caption can be the punch line, and vice versa. The layering of expectation and fulfillment of that expectation happens as the eye travels from one to the other and back. One of my favorite *Far Side* cartoons, the one-panel comics by Gary Larson, depicts a farm covered in limp chicken bodies—above which a sign reads "Boneless Chicken Ranch." The joke works whether you start with the appearance of catastrophic chicken massacre or by reading the illogical sign above the farmyard.

One element of physical comedy that is rarely addressed is skill—we know what bodies can and cannot do, what is unusual, and what is hard for our own bodies to execute. Think about Charlie Chaplin roller-skating blindfolded at the edge of a balcony, or dancing gracefully with a balloon while dressed as Adolf Hitler. Mabel Normand, the first silent comedian to throw a pie, was known for terrifying stunts escaping down a two-hundred-foot rope ladder from a balloon. Martial artist/comedian Jackie Chan manipulates highly unusual objects in his fight choreography. There is, of course, a lot going on comedically here besides the skill aspect, but the skill involved adds yet another level.

One of my favorite assignments in my History of Comedy class is the vaudeville assignment. We discuss the ways that vaudeville and other types of variety theater like burlesque, cabaret, and music hall have an incentive to delight their audiences. Vaudeville acts were designed to pull audience attention, to engage. They were honed over time in front of many, many audiences and the goal was to get as much attention for your individual act from the audience as you could. Audiences are drawn to unusual or difficult physicality. The laughter that is generated here is also that of discovery or delight.

A comedian uses these skills in a different manner than an athlete or a dancer. The comedian plays with our expectations of what might happen—they exaggerate difficulty, surprise us with success, or make the impossible look simple. Just this past week, my students did an act that involved throwing an apple and catching it with a fork. Once the apple was impaled on a fork, it was thrown to someone else who caught it on another fork. It went back and forth until the apple resembled an odd kind of space satellite spiky with the handles of silverware. There is tension and release here as well as incongruity—we know what apples and forks are for, but we have never expected to see them used in this fashion. There is also our awareness of the seeming physical difficulty of this act, which appears possible for us to replicate on our own but not probable.

It's important to note that for physical comedy, we can use all five original senses, of which visual comedy is just one. Aural comedy includes sound effects, wordplay, and wit. There are words and sounds that tickle our ears—they just seem funnier to us than other words and sounds. My family used to make my daughter Nora laugh hysterically just by repeating a specific list of words: *bosom*, *cubicle*, *frequent*, *boating*, and *tufted headboard*.

In Neil Simon's play *The Sunshine Boys*, an old vaudevillian, Harvey, explains his theory about the sound of the letter *k*: "Fifty-seven years in this business, you learn a few things. You know what words funny and which words are not funny. *Alka Seltzer* is funny. You say 'Alka Seltzer,' you get a laugh. . . . Words with *k* in them are funny. *Casey Stengel*, that's a funny name. *Robert Taylor* is not funny. *Cupcake* is funny. *Tomato* is not funny. *Cookie* is funny. *Cucumber* is funny. *Car keys*. *Cleveland . . . Cleveland* is funny. *Maryland* is not funny. Then, there's *chicken*. *Chicken* is funny. *Pickle* is funny."

Richard Wiseman from the University of Hertfordshire found that people on his LaughLab website rating jokes about animals preferred the one that had the most *k* sounds in it.[2] It is possible that this is due to the association with taboo words: After all, the *k* sound also appears in four of the words in George Carlin's routine "Seven Words You Can Never Say on Television."

Certain perfumers and chefs coordinate their ingredients with wit or surprise in a manner that is comedic. I was lucky enough to eat at the Chicago restaurant Alinea, where I consumed a version of a peanut butter and jelly sandwich that was a single skewered peeled grape dipped in peanut puree and wrapped in a skin of toasted brioche. The phenomenon of jellybeans with flavors like "dirt," "earthworm," and "earwax" could also be said to provide a comedic experience.

I suggest we consider additional senses here as well, such as proprioception, time, and agency. Proprioception is our sense of our own body in space—how it moves and what it can do. Animated films will frequently play with that sense of proprioception. When we see a cartoon character's eyes bulge out of their head as if on springs, we have an awareness that bodies don't normally work like that, but they also "feel" as if they do. It is often difficult to analyze this type of physical comedy directly—the logic of this comedy is kinesthetic. It is based in our felt sense of our own bodies in space, how we move and behave and how other bodies should also move and behave: what it feels like to slip and fall or how the texture of cream pie would feel smashed onto the skin of our face. The recognition that sets up our expectations is often not cognitive and perhaps not even directly conscious.

As human animals we have an awareness of the speed at which humans should move, and anything that moves at a different rate is put into the category of "nonhuman." Comedy makers of the early silent film era saw an indirect benefit from the difficulty of matching the speed of any given film's exposure to the speed of a projector. The speed of the physical movement was always a little bit off, and thus easily used as a comedic effect.

We have another sense of time—how long things generally take or how much time has passed. Comedy can take advantage of that temporal awareness by shortening or lengthening our sense of how long a given activity takes. The "Chinese Restaurant" episode of the sitcom *Seinfeld*, in which the characters spend nearly the entire episode waiting for their table, not only uses this element but also plays with two different versions. The characters are restless with their long wait (despite repeatedly being told that it will be "five, ten minutes"). The viewing audience has an added tension given how long television characters normally wait for a table (usually no time at all).

Agency is our sense of whether we are moving ourselves or being moved by someone else. The laughter in comedies like *Meet Dave* or *Weekend at Bernie's* seems to be related to our understanding that bodies that aren't in control of themselves are funnier. Whether the body is actually a spaceship being piloted by aliens or a corpse propped up by former employees, we know that it is not moving itself but is instead being moved. A classic bit of physical comedy used by multiple comedians over the years is the person who is so drunk that they must intentionally and deliberately move themselves to do the simplest of activities like walk down a street or open a door.

Which brings me to what might be the most simple and surprisingly powerful sort of physical comedy: recognizable human behavior.

We love to watch people behaving the way people actually behave but in the slightly artificial environment of a stage or screen. There is a sort of deep recognition to this kind of comedy. As Sid Caesar said, "There's humor in the little things that people did. If you showed them how they looked when they did what they did, people would laugh."[3]

One of the tenets of the kind of improvisation I teach and practice is that in every exercise or game there is what master teacher Viola Spolin calls a "point of concentration."[4] The idea here is that an improv performer puts their attention on something they can actually do, something accomplishable, even (or especially) when the story is imaginary. You are working to keep your imaginary ball the same size and shape it was when you started. You have to make eye contact with your partner in order to talk, etc.

When an improviser is doing this, some aspect of artificiality goes away. From an audience's viewpoint, we sense that the performer is doing something rather than pretending to do something. This kind of presence is subtle and ephemeral, but it's also riveting and often very funny. Perhaps it is as basic as the fact that we are deeply fascinated with other people but are rarely given permission to watch what they do in any kind of detail. It is intimacy with people we don't know (recognition and pain, anyone?). And as long as we put it in a context where we feel safe for ourselves and the characters, it is one of the most natural and deep kinds of comedy there is.

Character

This brings me to the third component of comedy: character.

In general, verbal jokes don't travel well. Not geographically—most puns don't translate from one language to another for example. And not temporally—setting up an expectation requires that we have shared knowledge, experiences, and language, and the further we get from any given time, the less the jokes from that period have meaning, let alone connect in a way that makes us laugh. An old SCTV sketch has Joe Flaherty and Dave Thomas in a parody commercial touting a recording of "Shakespeare's Greatest Jokes"—and if you act now, "we'll send to you this volume of footnotes, to help you get the jokes you get."

But characters appear to be, if not eternal exactly, then definitely translatable across time and space. There are archetypes—characters we see again and again in variations across countries and across eras. These archetypes show up in ancient Greece and Rome, in Africa, the Indigenous peoples of the Americas, in East and Southeast Asian cultures. It appears that while what human beings know changes across time and geography, many of the essential elements of what human beings are and do is remarkably consistent.

The miserly old man appears first in ancient Greece and Rome, and then again in nearly the same form under the name of Pantalone in the commedia dell'arte in Renaissance Italy, before turning up in modern American cartoons as *SpongeBob SquarePants*'s Mr. Krabs and *The Simpsons*' Mr. Burns or in a live-action gender switch as Lucille Bluth in *Arrested Development.*

Perhaps the first and most widely spread comic character archetype is the Trickster. This character tends to be lower status, amoral, and wins or gets out of sticky situations through guile and cunning rather than through strength or fighting. In ancient cultures, the Trickster was often represented by an animal or insect—Anansi the spider in West Africa, Coyote in North America, foxes or monkeys in many Asian or East Asian cultures. Tricksters are self-serving rule breakers who undermine the structure of the system. They disguise themselves, improvise with things that are to hand, and often (if briefly) lay bare the foolishness and faults that also reside in the rich and powerful. Bugs Bunny is a more modern Trickster, as is Eddie Murphy (especially in his early film work), not to mention pretty much the entire ensemble of the television comedy *It's Always Sunny in Philadelphia.*

If jokes are predicated on the reversal of expectations, character comedy is based in the confirmation of expectations. Once we get to know a character, the joy is in watching them behave in the way we expect them to behave and in watching them do what we know they will do. This is the essence of television sitcom. We come to closely know a specific character or ensemble of characters. The premise of any given episode sets our favorite characters into motion; they get a new job, take up a dare, launch a scheme. We immediately begin to predict the difficulties they will get into. We know that Leslie Knope will try to do the absolute rightest thing possible even when any sane person would abandon such a plan. We watch Homer Simpson's inexplicable success in some new job or position knowing that his innate laziness and short attention span will ultimately trip him up. When Lucy Ricardo gets a job in a chocolate factory, the laughs that come from watching Lucy and her best friend Ethel as they stuff their faces, their shirts, and their hats with unwrapped chocolates owes some of its pleasure to the precision and adept physical comedy of the performers. But more is due to the fact that we love and know Lucy and anticipate that her strong belief that she can conquer any situation through sheer persistence and energy will result in a specific kind of wonderful mayhem. And that anticipation is rewarded—character comedy in a nutshell.

We love comedic characters in much the same way we love astrological signs or those four-letter Myers-Briggs types. We have a sense that human behaviors are often defined by a clear but narrow perspective on the world. Our experiences suggest that those perspectives fall into a set of similar types and categories. Comedic characters confirm this experience we have of the world, and actively validate our expectations with exaggerations of the behaviors we have observed in our daily lives.

Both tragic and comedic characters have flaws, but the flaws of comic characters are the first thing we are presented with when we meet them rather than discovered later. In this they resemble a common human experience. We look at ourselves in the mirror and focus on the imperfections—the too-large nose, the bushy eyebrows, the rounded belly—and create an internal vision of ourselves that is not unlike a carnival caricature. Comic characters take those exaggerated flawed versions of ourselves and others and bring them to walk in the world.

Even comic characters with wealth, status, and power are brought down to the place of the quotidian and everyday. In the pilot episode of *30 Rock*, Jack Donaghy's certainty in his own decisions and opinions is immediately undermined by his lack of any useful knowledge on which to base those decisions. His title, "Vice President of East Coast Television and Microwave Oven Programming," is not just incongruous—it also nails his perspective as someone who can oversee two completely incompatible areas for General Electric because he knows essentially nothing of either of them. Underneath his clarity of purpose lurks all-too-human imposter syndrome.

We can think of comedic characters in performance as existing roughly in three dimensions: persona characters, archetypal characters, and three-dimensional characters.

Persona is the embodiment of a specific comedian's point of view or angle on the world. For a stand-up comedian, their persona is often simply the stage manifestation of how they present themselves, just a slightly exaggerated version of who they are in their daily life. But the curation of a good stand-up persona is a fairly complex process. In everyday life, we all play a variety of personas, depending on the given situation in which we find ourselves: concerned parent, flirtatious date, efficient employee. And we play even more complex and varied personas with those who know us best: mischievous prankster, hopelessly unskilled human putting together IKEA furniture, possessor of unlimited knowledge of the Star Wars universe. In first-person comedy, personas create expectations for, and frame, jokes and stories presented to the audience. A stand-up persona needs to intersect with audience expectations of us based on how we present in the world. It also usually references personal chosen identity, how we wish to be seen. And (most importantly) it needs to be congruent with and support the content and style of comedy we choose to present. In this kind of comedy, the audience is strongly aware of the performer and often conflates the persona with the performer. They may assume that the persona displayed is authentic and that the performer is providing real information from their experience rather than constructed joke-driven stories.

The second is a simple archetypal character used most often in sketch comedy and is appropriately a kind of a sketch themself in the sense of being drawn simply without much added detail or depth. This kind of character is defined by one or two traits and has one simple and clear but exaggerated perspective. John Belushi's Samurai character from the early days of *SNL* has a variety of jobs, but within those jobs his perspective is that he is always looking to cut things into pieces with a sword. Like Cecily Strong's "Girl You Wish You Hadn't Started a Conversation with at a Party" or "One-Dimensional Female Character," he doesn't even have a real name, but he does have a clear purpose. This sort of character might show up in a longer narrative film or play but usually briefly in service of a joke or plot twist.

Also, because, in general, this kind of character is transparent, we are very aware of the performer underneath.

Finally, there are detailed three-dimensional comic characters. These characters still have strong comedic perspectives and flaws and may have essential strong wants, but they have layers to them that can be revealed through and sustain longer comic narratives. They still demonstrate something about a given comedian's point of view or comedic voice, but that comedian is obscured by the mask of the character. These characters are not necessarily realistic, but they can inhabit multiple realities and occupations. They can pursue different objectives depending on their situation. Groucho Marx is always Groucho whether we see him as Professor Quincy Adams Wagstaff creating havoc on a college campus in *Horse Feathers* or Rufus T. Firefly the unlikely leader of the nation of Freedonia in *Duck Soup*. Mae West can act as a con woman posing as a music hall star or a lion tamer in the circus, but she is always the same sexually provocative dame looking for a man to "come up and see me sometime."

In more modern comedies, these characters maintain their essential comedic qualities but have the ability to grow, change, and make discoveries about themselves, especially over the course of longer modern-style sitcom narratives. Lucy Ricardo approached every new challenge with a deep belief in her ability to accomplish anything she set her mind on, while never learning to second-guess her lack of competence. But in *The Mindy Project*, Mindy Lahiri—played by show creator and head writer Mindy Kaling—can transcend a natural self-centeredness and lack of boundaries to build better relationships with the people she loves. Even an over-the-top character like Moira from *Schitt's Creek* discovers layers of connection and humanity under her (admittedly very thick) facade of extravagant artificiality and superiority.

Narrative

There are certain forms of narrative that are unique to comedy. The revue sketch, the farce, and the sitcom share a common narrative device: A simple problem, misunderstanding, or discovery is heightened credibly and logically but not rationally.

Improvisers are taught to create this sort of comedy by playing what is known as the game of the scene. Once they have established a clear exposition, they seize on the first unusual element of the scene and explore and heighten that element, asking themselves, "If this unusual thing is true, then what else is true?"[5]

A simple example of this sort of game-based scene is the vaudevillian Abbott and Costello sketch "Who's on First?," where Lou Costello is repeatedly confused by ball players with last names that correspond to common questions and phrases.

Early film shorts and cartoons apply a version of this process to simple activities and environments with premises that rely on a seemingly simple task that is somehow impossible to complete. In their Oscar-winning short *The Music Box*, Laurel and Hardy are tasked with delivering a piano to a house, which shouldn't be too difficult . . . until they discover that the house is at the top of a steep flight of stairs. At each point where they appear to have success, some small reversal occurs that causes the entire process to begin again.

A classic stage or film farce will set multiples of these games in motion simultaneously so that each builds its own logic while also intersecting with—and thus heightening—other games. As John Cleese says, "The perfect farce script is like clockwork; the writer winds it up by carefully establishing certain credible premises, and then lets the whole thing unwind with inevitable but startling logic."[6]

The key to these sorts of structures is that while the characters may be aware they are speaking or behaving in a way that is fundamentally irrational, they must also have a strong and recognizable reason to continue to "play" or attempt to "win the game" in the moment of action. The classic sitcom ensemble intersects neatly with this requirement, providing characters with clear flaws and narrow comic perspectives on the world that can provide motivation for irrational behavior. It's notable that one way to write sitcom using this structure is to do so backward. I will go into this in more detail later in the book, but in short, creating a plot for an episode of *I Love Lucy* might start with the question "What do I want to see Lucy do?" and then, step by step, create a logical progression from an answer to that question. For instance, I might say I want to see Lucy stomp grapes, and work from that climactic moment back to its source (in this case, a chance meeting with an Italian filmmaker on a train).

One of the oldest sorts of comic narrative does not follow a traditional "story" pattern. Variety narratives, such as vaudeville or music hall shows, structures for improvised comedy, classic sketch revue running orders, and stand-up set lists are forms of comedic narrative. All of these have an intentional structure that seeks to create a specific kind of comic experience for an audience. This kind of comic narrative uses variety of style, energy, speed, and size to take the audience on a journey that may not have a direct sequence of causality but nevertheless builds and creates an integrated experience.

Longer comedic narratives will often use (or, in the case of parody, directly borrow) traditional dramatic structures. Even then, a variety structure is still visible underneath, as in the anarchic comedies of the Three Stooges or parody films like *Airplane*. A comedy that uses a more dramatic-style narrative will usually strongly feature the other comedy components.

Comedic narrative often uses an extended or repeated joke structure. Like a good joke, a comic narrative sets up an expectation of what will happen in the story and then reverses that expectation or confirms it in a manner that is in some way surprising or novel. Think of a Road Runner / Wile E. Coyote cartoon short. The expectation is set early that the coyote wants to catch the roadrunner. From then on, the narrative consists of the coyote laying ever more complex or unusual traps (setups) that then fail (reverse) in ever more interesting and unusual ways. The fact that the traps fail confirms our expectations, but the comedy is also in guessing and being surprised at the exact ways they do so.

Unlike in jokes, the reversal in a comedic narrative rarely reverses expectations entirely. We don't discover that we are following an entirely new story at every turning point. The coyote doesn't catch the roadrunner and eat it. Nor do any of the coyote's mishaps with various traps, explosives, or falling anvils lead to his permanent death or dismemberment.

The reader is rarely confused or unsure at the outset of this kind of comedic story: Clear exposition sets up expectations. Again, those expectations can and often are mistaken or reversed, sometimes quickly, as in James Thurber's "The Secret Life of Walter Mitty," whose opening paragraph catapults the reader onto a navy hydroplane entering a hurricane—only to reveal in the next paragraph that all of this action is taking place in the mind of a dreamy middle-aged man driving a car. But once the pattern of daydreaming has been established, it can repeat and create tension through delaying the expected shift from fantasy to real life and back again.

Steven Kaplan defines film comedy as requiring the presence of a central comic character, “Comedy is about an ordinary guy or gal struggling against insurmountable odds without many of the required skills and tools with which to win and yet never giving up hope.”[7]

One clear sign that we are in the audience of a comedy is a distinct and novel point of view. Charlie Chaplin has been quoted as saying “Comedy is life viewed from a distance.” Elaine May agrees that distance is important but suggests the opposite direction: “The difference between comedy and romance and tragedy is that in comedy you do every detail and in romance and tragedy you do a sweep. If you kill yourself in a drama, you take the gun and you shoot yourself. If you kill yourself in a comedy, there are no bullets. You have to go buy some. You don’t have any money; you have to borrow some. You have to have your ID. It just goes on.”[8]

Point of View

Point of view is the component of comedy that describes the outside perspective a comedian brings to their work. We could also call this their voice. The physical manifestation is their persona. Of course all narrative to some extent or another has a point of view—first-person, omniscient, third-person. Most films are shot clearly from a perspective. But the way point of view manifests itself is functionally different in comedy than in drama. A comedian provides us with a consistent awareness that someone is telling the story and their voice is speaking directly to us. It is telling us how to play, trying to make us do something (laugh, among other things). It is manipulating us and intentionally sharing a perspective.

Comedy is a dialogue with the audience. It can be direct and presentational, as in stand-up; it can be loose with a level of cocreation, as in improvisation. In the case of narrative comedy in films, theater, or television, that dialogue may be more indirect, but it is always definitely there. This is what physical comedian John Wright calls “complicity with the audience.”[9] The audience, whether physically present (as in a theater or comedy club) or virtually present (while watching at home) has a role to play. But who exactly are they playing with?

When an actor is playing a part in a comedy, there is an awareness of the performer inside the character that we don't get in a dramatic role. In comedy, we see the humans behind the characters. This is true even in the cases of the great character performers who disappear into their characters, like Catherine O'Hara, Lily Tomlin, or Whoopi Goldberg. We still know there is someone who is commenting on the character as well as portraying them.

A comedian functions like a camera—showing the audience the world from a particular angle and through a particular lens. That angle and lens is formed first by the experiences, knowledge, interests and preferences of the individual comedian. They are providing their understanding of what is true, what is painful, and their own distance on those things. But it is a curation of those things designed to provoke humor in an audience.

Persona—as I mentioned earlier—is the intersection of character and point of view. It is an intentionally chosen manifestation of the comedian's frame and filter, but one shaped by how audiences perceive them in performance as well as being the right vehicle for the comedian's material.

Parody is a point of view turned onto an author, work, or genre for comic effect. Satire is taking a POV and focusing it outward to expose and criticize stupidity or vices, particularly in the context of contemporary politics or other topical issues.

Groups of comedians collaborating together will often have a collective point of view that is distinct from the perspectives of the members of the ensemble in their solo work. Writing jokes for a late-night host's monologue or a network sitcom requires an ability to write in someone else's point of view. We love our favorite comedy shows because they have a specific voice and perspective on the world—often one that matches our own.

The creator of a character is showing the audience something about humanity. "See how people who are parents do this thing?" "See how this type of person behaves when they have power?" Characters also have their own point of view. It's likely that the character's point of view is different than the creator's. So you have POV within POV—and if the characters are writers who write characters who have points of view it could go on and on into infinity—a kind of comedy version of the recursive Droste effect.

All comedy has a point of view of some sort. One signal quality of comedy is the audience's awareness of framing and filtering. This is the essential thing behind the doubleness I described in the section on visual comedy. I see something, and some other "I" sees it too but sees it from a different angle and in a different way. This other "I" could be another person, it could be ourselves in the past or future, but a significant part of our experience of comedy is in this sense of multiple versions of the same story happening simultaneously. We discover that what we thought was true is not quite true, or that as in an optical illusion, where, say, the silhouette of two faces turns into a picture of a vase and then back again the longer we look at it, there is another way of seeing that changes the picture itself. Or conversely, we discover that a thought, experience, or observation of the world that we assumed to be uniquely our own is shared by someone else.

Modern Western comedy seems to value point of view more highly than at any other time in history. A significant change occurred in American comedy in the mid-1950s with comedians like Mort Sahl, Lenny Bruce, and Dick Gregory, whose material was funny not because of the jokes they told but because of how their point of view informed the material they performed. Steve Martin took it even further when he created his stand-up act in the 1960s and '70s, providing the point of view of "joke" often without including any of the actual joke content. In our current comedy environment, it is possible for something to be funny merely because of how it clearly fits into the point of view of the person making the observation—no overt joke necessary.

You could say that old-school jokes, the ones people used to share with each other by prefacing the telling with "Do you want to hear a joke?," are one of the only components of comedy without a point of view. But even those have now been assigned a perspective and persona. Go online and search for "dad jokes" and you'll find hundreds of traditional jokes of the sort that populate "joke books," although a modern stand-up comedian would be mocked by audiences and pilloried by fellow comedians if they elected to tell those jokes in a club. Unless, of course, they elect to frame those jokes through an ironic point of view of some sort. For a classroom stand-up assignment, I once had a female student read a series of misogynistic jokes in a deadpan persona. In this instance, the comedy was in her choice of and point of view on the content of the original jokes.

While it is useful to look at the components separately the component structure is more useful for analyzing existing comedy. They provide a variety of access points for thinking about how we create and revise the comedy we make. Our first clue that we are watching a comedic narrative is often the presence of jokes. Great physical comedians from Cantinflas to Gilda Radner also play memorable comic characters.

Part of the brilliance of the stand-up comedian Richard Pryor was his command of all five components simultaneously. In his film *Richard Pryor: Live in Concert* the jokes are abundant from an authentic and dark point of view as he takes his audience through the story of his heart attack. He realistically physically embodies himself writhing in pain on the ground. While doing so, he switches effortlessly between three different characters: his terrified persona, God's not particularly attentive telephone operator ("I'll have to put you on hold"), and his angry heart ("Were you trying to talk to God behind my back?").

My personal favorite moment of the concert film though is a piece of deftly observed and executed physical comedy. Pryor is telling a story about hunting with his father, making the sound effects of sticks crunching beneath their feet as they stalk a deer. In a neat narrative twist, he adds in a sound effect that briefly calls back an earlier bit about a horny squirrel monkey. And then suddenly, he is still. All by himself, dressed in his sweat-stained silky red shirt and black pants, he is also the essence of a deer, about to take a drink and then suddenly suspicious and aware of being watched. All five components of comedy come together, and the joke is the least important part.

Or is there really even a joke there at all? Does there need to be?

4 THICK AND THIN COMEDY

In his book *Ha!*, Scott Weems describes a study by the Stanford psychologist Andrea Samson, who

> instructed subjects to view cartoons that either included background incongruities or omitted them entirely. For purposes of experimental control, two versions of each cartoon were used: an "extra-incongruity" one and a realistic one. Subjects saw mixes of each and were tasked with rating how funny they thought each was. For example, one cartoon showed a mother and father penguin standing in the Antarctic wilderness, celebrating with wild gesticulations: "He just spoke his first word," one says. "Great, what is it? Mama? Papa?," says the other. The second panel shows both penguins standing next to their offspring, who is exclaiming, "Damned cold!" In the realistic version, the words remained the same, but the penguins were replaced by Eskimos.[1]

As a comedy maker and teacher, I find this study interesting but also a bit frustrating. It is useful to understand that a joke or piece of comedy can be funnier if there are additional comedic elements. But my experience as a maker of comedy is that you can't just add an unrelated joke to a sketch or an unusual element to a cartoon and have the result be funnier. In fact, usually the opposite is true.

I would propose that rather than thinking of these as "background incongruities," we see them as part of a larger whole. The joke itself might be the base comedy. But the visual comedy provided by the penguins isn't extraneous—it is part of what makes the joke work. The penguins bring layers to the comedy: The picture itself is funnier because penguins are generally seen as especially comic. Among other reasons, we recognize a kind of human shape in penguins, but they are also distinctly birds. There is added incongruity because these particular penguins can speak. And finally, unlike the people in the neutral cartoon who are wearing clothing, the penguins are out in the cold without any observable insulation. They have it, of course, but we can't see it, so there is an additional pain element of thinking about whether/when penguins really do get cold.

The comedian in me also wants to point out that the language of the joke in this experimental cartoon has a fundamental flaw in it. The baby (whether penguin or human) didn't actually say their first word, they said their first *words* (plural). If you change the dialogue to read, "He just spoke his first words," and "What were they? *Mama*? *Papa*?" the specific logic/recognition in the joke works better. And weirdly, it doesn't matter that the second parent gets that logic wrong. What matters is that the setup "baby's first words" agrees grammatically with the punch line "Damned cold."

The change I made to the joke's wording makes it work better. Switching to penguins from Eskimos also makes it funnier and work better. Especially since using "Eskimos"—a stereotypical depiction of the Indigenous peoples who inhabit the Arctic regions of the North American continent—may have made the original cartoon less funny to many viewers.

If we are searching for how to make things funnier, we need to think of comedy as not being just one thing at a time or a hierarchy with a single joke at the top of the heap. I would suggest that it is more useful for comedy creators to think of each moment of comedy as consisting of multiple layers. Some comedy is thin—that is, it uses just one or maybe two components in relatively simple ways. For example, a one-panel cartoon is a physical comedy joke. Thin comedy contains just one or two of the comedy components, and components such as narrative and point of view are less likely to be used comedically on their own. But thin comedy is not just defined by the presence of only one comedy component; it is also defined by the relative value or complexity of the elements of recognition and pain. Thin comedy uses one of a handful tactics, often surprise, shock, or incongruity, to create pain. The recognition in thin comedy is that of mistake or taboo.

You may have heard the old saying that puns are the "lowest" form of comedy. This isn't necessarily true, but a simple pun is a very good example of thin humor. The pain trigger is a mistake. You thought you understood a word based on context clues, but you got the wrong meaning. Or you heard a joke, and you weren't aware of a homophone that has a different spelling from the word you assumed you heard. The recognition in a pun is tied directly to that error: You discover that the word in question has more than one meaning.

Some examples of thin comedy across the different components include fart jokes, foul language, slapstick, sarcasm, non sequiturs, repeating what happened earlier to get a laugh without expanding on it. Or the kind of reference comedy that relies solely on simple recognition such as referring to well-known commercial tagline ("Where's the beef?!" Or "Can you hear me now?"). A stand-up visiting a town will drop the name of a well-known local suburb or part of town to get a laugh. In Chicago, Schaumburg is shorthand for "obvious parochial suburban location," which is helped by the fact that Schaumberg is a funny-sounding name, which thickens the comedy but only a little. Thin comedy generally doesn't wear well. You might laugh very hard at a thin joke the first time you hear it, but it will often be significantly less funny the second time around.

Thick comedy uses multiple components at the same time, and more complex filters that convey value, like irony. Thick comedy generally rewards multiple viewings or listenings either through the discovery of previously unnoticed layers or because the pleasure of the initial laugh wasn't just tied to the discovery of new information. Recognition in thick comedy may be connected to a resonant truth about human behavior as opposed to a simple piece of information.

Examples of thick comedy include satire, highly skilled physical comedy, jokes that come out of an understanding of character motivation or history. A "thick" callback sheds new light on some earlier aspect of a joke or narrative moment rather than just returning to it.

This isn't a binary. Think of comedy as existing on a spectrum from thin to thick. A visual joke is a little bit thicker than a pun because it uses two components. A pie in the face is a thin piece of physical comedy. It's thicker if we add the component of character either of the one throwing or the one receiving that pie. A comedian telling a "dad joke" to an audience in a club is doing something different than a dad does when he repeats that joke to his family. For the comedian there is an intentional point-of-view frame around the choice to tell the joke in that space to that audience, and that makes the club moment of comedy thicker. Very thick comedy like the work of satiric comedic filmmaker Taika Waititi may contain so many levels and layers that it ceases to pull laughs even while the overall effect remains comedic.

Credit for this way of framing comedy goes to my colleague Jennifer Ellison, Second City's creative director and an adjunct professor at Columbia College Chicago and DePaul University. At a conference about the connections between behavioral science and humor that we put together at The Second City in 2016, there was a discussion of the difference between comedy that "works"—that is, comedy that gets a laugh from its intended audience—and our personal perception of "good comedy"—comedy that is better or richer in some meaningful way. Jen drew from her background in teaching ethics and the philosophical idea of thick and thin concepts. Certain words are descriptive, and other words contain a deeper sense of evaluative meaning.

Some comedy is just meant to get a laugh from an audience and other comedy communicates deeper value and meaning through its use of multiple components, especially those of character and point of view. Jen is quick to point out that in her experience, thin comedy is not necessarily better than thick. Rather, they both have functions and uses:

> We require a whole spectrum of thick and thin in order for us to enjoy longer-form comedy. It's more meal based than it is snack based. A snack is like a knock-knock joke. Something that is more meal based is something like a comic film. Those require some things that are thinner and some things that are thicker like the ways in which the characters interact with each other and their thoughts and feelings about the world

> around them and how that expresses the larger idea of the film. It's both. "I'm going to do this dumb joke about butts" and "This is the way I feel about my own inability to grow over time à la *Groundhog Day*."

In a Second City show, we use short joke scenes called blackouts throughout the revue. We use blackouts for several reasons—to showcase a cast member who hasn't been seen in the show for a bit, to cover for someone who needs to do a complicated costume change, or just to vary the energy of the show. But one specific reason we will use a blackout is to get the audience thinking as a unit. When an audience laughs together, they are having roughly the same thought at the same time. Of course, we can't be sure that everyone is thinking the exact same thing, but with what we call a "hard laugh"—a loud, immediate laugh from the entire audience—they are certainly having the same response to a specific stimulus. This audience unity is very useful if we are about to introduce a more challenging or complex piece of comedy. Sometimes the best way to do that is to use a thin joke or a thin joke element. Sheldon Patinkin, a founding Second City director and longtime head of the Columbia College Theater Department, used to say, "Sometimes a groan is as good as a laugh." In other words, an obviously thin joke that the audience knows and has heard before will still provoke the same simultaneous response.

A thin joke repeated loses its novelty and will no longer make its audience laugh, but you can create a barrage of thin jokes or add multiple toppers that build off one initial punch line and, with skill and timing, create something thicker. You can use the fact that a joke is familiar and easy and repeat it in a way that turns it into a game. *The Muppet Show* used to pride themselves on this: If a joke was thin, they would repeat it until it became a running gag, something the audience was looking for and anticipating. The experience of looking for that shared joke became a source of the audience's laughter and as a result, a thicker experience.

Having awareness of thin elements can make you a better comedy creator. Expletives and foul language may trigger shock laughter on their own, but it's often thin comedy. Jerry Seinfeld consciously took all of the swear words out of his comedy monologues, theorizing that if the joke didn't work without them in it, then the joke didn't work.

This is different from how 1950s stand-up comedian Lenny Bruce used foul language. Bruce was making his audience aware that he was a rule breaker in an era in which rule breaking was desperately feared. His intentional use of "obscene" language was designed to demonstrate the effects of that fear. Unlike the comedy Seinfeld was working on, Bruce's use of foul language was not thin and joke based. It was thicker, with a strong and topical point of view in addition to the content of the joke itself.

There are certain sketch premises that I refer to in rehearsal as "magical ponies," from a scene created in one of my classes. The performers were playing magical ponies that ate magical oats. That was the entire premise. Paper thin. But every time we put that sketch up in rehearsal, the rest of the cast would die laughing. There was a bit of comedy to be mined from the narrative premise, but what really made it funny to the ensemble was the playfulness of the participants and what their castmates knew about the personalities of the performers.

Thin comedy relies heavily on an entire audience having roughly the same experience at the same time. If a sketch has only has one simple game and a significant segment of the audience is confused by that game, the piece won't get a strong response. The "Magical Ponies" sketch played to resounding silence from the audience when it was put early in the show but got significantly more laughs when I moved it toward the end of the act. The comedy was automatically thicker because the audience had seen the performers in other contexts and had started to get to know their point of view and (like the other members of the cast) understand how and why this particular sketch connected to that point of view.

In practice, it isn't necessary to use just one component of comedy in order to provide the required elements of recognition, pain, and distance to create laughter in your given audience. Steve Martin's stand-up act in the 1970s could have been perceived as too painful because of the tension he created by removing traditional punch lines and relying on the failures of his persona, but the presence of familiar vaudeville-style physical comedy created both recognition and distance. Audiences may find taboo-based comedy off-putting or offensive, but distance can be provided by the presence of a familiar and safe performer or character. The comedian Moms Mabley was doing fairly explicit sexual jokes with a decidedly feminist edge during the early part of the twentieth century. The sassy old lady character she assumed provided both distance and recognition that allowed her audience to laugh.

When I directed the final show for comedian John Reynolds's class in the Second City Conservatory Program, we had an ongoing issue. John is now known primarily as a comic actor in shows like *Search Party*. His comic sensibility as a writer is very dark, offbeat, and relies heavily on taboo and non sequitur. He pitched sketch after sketch in class that I could see would be very funny in a room full of people who closely shared his sensibility but was likely to be off-putting to most. I struggled with how to help adjust his ideas to create comedy for a general audience that didn't have the very specific ironic distance on taboo subjects that John enjoyed. I like John and while the kind of comedy he liked wasn't my personal taste, what *was* funny to me was understanding why it was funny to him. It was a kind of metacomedy; he was enjoying the idea of forcing an audience to sit through something uncomfortable. Not unlike Eric Andre, he was making comedy that was most interesting to think about after the fact rather than enjoy in the moment. And understanding that is how I solved the puzzle as a director. Within the context of each sketch premise, there was very little way to give an audience enough distance to enjoy the absurdity the way John enjoyed it—especially since many of the sketches were ironically referencing very disturbing items from contemporary news.

But what I could do was to create distance by adding layers of character and point of view. So I had John write a short monologue in which he told the audience that he was deeply angry with me, his director, because I had refused to put what he considered his best work into the show. He then sat down and read for them the list of (actual) premises he had pitched to me. The audience loved it.

Let's break this down so we can see all of the layers. He started with several initial thin sketch premises that would likely shock the bulk of our audience. It might get some laughs for that reason (and maybe get louder laughs from one or two audience members). It would be very difficult to sustain those laughs throughout the sketch. By having John read the pitch to the audience rather than performing the sketch in full, we made the idea thicker by clearly filtering the premise through his onstage persona (and thus added distance). Each premise read was a joke with the implied setup "What is the darkest/worst possible idea for a sketch?" We piled on other equally shocking pitches and ordered them so that they got progressively more offensive. The audience was laughing not just at the shock but also at the escalation of absurdity and awkwardness. They got to imagine the pain of another audience being forced to watch these uncomfortable scenes (thus generating a kind of internal comic narrative).

The audience got to recognize and enjoy a character version of John (much more obtuse about why these sketches wouldn't work than in real life) and imagine how I and the members of John's ensemble might have tried to handle having to watch these scenes in rehearsal every week. This particular ensemble included Shantira Jackson, who went on to write for Amber Ruffin (among others). Shantira's sensibility is both more sincere and deeply sillier than John's. You could imagine making eye contact with Shantira during class and sharing the thought "What is going on with this dude?"

More characters and recognition on multiple levels. There was a brief hit of pain from each absurd or transgressive idea but also the incongruity of imagining those sketches on the stage. I would add that I think there was some even deeper recognition at work. One of the things I personally enjoyed about the sketch was that all of the pitches he listed were ones he actually had pitched in class. The audience got to enjoy genuinely getting to know John's ironic point of view, but from a truly safe distance.

It's important to note that I didn't "fix" the jokes—I adjusted them to the taste of the audience who would be coming to watch this particular show. There are undoubtedly audience members who enjoy John's comedy straight up without any of the distance I created. To be effective at creating comedy, we need to pay attention to the way our personal taste informs how we feel about the comedy we watch.

Taste, Hack, and Watching Comedy as a Comedian

One way to become funnier is to study the work of other comedians. For most of us it was one comedian or set of comedians that got us interested in making comedy in the first place. We watched Carole Lombard in a 1930s screwball film comedy or George Lopez do stand-up because our dad made us watch them (so many of us had our first comedy experience thanks to our dads). Or we discovered a particular comedian on our own on TikTok or YouTube—a lot of my students have a deep and abiding love for Bo Burnham or Quinta Brunson because they found them online early on. And we got interested. How did they do that? Could *we* do that?

It's useful to check out comedy beyond our initial personal favorites. Watching and listening to comedians from other eras and other disciplines can open up all sorts of avenues for our own comedic work in terms of forms and styles. I've had students who thought they were comic actors fall in love with stand-up after watching how Phyllis Diller combined one-liners with an over-the-top persona or standups who had their minds blown by the physical clowning of early silent film. As a comedy maker, I find that having a broad and deep knowledge of comedians and comedy styles has practical value. When I come up against a comedy "problem"—when there's a joke or a premise that I know has potential but I can't quite figure out how to execute it—I can think of another comedian whose work I know and ask myself how they might solve the problem. That opens up a whole slew of options I didn't have before.

We all have personal comedy preferences. Some people really like humor of tension and discomfort. Others—for example, me—don't. I can fully recognize the artful way the comedian Ziwe satirizes the lies people tell about race and gender through the deadpan verbal traps she builds when she interviews real-life guests on her show. Or how sketch comedian Tim Robinson stacks absurd discomfort upon discomfort until his characters explode. I get how that reflects something humans experience in the world right now. Both comedians create really good comedy. But it's not what I watch when I want something that I know will bring me pleasure. I like my comedy just a little bit nicer, more personal, and full of referential jokes that reflect the art, news, and literature I consume.

Your personal comedy taste is informed by your family, friends, mentors, and the values of your community. My father took me to see showings of 1930s witty comedies *The Thin Man*, *His Girl Friday*, and *To Be or Not to Be.* I wasn't allowed to stay up late to watch *Saturday Night Live*, but I had "cool" friends in grade school who introduced me to Gilda Radner and Jane Curtin. A box of paperback books I bought at a garage sale—yes, I was a weird kid who bought books at garage sales—was where I discovered writers like Dorothy Parker, Fran Leibowitz and "housewife humorists" like Peg Bracken and Jean Kerr. In middle school I aspired to be part of a crowd that could quote large chunks of Monty Python sketches at the drop of a hat, and my high school boyfriend worshipped the Marx Brothers. Later I watched Nichols and May, and was reinforced in my preferences by my professors in college and my early mentors at The Second City to view certain kinds of comedy as better and more worthwhile. Despite some early exposure to Dick Gregory and Whoopi Goldberg, most of my comedy taste was influenced by watching white comedians.

I prefer comedy of wit and certain sorts of satire, but that doesn't mean that other types of comedy are bad or less worthwhile. As a comedy history teacher, I've struggled with the way that academia has generally praised "high" comedy (comedy of wit and manners and social or political satire) and decried "low" comedy (comedy of the body, falling down, comedy about sex or bodily functions). One reason for my discomfort is that what is termed "low comedy" is often the comedy of the poor and the oppressed peoples of the world. I was lucky that my comedy education involved quite a few female comedy role models, and I do my very best to provide a variety of comedians and comic points of view to my students, but at the same time, I'm aware that the examples in this book reflect my own taste and the comedy I know best. Even after all the cuts I've made as I've edited, I'm pretty sure that there's still a bit too much Groucho and Seinfeld.

If you view comedy through the lens of the comedy triad, it's clear that what is funny is relative. It is reflective of each person's experiences and knowledge, their traumas (or lack thereof), and the coping mechanisms they have developed. But our personal taste in comedy is more than just what we find funny or laugh at.

In 2007, the writer and professional provocateur Christopher Hitchens wrote an article titled "Why Women Aren't Funny."[2] This one article spawned a series of editorials, blog posts, and (at least in my little corner of the world) many, many panel discussions in which the question posed by the article was gnawed over exhaustingly. It's a little embarrassing that we all took it so seriously, because the answer is very clear. Since comedy is relative, it's not that women aren't funny—it's that women aren't funny *to Christopher Hitchens and others like him*. Those men (and some people who are not men) aren't interested in the experiences of half of the people who share their world. They don't know or care about what other people recognize or find too painful. It is also no surprise that the people who are not in the most dominant parts of a society are going to have a pretty good grasp of what might be funny to those in power. Understanding what is recognizable, painful, and safe for the people in charge is a strong and appropriate defense mechanism, and when you understand the joke, you are also likely to find it at least mildly funny.

I believe it's important to differentiate here between comedy that "works"—meaning that it gets a laugh from its intended given audience—and comedy that is "good" (or "bad" for that matter). There is a righteous (and I believe somewhat appropriate) dislike in the comedy community for "hack" comedy. At base, hack is types of jokes or specific comedy tropes that are done too often. But getting any given set of comedians to truly define "hack" is difficult if not impossible. There is always a group that staunchly defends the position of "as long as they laugh, it's good." It's possible to take an obvious overused joke and then play with it until it both represents the original joke and also its opposite, irony squared. There are comedians who do that brilliantly. But that's not really "hack." True hack reveals some level of disdain for the audience beyond using elements that are tired or formulaic.

I do think there is value in having criteria to evaluate comedy beyond our personal relative taste. The most obvious is laughter. Did we laugh? Did the audience laugh? It's not a bad metric. After all, laughter is a measure of whether a joke or moment "worked." And any comedian worth their salt places a high value on jokes or moments that create a hard laugh. When you get one of those, you know you have succeeded in getting your audience members to have roughly the same response at the same time and that the response is at least partially involuntary. The balance of recognition, pain, and distance in that comic moment or joke have come together in a way that works for many people in apparently the same fashion. You can use those laughs to build a repertoire of comedy that does the same thing not just for that one audience but for multiple audiences over time.

Is a joke that gets a hard laugh from a variety of audiences the best joke? It isn't true of my favorite joke, and I'll guess that it isn't true of your personal favorite joke. Your favorite joke is one that feels personal to you—it hits you right at your personal points of truth and pain and distance.

There is such a thing as getting too many laughs. A few years ago I directed a particularly smart and funny Second City touring company. They were so driven to wring every bit of laughter that could be had out of every moment of every single sketch that the audience's huge level of enjoyment of individual moments got in the way. There were lots of laughs, but the experience ended up feeling incomplete because the audience (and the cast) lost the sense of the whole. Telling a group of young comedians to "get fewer laughs" did not go over very well. But when they did, the show was more effective. A good sketch show, stand-up set, or comic play needs to contain ebbs and flows. Giving an audience opportunities to take a break as well as laugh hysterically actually builds laughs over the course of the performance.

There are lots of laughs we may not want to get—a laugh at the expense of someone else. The "blood in the mouth" laugh is one where the audience is laughing at the wrong person or thing. It's a laugh that the comedian didn't intend to get, or at least not for that reason.

In the late 1980s and early 1990s there were a number of one-man stand-up-style shows, with names like *Don't Bother Me in My Man Cave*, making the rounds in small professional venues. This is not a real title—in fact, I'm pretty sure the term *man cave* didn't come into general use until much later—but you get the idea: straight white male comedians purporting to be making fun of men by channeling a series of sexist characters. I recall sitting in the audience of one of these shows and coming to the realization that there was something wrong in the response of the audience around me. The audience wasn't laughing at the chauvinist character—they were laughing at the jokes the character was telling. And the butt of those jokes wasn't men at all—it was women. The performers in this case had deniability ("I didn't tell that joke; my character did"). But the effect on the audience was the same as if the performer had told the joke himself.

I find that learning how to think about, analyze, and evaluate comedy of all kinds gives my students tools that are useful when they create and revise their own work.

Analyzing Comedy Someone Else Has Created

First, do some objective analysis of the work in question. Ask these questions:

- Which of the five components of comedy are being used?
- What kinds of recognition and pain show up?
- What techniques are used to provide distance for the audience?
- What filters and framing does a comedian use to define their point of view?

Let's start by looking at Jerry Seinfeld's often-imitated "Airport" set. He's a notable joke writer, and jokes are at the core of this piece. Almost no physical comedy besides his distinctive vocal rhythm (lots of repetition of words and phrases) and musicality (listen to how he hits high notes at a number of places and how he uses it to punch jokes). The narrative is linear and direct—he takes us through airport security, into the airport, and eventually on to the plane just before takeoff. Most of the character information is observed from the outside. What really distinguishes Seinfeld is his point of view. I would argue that his framing is extremely close up. He is obsessed with minutiae: The entire set is a series of extreme close-ups (the zipper on the security guard's pants, the faucets in the airport bathrooms, the slot for used razor blades in the bathroom on the plane). He commonly uses the joke filters of exaggeration and misplaced focus. His personal filter is one of general annoyance or crankiness, which is reminiscent of the complaining tone of classic Borscht Belt comedians.

The points of recognition in Seinfeld's act are obvious—he is discussing a fairly mundane experience common to anyone who travels in the modern world. The pain points are similar, the many tiny cuts of discomfort and annoyance that accompany air travel. His skill, the specificity of his point of view, and the low stakes of the topics at hand all create distance for the audience.

Once you have done this, you can look at the audience response. If comedy is created intentionally to provoke laughter or humor responses in a specific audience, then it's appropriate to ask whether and how this has been done. To be more specific, ask these questions:

- Did it make the audience laugh?
- Does it appear that the audience laughed when and where the comedian(s) intended?
- What kinds of laughs did the piece get? Did it get hard laughs from everyone, or were the jokes most appreciated by different or smaller pockets of audience members?

There's nothing wrong with those smaller laughs, by the way—most of our favorite jokes are the kind that don't play well for the largest audience. At Second City, there is a wooden bench on the side of the Mainstage theater where the directors and other performers sit to watch shows. You don't want a show full of "bench laughs," but the jokes that got a response from the bench are some of my personal favorites in shows I have created.

Now dig a little deeper and look at the delivery and execution of the material. Ask:

- How was the timing and delivery?
- Was the physical comedy or acting skillful?
- What about the use of components that made the comedy thicker, like wordplay and wit?

Finally, pay attention to your own subjective response to the comedy. Ask:

- Did it feel true or recognizable to you personally?
- Did it surprise you or make you feel uncomfortable?
- Did it feel novel or had you heard similar comedy before and it felt tired?
- Did the context it was presented in provide enough distance for you personally that you felt comfortable laughing?
- How much does it match your personal preferences in terms of comedy?

This method takes into account the fact that comedy is relative and that very good comedy can be made that we don't personally find funny or enjoyable. And vice versa: A joke that makes an audience laugh (it works) may not be what I consider after some thought and reflection to be a "good joke."

Now, let's imagine that I take you out to a comedy club in the suburbs of Chicago to see a comedian neither of us knows perform a set as part of an evening of stand-up, with the intention of analyzing and critiquing the comedy.

This comedian's set consists of thin jokes that use very basic elements of recognition (women and men are different) with the bulk of the pain elements coming from taboo (using derogatory or shocking language). There are few other components involved other than jokes and a rudimentary narrative. The point of view and related persona do not feel specific or unique to this performer (he is a white man dressed in jeans, a T-shirt, and a plaid button-down), and while his "crowd work" interactions with audience members elicit laughs, they don't expand our sense of him or them as human beings. The jokes are told semi-skillfully. The timing is good, enough so that the punch lines come as something of a surprise.

The audience laughs, and that social element along with the alcohol we're drinking (there is a two-drink minimum at the club) means that we do too, but the laughs aren't particularly hard on either our part or the audience's. The comedy is recognizable to us, but primarily because we have heard similar jokes before. It doesn't feel novel, it feels old and tired. There aren't any jokes that feel directly stolen from someone else, but it does feel a bit derivative of a number of other comedians. And while we laugh, we are also aware that the objects of this comedy aren't particularly deserving of ridicule, so we don't feel particularly good about our laughter after the fact.

This was comedy that worked, but it wasn't good comedy. It also definitely wasn't to my taste even though I laughed in the moment and there were people at the club who appeared to be enjoying themselves. On the way home in the car, we can discuss why we didn't enjoy the show in a way that dug deeper than just talking about whether or not we laughed.

And we come to the agreement that yes, in this case, it was "hack."

But if we really want to dig deep into comedy analysis, the next step is to look at how comedy has been discussed and analyzed over the centuries.

5 HUMOR THEORY

My freshman year of college I took a theater survey course titled Comedy and Tragedy (way more tragedy than comedy, since in academia comedy is often treated as something that happens only after you have waded through all the "important" stuff). During that class we read a selection from Henri Bergson's classic essay "Laughter" in which he theorizes that laughter results when human beings behave rigidly, like machines. We didn't spend much time discussing the essay, and my eighteen-year-old self, whose ultimate goal was creating serious works of absurdist theater in basement cabarets, shrugged and thought, "I get it, but I'm never going to use it."

Later when I was working on the initial curriculum for the Comedy Studies program, it seemed important to include some basic humor theory. As a start I revisited Bergson and I found his work to be significantly more interesting than I had at eighteen. Bergson clearly illuminated one aspect of humor and laughter which seemed to me to be useful. But now, as a practiced comedy maker, I could immediately come up with multiple examples of comedy that didn't fall within the boundaries of this particular theory.

I could make something of a case for all humor as involving people behaving in a rigid, machinelike way. It is a good fit with certain comedy components. It agrees with my understanding of comedic narrative as one that proceeds logically but not rationally. It works for thinking about comic character as being defined by a narrow but extreme perspective. The argument starts to break down when I try to apply it to jokes. I suppose you could say that a joke is setting up one rigid perspective and then replacing it with another. But the error that is the essence of many jokes is far more human than machinelike. It's less about rigidity and more the sloppiness of all-too-human bias. More importantly, Bergson's theory only supports one aspect of what you need to revise a joke: Making it more logical can help if that is the issue, but the solution might just as easily be to invoke an emotion. It is in the realm of point of view that I find I have to stretch Bergson's theory until it really isn't useful anymore, unless his argument is that all comedians are pointing out rigid thinking in the world. Some certainly do. However, it takes a lot of work to connect machinelike qualities with the giggles elicited by watching Amber Ruffin sing a song about her love of joking about white women's butts or the audible enjoyment my students get out of a well-placed *Wizards of Waverly Place* reference (a Disney channel sitcom from the early 2000s that's highly recognizable to college students circa 2025).

It's definitely much less recognizable to our modern eyes. Machines don't define the twenty-first century in the same way that they did in the past. When Henri Bergson was writing in the very early part of the twentieth century, two things were going on. Society was right in the midst of the most intense part of the Industrial Revolution; machines had changed and were actively changing nearly every aspect of society. It was also the era of early silent film comedy. Machines and machinelike behavior were both very recognizable to him (and to audiences of the time) and highly useful for the type of physical comedy that silent film frequently relies on.

In a more traditional academic book, this is the section where the authorial game is to go through all of the traditional theories one by one and debunk them, show that they are in some way flawed, and then present how my theory is superior or fulfills certain criteria better than these previous theories. I'm not going to do that.

I'm interested in doing research on past thinking about comedy and humor because I want to see if it is useful to those doing the work of making comedy today. What I found as I dug into the areas of humor theory is that there is a lot to be taken from what thinkers in the past have conjectured and written about this topic even if these theories don't apply to every situation or instance of comedy making. We can apply some aspects of all of these theories to either create, analyze, or revise created comedy depending on the situation. Understanding humor and laughter theories can lead to new ways of framing an approach to the comedy we want to make.

The theories I'm going to unpack here are a set of tools a comedy creator can use in different ways at different times. All the tools are useful depending on the situation, the kind of comedy the creator wants to make, or the comedy problem they are trying to solve. Some of these tools will function better for certain people and not others. Some might find that using the lens of one particular theory is especially helpful to them in generating comedic material. Later, a completely different theory could unlock a revision of that same material and make it work better for its intended audience.

A couple of thoughts before we get started.

It's important to understand that the theorists of the past were addressing many different concerns or areas of inquiry. Some were interested in why humans laugh. Others were interested in the uses or societal value of laughter and humor. Still others wanted to find the one essential underlying key to all occasions of laughter (so not just responses to jokes but also why we laugh when we are tickled or uncomfortable). Often their views of laughter and humor were based in their observations of just one of the comedy components. One theorist might have come to a conclusion about laughter by considering jokes and another to a contradictory conclusion in a theory prompted by observations of physical clowning. And really none of these theorists were directly interested in how to make comedy, just in critiquing or analyzing its effect.

Right after 9/11, Roger Rosenblatt announced in *Time* magazine that "the Age of Irony" had come to an end.[1] Indeed, irony, with its detachment and cold observation, was not a kind of humor that was wildly successful right after the fall of the Twin Towers. At the end of 2001, many people were experiencing the aftereffects of trauma—they weren't detached. Ironic humor no longer *felt* true. As with Bergson who was shaped by the age of machines and factories, most humor theory has a shape related to the place, people, and values in which it was debated and discussed. While most humor theory appears to be trying to answer the question "What do we laugh at?," it is even more so related to the question "What do we laugh at *right now*, and why are we now laughing at that thing?"

These theories have traditionally been roughly grouped into three categories, but those categories are more an after-the-fact creation than actual schools of thought. The thinkers and theorizers in any one category may have some points in common, but they also often contradict each other—in fact, if we were able to magically get all of these "like-minded" theorists from multiple centuries into a room together and invent a device that could simultaneously translate ancient Greek, Renaissance English, and nineteenth-century German, I have no doubt they would begin furiously arguing as opposed to seeing themselves as being in any sort of agreement. It's important that we not see the theory titles as monolithic. Thinkers who have been placed in one category may have some interest in or focus on elements of another category.

I find that the focus for many of these theories is on the aspect of pain that is present when we laugh or feel humor—possibly because the goal was to figure out if laughing at that specific kind of pain means something about humans and the human condition. Many theories include elements that provide distance. Almost none highlight recognition, although you could argue that it's implied somewhere. You can make a good case for most of these theories, but as with Bergson, you have to really stretch to make one theory fit all situations of humor and laughter. Fortunately, I'm not looking to do that. I'm interested in creating comedy, and I'm proposing that we approach these theories by viewing them through the lens of my own theory of comedy and then use the insights behind these theories to manipulate our three primary elements as we create or revise comedy of our own.

Superiority Theory

The essence of this theory is that human beings laugh at the failings or pain of other people. Laughter and humor results when we compare ourselves to someone else and see them as less than ourselves. Whenever we laugh, we are making fun of someone else, taking them down to lift ourselves up.

Superiority theory is the oldest articulated theory of humor and laughter. There are early references to it in the work of Plato and Aristotle. According to Plato, "Laughter feels good, but the pleasure is mixed with malice toward those being laughed at."[2] And to quote modern humor theorist John Morreall, "When Plato imagined the ideal state, he wanted to severely restrict the performance of comedy. 'We shall enjoin that such representations be left to slaves or hired aliens, and that they receive no serious consideration whatsoever. No free person, whether woman or man, shall be found taking lessons in them.' 'No composer of comedy, iambic or lyric verse shall be permitted to hold any citizen up to laughter by word or gesture, with passion or otherwise.' "[3]

In *Nichomachean Ethics* Aristotle speaks specifically of comedy as "a representation of people worse than us, not in the full sense of bad, but what we laugh at is a subdivision of the ugly/shameful."[4] Interestingly, he also goes on to say that it should also involve "no pain or harm," thus including distance.

Later Thomas Hobbes took this point further, arguing that "people are prone to this kind of delight because they are naturally individualistic and competitive," and then saying, "Laughter . . . is caused either by some sudden act of their own that pleases them; or by the apprehension of some deformed thing in another, by comparison whereof they suddenly applaud themselves."[5]

Part of the argument here is that laughter is bad for you, something that moral or good people should not participate in. It is associated with our lower or more base instincts. You may have noted that Plato also associates humor with "the other": It's OK for those from the lowest classes or foreigners to create comedy, just not citizens. And they aren't allowed to make fun of the citizens, only of themselves. Throughout much of the early Christian era, there was a general feeling that laughter and humor was something to be avoided or downright sinful, as in Benedictine law, where nuns and monks were not only discouraged from loving "prolonged or boisterous laughter" but were also forbidden from provoking it through "buffoonery, idle words, or such as move to laughter."[6] We should not take this to mean that those of the early Christian era tried not to laugh. More than likely it was true then (as it is now) that some people were preaching about not making fun of others while the general public was laughing at people kicking each other in the butts and falling down.

Superiority theory has a lot to teach the comedian. Human beings are fascinated with other human beings: We watch them and pay attention to them. Anyone who went to high school—or worked in a comedy theater or club for any length of time, or an office, or, OK, pretty much anywhere—is familiar with the ways that individuals jockey for social position within a group. Losers of these dynamics are subjected to derisive laughter. Adults may be less obvious about it than teenagers, but they remain keenly aware of who is winning or losing in any given social interaction. The comedy in the sitcom *The Office* is driven by these dynamics at the micro level of a suburban paper distributer just as late-night comedy roasts the losers on a grander political stage.

It's rare in slapstick that the targets of violence don't in some way deserve what they get. The harassing authority figure is the best person to slip on a banana peel, get a kick in the pants, or a pie in the face.

Competitive put downs or roasting goes back at least as far as ancient Rome. Flyting, a ritual competitive insult game, was practiced in medieval Norse and British societies. Nigerians participate in something called Ikocha Nkocha, one of a dozen African insult games that show up in North American Black communities as the Dozens.

The bulk of character comedy is based on seeing other people fail or make mistakes. In *The Comedy Toolbox*, Jon Vorhaus argues that an essential aspect of comic characters is that they are somehow blinded by or defined by their flaws. A perfect hero is rarely a comedic character unless they are so perfect that it becomes a flaw, as with Gaston in the Disney version of *Beauty and the Beast.*

There are direct connections between superiority theory and parts of the recognition/pain/distance triad. Pain is everywhere—misfortune, failures, falling. There is recognition of human flaws and their effects. But for me one of the chief values of superiority theory is in its relationship to the element of distance. It explains why and how we can hear of one person's failures and feel sympathy and then hear about another's and laugh. We feel superior to the person we're laughing at and perhaps even as if the object of our laughter is not fully human. Or at least not as human as we ourselves are.

One of the simplest notes I give on comedic sketches or longer pieces is that if a character is going to experience multiple misfortunes, the piece will be funnier if you first demonstrate that the character deserves punishment of some kind. You can make them mean or cruel, but you can also simply give them a fault they have elected not to correct that then comes back to bite them in the ass.

A clear element of the sitcom *30 Rock* is that the characters are nearly always aware of the potential pitfalls of whatever dubious scheme they are about to embark on. Their resulting failures are then more enjoyable than cringeworthy. We know that Liz Lemon made the deliberate choice to get a flu shot when she knows the rest of the crew does not have access to one and is therefore violently ill. When Liz inevitably gets caught faking that she has the flu (turns out the vaccine causes a rash that she is unable to hide), we laugh at her pain because she knew what she was doing and did it anyway. She deserved it.

My chief issue with Superiority Theory is that it only covers and focuses on the kind of humor and laughter that centers people (or, I suppose, personified animals, like Bugs Bunny). For comedy about characters and physical comedy performed by human bodies, it makes sense that the laughter is directed at another human and that the audience compares themselves to and feels superior to that human. But for comedy that addresses ideas and objects, it is better to look at the second primary theory of humor.

Incongruity Theory

The second major umbrella area of humor theory is generally termed Incongruity Theory.

Incongruity Theory posits that humor or laughter results when two things or ideas occupy the same space in a way that is highly unusual or doesn't make initial intuitive sense.

Play with a baby for any period of time and you can see incongruity theory in action. Babies adore it when you put your shoe on your head or your hat on your foot. They laugh convulsively if someone pretends to eat their little toes and not just because it tickles but because they know that baby toes are not food for human adults.

Incongruity Theory is probably the most currently widely accepted theory of laughter and humor in philosophy and psychology. It isn't a new idea. Aristotle mentions incongruity as a cause of laughter.

Immanuel Kant, Søren Kierkegaard, Arthur Schopenhauer, and scores of others have written and theorized in connection to this concept.

A pun is an example of incongruity in a joke form—a single word with multiple meanings or a homophone (a word that sounds like another word but is spelled differently and has another meaning—for example, *paws* and *pause*) is used that tricks the listener into making an incorrect assumption. For example, there are two possible meanings of the word *bright*—both a shining light and intelligence. In the Phyllis Diller joke "Light travels faster than sound. That's why some people seem bright until they speak,"[7] the humor is in the instant of rediscovering that those two meanings can coexist in one word.

A great deal of visual comedy is incongruous—objects that are the wrong size or in the wrong place. Many of the examples I cited in the section on visual comedy fall under the incongruity umbrella, such as dogs in clothes or Harpo Marx answering a question by honking a horn in a way that feels like speech while simultaneously not being speech.

My old friend Henri Bergson is most frequently put under the umbrella of incongruity, since his theory suggests that two things that appear to be incongruent are true at the same time—a man is also a machine.

There is a scene in Charlie Chaplin's film *Modern Times* that illustrates Bergson's concept of incongruity comedy perfectly. Chaplin is working in a factory repetitively tightening bolts on an assembly line. When the line freezes, he continues to do his job as if he were simply a robot whose only purpose is to tighten bolts: Everything that looks like a bolt is tightened with his wrenches, including the bolt-like buttons adorning the rear of a lady's skirt as she walks by him. This is a thicker moment of comedy that moves beyond the robotic to reference the character mischief that Chaplin's Little Tramp was well known for—doing slightly vulgar or dirty things with an innocent excuse.

The Russian philosopher Mikhail Bakhtin has a take on Incongruity Theory that specifically looks at the upending of social norms during the traditional Carnevale festivals associated with certain parts of the Roman Catholic calendar. An example of this in the United States is Mardi Gras as celebrated in New Orleans (and to a lesser degree elsewhere) just before Lent. One signature of these festivals are elements that turn social status upside down: Lowly peasants are made "king for a day"; rigid social hierarchies are erased or disguised with masks and costumes.

It is worth noting here that Bakhtin's theory also contains and supports elements of the Superiority Theory. Awareness of status and the value that societies place on status is central to what is funny about the reversals of carnival. When the peasant is made "king," the people at large get to indulge in feelings of superiority over their new "ruler"—and likely this provides an outlet to genuine but suppressed feelings about the actual ruler.

An adaptation of the Incongruity Theory introduced in the late twentieth century by John Morreall (usually called the Incongruity Resolution Theory) adds an element suggesting that incongruity is generally not enough to induce laughter or humor without an additional element of coherence. We laugh not when two things are first put together that don't make sense but later, when we make some form of "sense" from what we first perceived as nonsense. In this version of the theory, our laughter is triggered not by the puzzle ("Why would this strange thing happen?") but the solution to the puzzle ("Oh, I thought it was this, but instead it was that"). What we thought was illogical becomes logical when seen in a new light, from a different angle, or with a new level of understanding.

Thus, in the earlier joke I included that hinges on two meanings of the word *bright*, the laughter is created not by the fact that the word *bright* has two meanings but that the audience was tricked into assuming one meaning of the word because of the context it was presented in, very briefly confused, and then pleased when they recognize the misdirection.

Some form of incongruity theory is the most generally accepted theory for why we laugh. In the humor theories that are posed and/or researched by social and evolutionary scientists, it seems to lay the groundwork for at least a partial understanding of the underlying brain mechanisms of laughter and humor. Incongruities seem to be central for an enormous amount of humor of one kind or another. And as with most of the primary theories you can make the case that Incongruity Theory covers all aspects of humor, although it's a stretch and at the far edges starts to be a bit strained.

You could say that we laugh at comedians who use foul language or taboo subjects on stage because it is incongruous or surprising to us to have those subjects mentioned in a venue where they would not normally be brought up. But the laughter generated by an obscenity is generally much larger than that generated by a non sequitur and from the comedian's perspective it is different in quality.

For Incongruity Theory, as with Superiority Theory, recognition is assumed or implied. If I know who normally hangs around in living rooms watching television, then an incongruous cartoon of giraffes sitting around in a living room watching television might be funny to me.[8] Incongruity Theory functions particularly well for comedians if you think of comedy as breaking or reversing expectations based in recognition. Setting and building expectations is one of the major and useful comedy tools.

The Incongruity Resolution Theory also contains a kind of implied recognition, that of a logical solution. We start with something that is confusing and thus mostly unrecognizable and discover that we understand and recognize it after we see it from a different angle. For there to be incongruity, there must be an understanding of congruity. What do we expect to happen? What is our (or our audience's) assumption of what "normal" looks like? What mental pattern is being disrupted? Role reversal implies that an existing or expected hierarchy is being turned around.

The concept of incongruity is a useful and practical tool for comedians. Putting two things that don't belong together in the same space is a simple and easy first step to finding something that could be shaped into comedy. One quick-and-dirty way of creating a comedic character is to make a list of adjectives (angry, sloppy, spiky, graceful, bubbly, elegant) and then randomly combine them with a list of occupations (plumber, priest, elementary school teacher, king, waiter, rock musician). So you might have an elegant plumber, a sloppy king, or a spiky priest. (A more detailed version of this exercise appears in the "Creating Comic Characters" chapter.)

A common parody trope is to superimpose one style or genre on top of another—for example, the successful parody novel *Pride and Prejudice and Zombies.* Companies that create fully improvised musicals often start by asking for a dramatic film or story. *Anything Dramatic! The Musical* provides an easy and immediate incongruity between a serious story and the stylistic tropes of musical theater that is sustainable for an extended period.

Silent film comedy will often use the simple but impossible task, as in the iconic parking scene from *The Pink Panther* (2006) that exploits the incongruity inherent in the difference between the simple task of Jacques Clouseau parking his tiny car in a huge spot and the absurdity that he still hits both cars in the spots next to him multiple times, causing severe damage to each.[9]

If we include expectation and reversal of expectation, there are even more ways for comedians to use and manipulate incongruity. The comedian Sarah Silverman started her career by setting expectations with her sweet "nice Jewish girl" persona and then reversing those expectations when her act included shocking and taboo material.

What Incongruity Theory doesn't do is provide for the context in which the incongruity is placed and how that context affects whether and how funny any given incongruity is to any given viewer. Audiences don't just laugh more when a performer references a taboo onstage. It depends on the specifics of the reference itself, on the audience's age and political/social leanings, on how deserved or meaningful the taboo is in the context of what else is going on. It isn't just the incongruity that triggers the laugh. The laugh is also affected by the mental and emotional distance that any given audience has on the content and meaning of swearing or obscenity.

A great example of this is from a classic Second City scene that (at least internally) goes by the name "Gump," originally written and performed by Adam McKay and Scott Adsit in the early 1990s. The premise is that a member of the HR department at a large corporation must deliver the results of an intelligence test taken by a high-level VP. In the language of the sketch, the test indicates that the VP is "legally retarded." One of the major drivers of the humor of the sketch is the incongruity of that phrase. Adsit's character, the VP, Mr. Grissom, responds to the news by asking, "When you say legally, do you mean I'm going to be arrested?" There is a deeper incongruity: At this point in time, the term *retarded* was simultaneously a medical diagnosis and a playground slur, which is heightened by the status stretch of a low-level corporate employee being forced to use the term directly to his high-level superior.

When the sketch was initially performed, it was well received, and requiring a character who didn't want to use the term to say it was a strong driver of laughter from audiences.

But gradually the audiences stopped laughing so much. Because of its modern connotation as a slur, the word was retired as a diagnosis, and due to the efforts of those with development disabilities and their families over a period of time, use of the word in public was stigmatized. What had originally felt to audiences like a specific and enjoyable incongruity now felt uncomfortable and cruel. The incongruity was still there, but the feeling was different and infinitely less funny.

There is a long history of the various diagnoses for people with developmental disabilities eventually becoming jokes and slurs. The term *moron* followed a similar path. It seems that every time the medical establishment revises these diagnoses, they are only a few steps ahead of those who would use them to punch down.

Henri Bergson does address this phenomenon in *Laughter*—recall that earlier I mentioned that thinkers about humor and laughter are not grouped cleanly into these theory categories. Although Bergson believes the primary reason for our laughter is the idea of a human being behaving rigidly and like a machine, he also explores something else that could be said to be part of Superiority Theory. He points out that to laugh, people often need to suspend their feelings. That disconnection isn't universal—it is very much time and context dependent and is an important piece of what comedians manipulate when they use the recognition/pain/distance triad.

Tension and Release Theory

The final of the "big three" humor theories is promoted by Sigmund Freud in his book *Jokes and Their Relation to the Unconscious*.[10] Known as the Relief Theory or as the Tension and Release Theory, it suggests that laughter is a way of releasing tension or energy that builds up through discomfort of a variety of kinds. Unlike Incongruity Theory, this is largely a theory of laughter rather than of humor. There's something about laughter—its uncontrollability, the fact that it is an active physical manifestation of an inner feeling or experience (not unlike tears, but more surprising)—that has fascinated people over the centuries, bringing up slightly different questions from the feeling of humor.

Freud proposed that certain topics or situations create an actual physical buildup of energy, often because of repression of feelings or emotions (he believed these feelings were most often sexual or hostile), but also through trying to understand something difficult or unusual. John Morreall explains, "According to Freud, most prepared jokes and witty remarks are about sex or hostility, because those are the big urges which society forces us to repress."[11]

Freud also takes on physical comedy. He suggests that what makes clowns funny is the disparity between the energy that we ourselves would use to do an action and that used by a clown to do the same action. What we perceive as easy and using little energy, the clown makes extraordinarily difficult, or, in the case of skilled physical clowning, what we know to be difficult appears effortless. Freud suggests that audiences experience that difference physically and it creates a genuine buildup of "energy packets" inside their bodies. Laughter then allows for a physical expression that releases the built-up energy.

While the physical mechanics implied in Freud's theory are questionable, tension and release illuminates new aspects of the recognition/pain/distance triad. As with most humor theories, the recognition aspect of this theory is implied—things we recognize as true and also recognize as wrong or bad or incorrect are what are suppressed. But Tension and Release Theory highlights kinds of pain used in comedy creation that are hidden or played down in the other theories of humor. There is comedy of the body of the sort that is thought to be inappropriate or vulgar, such as pooping, farting, and sex (with all of the various animal implications). Comedy exploits taboo, from simple taboos against foul language to more complex societal taboos against speaking lightly of death and religion. The presence of these taboos does create discomfort and tension.

There are other aspects of discomfort used frequently in the production of comedy that are not necessarily taboo or repressed. Comedy theaters famously choose to make their audiences a little bit uncomfortable; the seats are hard, the audience is packed in close together, and the room is cold, because experience tells us that a warmer and more comfortable crowd laughs significantly less.

Relief Theory highlights that humor and laughter contain not just pain but also the anticipation of pain. Comedy of incongruity usually takes place in the same space at the same time as in a picture or a character. Tension and release illuminate the experience of comedy as taking place in a linear fashion over time. In doing so it gives comedians different tools, ones that work well in the components of comedy outside of jokes. This is particularly true in comedy of character and narrative.

Familiarity with a character generates expectations about their future behavior. In a comedic narrative, a character is put into motion in a given situation. This generates expectations of how the situation will play out, but there is ongoing tension: Is our initial guess as to how the character will behave correct? What will the results be? The wait to see what will happen, as well as how long it takes, and in what manner it will play out, creates tension.

Animated cartoons are masters of this. In a *Road Runner* short, Wile E. Coyote sets up a trap, and we wait to see how the trap will actually work. A boulder is poised at the top of a hill. We know it will eventually come down, and our experience with these cartoons tells us it will land on the coyote rather than his intended prey.

The absurdist physical performers in Blue Man Group provided raincoats at the start of their performance for those sitting in first couple of rows of seats. This serves not just to protect audience members from getting wet during the performance but also to generate the expectation that water or wetness is coming. Waiting for that event builds tension and creates a heightened response to even unrelated moments of comedy. When the anticipated event comes there is a kind of a distance or safety—it is done, it is finished, the discomfort of waiting is resolved. Laughter most often results.

In his book *Born Standing Up*, comedian Steve Martin discusses how he played with tension and release in his stand-up act. "What if I created tension and never released it? What if I headed for a climax, but all I delivered was an anticlimax? What would the audience do with all that tension? Theoretically, it would have to come out sometime."[12] He discovered that his audiences did indeed find their own places to release the tension through laughter. Eventually, he would use this discovery to manipulate his audiences further—finding the places where the audience generally released their own tension and then building to those events as subtly or unusually as he could.

The early (and most commercially successful) of the anticomedian Andy Kaufman's stand-up performances built tension through deliberately terrible or uncomfortable performances: A clearly nervous, awkward man stands next to a record player waiting to perform, or a naive stand-up with a poor grasp of the English language does hackneyed imitations. Then, just at the point at which enough tension has built up that the audience is ready to turn on Kaufman and leave or start booing, he releases the tension spectacularly. He would perform an impeccably timed lip sync to a section of cartoon theme song or reveal a pitch-perfect Elvis imitation. As he became better-known, he was able to build tension for longer and longer periods of time. Audiences were willing to wait to see the eventual release, which occasionally never came or happened only in retrospect when they discovered that they were the butt of a deliberately long and excruciating practical joke.

Throughout the first part of her stand-up special *Nanette*, Hannah Gadsby tells jokes that play off the tension of how she presents as a queer woman and what that means for her as she moves through the world. With each joke she releases tension through complicity with her audience, calling out the device explicitly. She creates safety through her own comfort with herself, confirming through a nod and a wink that though she has brought up a difficult topic resulting in audience tension, she is OK and therefore it is OK to laugh and ease the tension. At the end of the special, however, she critiques this exact quality of comedy itself by suggesting that in providing this release she has done a disservice to true aspects of trauma from her own life.

Certain comedians create expectations either through their physical presence or their reputations. I have noticed as a comedy director that audiences will zero in on certain performers and play close attention to what they do. Chris Farley was one of these performers. Before he was famous, I would watch him perform in The Second City touring company, and there was something in his onstage presence that created an expectation in audiences that built tension and generated laughter even when he wasn't actively attempting to do anything funny. Similarly, comedians who are known for saying and doing the unexpected or the taboo will often elicit laughter with relatively innocuous jokes. The tension of what "might" happen infects the audience regardless of the actual presence of a shock or taboo.

I would argue that audience tension likely generated additional laughter for Lenny Bruce during the time he was frequently getting arrested for breaking local obscenity laws. The audience would be waiting—first, to see if Bruce was going to do or say something illegal, and second, to see if a cop would stop the performance. In a clip of Bruce from one of his rare television appearances, he tells the audience he is going to say a word "that starts with an *s* and ends with a *t*," immediately triggering enormous audience tension that he is going to say a word that (as George Carlin would remind us years later) "can never be said on television." He does what he promised, but in this instance the word is *snot*—not the obscenity foremost in the audiences' minds. The tension created releases a laugh much stronger and more heightened than what would come from the incongruity present in the joke. The clip itself is much less funny to a modern American audience both because certain kinds of foul language are now commonplace on all but broadcast television and because the tension of live television is missing. (Of course, since the clip is on YouTube, it would most likely notify us in advance of the presence of a slur with a headline along the lines of "The TV appearance that ended the career of Lenny Bruce!!!!!!!")

A modern example of this is the comedian Eric Andre, whose work includes disturbing practical jokes filmed in front of unsuspecting strangers and aggressive audience interaction within his stand-up. Andre described his comedy in the *New York Times* as having "an element of sleeping danger. You want there to be something at risk."[13]

In comic acting, it is often the job of a particular character to "release the laugh"—signaling to the audience that what they see is indeed laughable as opposed to uncomfortable or pitiful. George Burns and Gracie Allen's comedy partnership was built on the premise that Gracie's mistakes were charming and understandable, and this was achieved because George released the tension in the audience created by her errors through his pleasure and patience with her mistakes. More modern comedies of awkwardness like *Abbott Elementary* use the conceit of the mockumentary, allowing for a fairly realistic acting style in the midst of highly uncomfortable antisocial behavior because the tension is released by the subtle presence of an unseen cameraperson.

Another way to create tension in a comedic piece is by announcing or implying that something will happen later in an act or sketch and then withholding it as long as possible. Or forever, as in Kristen Schaal's early bit where she announces a duet with a singing and dancing bird that never arrives. A narrative premise in which a character has a secret from another character builds tension, and this often works whether the audience knows the secret or not. In one of my favorite exercises to teach in improv classes, I give two students each simple "wants" to play along with a strong reason to not directly reveal those wants. For example, one person knows that their coworker is going to be fired in two days and has been told not to reveal the information, while the about-to-be-fired coworker has just discovered through DNA testing that the first coworker is their long-lost sibling given up for adoption many years ago. There are rarely any actual jokes in these improvisations, but they generate a great deal of audience laughter. It is the combination of character behavior along with the tension generated between the two players by their competing secret agendas that creates the comedy.

Tension and release can and often should affect the exact timing of the way a particular joke is delivered. Once you know what your setup and punch line are, it can be useful to play with the distance between them, add more words or a pause in your delivery. You may find that you get a bigger laugh from your audience by creating that extra bit of delay. It's also valuable to be aware of how or whether you have released a laugh. Through the tone or rhythm of your delivery, did you indicate that the punch line happened? Or did you indicate that there might be more? Listen to comedians like Phyllis Diller, Redd Foxx, or Henny Youngman. They will speed through the initial setup, slow down just a touch as they near the end of a joke, and then take a deliberate and noticeable pause after the punch line to make sure they have released the laugh.

Benign Violation Theory

The social scientist Peter McGraw, building on previous work by Tom Veatch,[14] proposes that humor occurs when and only when three conditions are satisfied: (1) The situation is a violation; (2) The situation is benign; and (3) Both perceptions occur simultaneously. McGraw tested his theory at his lab in Boulder, Colorado, to see whether jokes or situations that demonstrated benign violation were viewed as humorous by readers and viewers, and his study found this to be generally true. Unlike some of the theories previously detailed here, Benign Violation Theory also seeks to explain all or most instances of laughter—not just laughter related to directly humorous situations but all kinds of social laughter, including that produced by tickling.

McGraw has done some very interesting studies that directly suggest that psychological distance is an important aspect of the humor and laughter response. I am struck by the use of the term *benign* instead of *distance* in his final theory.[15] *Benign* suggests something safe or, as *Merriam-Webster's* puts it, "of a mild type or character that does not threaten health or life." The language used in most other theories of humor and laughter posit something actually or at least potentially harmful (not mild or unthreatening) but focus on the fact that it has passed, resolved, or is not close enough to be a current threat.

I am interested in thinking about violation as a kind of pain. Again, in *Merriam-Webster's* violation is termed "an infringement or transgression." This suggests that here, as in Superiority Theory, there is a directly human element to humor and laughter. It requires an actor or action to take place and to be perpetrated with some sort of intention. This provides a context that supports the relativity of humor (the idea that different things strike different people as funny based on their experience and knowledge).

This theory also implies recognition: If something is a violation, it must be violating something—generally, a norm of behavior. This is a useful form of recognition for comedians to play with and subvert. What is "normal"? What are people "supposed" to do? What does everyone "believe" to be true? This provides a path for creating kinds of comedy not readily suggested by other humor theories.

An interesting premise generation exercise would be to start with a list of commonly understood social rules and then to play with breaking them in a way that feels safe. In a sketch from the British sketch show *Big Train*, for example, employees protest a new rule forbidding masturbation in the office. This is treated throughout the sketch identically to the way people complained when smoking was first banned in workplaces.

I once directed a show that had a sketch about the (then new) concept of "Casual Fridays."[16] A young and energetic manager has convinced his superiors to introduce the idea to his department, and he is excitedly waiting for the first of the employees to arrive. As each enters (in a classic version of what I refer to as a pile-on scene), they demonstrate a wide and increasingly upsetting (but still fairly benign) set of variations on violating the normal rules of casual Friday. The first employee enters in a Boy Scout uniform, and the audience discovers that as opposed to suggesting that employees wear jeans and short-sleeved shirts or khaki pants and polos, the directive has been to "wear what you would normally wear over the weekend." The employees have taken this literally. There is a fast-food uniform from the accountant who moonlights at McDonald's, and a swimsuit for the one who spends all weekend at the beach. Eventually the breaking point comes when a highly popular employee shows up in full Nazi regalia.

This sketch demonstrates how each of the traditional theories of humor can be present and useful in one short piece of comedy. We can find Superiority Theory, both in the manager's inept choice of directive and in the misunderstanding of it by the employees. There is incongruity between the expected Casual Friday outfits and what is worn. There is tension in the wait for each new entrance and a (mostly) benign array of violations of an understood social norm.

Evolutionary Theories

Scientists have also formed theories as to the evolutionary purpose of humor and laughter. What makes these theories fundamentally different from the philosophical/psychological theories is that ultimately these theories are asking a different question. The base question is not "Why do we laugh now?" but instead "What caused us as a species to develop laughter, and what does that tell us about the uses and value of humor and laughter to humans in practical and evolutionary terms?"

Most of these theories involve some idea of a protohumor, a behavior or ability that was useful to human survival and passed down genetically. This initially valuable adaptation would not encompass all aspects of how we currently experience laughter, humor, or comedy. But the history of human development suggests that it is common to find new uses for the simple tools that evolution provides. This is known as exaptation, a phenomenon where an existing process is repurposed for another use. It seems likely that the many ways we experience and use laughter, humor, and comedy exist because an initial cognitive trigger was useful for other social or evolutionary reasons.

When young human beings play, they are practicing skills they need for their lives. They often do so by engaging in a version of a real thing without actually doing it. A child might practice eventual parenting skills by playing with dolls or discover elements of engineering through building things with blocks. All sorts of young mammals learn to fight by engaging in play versions of fighting with littermates or members of their own packs or social groups. When doing so they use physical and sometimes auditory cues to let everyone know they are practicing and "playing" rather than actually fighting.

Studies of apes have noted that when these animals play at fighting, they exhibit a kind of smile or grimace and make a sort of panting noise that scientists have theorized might be a simian equivalent of laughter.[17] This suggests that laughter could have evolved from something similar in humans.[18]

A potential exaptation of this seems obvious and straightforward. If early humans signaled, through laughter, that something they were doing seemed dangerous but was not, they might have also laughed in other situations, such as thinking they saw a snake and then discovering it was a stick. It makes sense that there would be mutually shared laughter when several people discovered this lack of danger simultaneously. It's only a fairly short jump from having this mutual discovery to purposely creating things that use the elements of danger (pain) and safety/play (distance) along with shared experience (recognition) to generate laughter in a group. To make comedy.

A related theory is proposed in *Inside Jokes: Using Humor to Reverse Engineer the Mind*, by Matthew M. Hurley, Daniel C. Dennett, and Reginald B. Adams Jr.[19] Here the initial and underlying basis for humor and laughter is connected to an evolutionary reward for "debugging" the shortcuts that humans evolved as their brains grew and stored information in more complex ways. In this theory, humor results when a person commits to a mental model of their experience using a shortcut or heuristic of some sort and then discovers that they weren't correct. The idea here is that it is of value to the survival of the species to both use these shortcuts and also have a way of making sure that we enjoy testing them as opposed to just relying on them. When we jump to an understandable conclusion and then discover that there was a different and equally valid conclusion, the suggestion is that we receive a kind of internal reward that results in a response (laughter) and makes us feel good.

In this theory the primary kind of pain is a mistake. We made a mistake, and since it wasn't a fatal one, we laugh. As we discussed earlier, this is the core joke mechanism. A joke sets up an expectation of some sort that leads the perceiver to make a mistake, which is revealed in the punch line.

Hurley and his colleagues suggest that this fundamental joke mechanism is the basic element of humor and that over time all other sorts of humor were exapted from this initial evolution-based system. This theory seems to me to be directly congruent with the recognition/pain/distance triad. If humans initially laughed (and enjoyed laughing) because it was pleasurable to make a certain kind of mistake, it follows that there may eventually be related pleasure to watching someone else make that mistake (as in character or physical comedy).

Additionally, if someone else laughs at the same things we laugh at, under this model we know that (1) they use the same shortcuts we do, (2) we can assume they know the same things we know (recognition), and (3) they make the same mistakes we do (recognition and pain). Our shared laughter informs us that we belong to the same group or tribe. There is an additional potential exaptation at work here that could explain the phenomenon of laughter generated almost purely by recognition as well as providing an explanation of why we may laugh socially even when something isn't particularly funny to us.

The research about shared laughter supporting social bonding reinforces this idea. Studies have shown that we laugh more when the comedy we are watching is connected to something we are familiar with (i.e., something we recognize).[20]

A lot of interesting conclusions can be drawn here. Maybe one reason comedy tends to be "sticky" is that we remember it because it is related to insight. As I noted earlier, studies in China suggest that insight and humor appear to be processed in our brains in a similar manner. But comedy and humor are particularly complex and difficult to study scientifically because of the myriad of ways they manifest and the fact that any given joke or comedic moment is built out of multiple components. Not only that, but the effectiveness of any given comedy moment is also affected by where we experience it and who we experience it with.

6 COMEDY AND YOUR BRAIN

In 2011, I became obsessed with a book. *Thinking, Fast and Slow* popularized the research of economists Daniel Kahneman and Amos Tversky.[1] They were two pioneers of a field known now as behavioral science. The essence of their work is that although humans like to believe they make decisions rationally, that is rarely the case. In fact, human beings are most often irrational, and even more interesting, humans seem to be *predictably* irrational. Humans tend to make the same kinds of mistakes in the same kinds of situations. *Thinking, Fast and Slow* is in no way focused on humor or comedy theory. But if we are looking to use pain and recognition to make our comedy, it stands to reason that understanding the predictable mistakes (pain) that most human beings make (recognition) is a huge benefit to those of us who want to understand and make comedy.

Kahneman suggests that we should understand our brains as consisting of two systems. These systems aren't physically located in different parts of the brain—Kahneman is just providing a working metaphor for two different ways the brain functions. This division of labor seems to be designed to help our brains use the least amount of energy to accomplish any given cognitive task.

System 1 automates the things we need to do most frequently. It is the intuitive part of our brain. Our System 1 is comfortable with the familiar, and it works fast. Ever see someone out of the corner of your eye and know exactly who that person is? That was your System 1 at work. It saves you time and energy. You don't have to look at a dog, catalog all of its features (ears, whiskers, tail, nose), match those features up to a detailed list, and then decide "dog." The fast part of your brain has already done that for you, and it does it so quickly you aren't even aware it is happening. It uses the knowledge you have automated. If your third- and fourth-grade teachers drilled you on your multiplication tables, they were helping you automate that math information for use by your System 1.

Your System 2 only jumps in when you don't have a good guess or when something unusual happens. Your System 2 is the slow brain. It requires you to think through a process step by step. You may have automated your times tables, but in order to multiply three-digit numbers, most of us need to access our slow brain. We might even need to write the numbers down on paper, essentially taking the problem apart and breaking it into even smaller, more manageable pieces.

Your System 1 brain uses shortcuts—it improvises with what is at hand, but it is not particularly concerned with accuracy. It relies on your previous experiences and then makes a good guess. As a result, it is often wrong. Sometimes just a little bit wrong but not enough wrong for you to care or even be conscious of the error. And your brain is OK with that. It says, "I got it, good enough."

Not coincidentally, this also provides a good model for and understanding of how jokes work in the brain. It maps almost directly on our current definition of a joke: a setup that creates an expectation and then a punchline that reverses that expectation. You could think of a joke as (1) providing information that sets up your System 1 to jump to a conclusion (setup) and then (2) providing some form of new information that is confusing enough to trigger your System 2 into figuring out that your System 1 was wrong. Our brains find the resolution of the mistaken assumption pleasurable—and we get laughter or humor.[2] We associate a pleasurable experience with situations in which we check our System 1 brain with our System 2 brain. We are in essence testing our System 1 for glitches, and we receive pleasure for doing so in the form of amusement or laughter.

Biases and Heuristics

There is more here than just a better understanding of jokes. The common mistakes and tendencies described in *Thinking, Fast and Slow* are a gold mine for comedy because they also describe predictable ways that humans think and behave. The patterns of thinking that create these behaviors are known as heuristics and biases.

Behavioral scientists design experiments that show that under certain conditions, people tend to operate in certain ways and tend to make certain kinds of mistakes. That's what comedians do. We create our own kind of comedic experiments, predicting that in certain circumstances audiences will tend to create certain kinds of expectations, and that if we reveal those expectations are wrong, they will respond with laughter (or groans or applause). We also showcase the opposite. We create characters who are recognizable and funny to our audiences because they make mistakes of the kind they recognize in themselves and the people they know. It only makes sense for comedians to learn more about these biases and heuristics and apply them to our work.

I'm including three examples below along with a suggestion for how they might be used in comedy creation. In describing these biases I'm using the word *we* to mean human beings in general. Most humans appear to have versions of these biases. And for the most part the biases are unconscious. They operate without us being aware that they are influencing our thinking or behavior. What is especially interesting is that most of these biases continue to have this influence even after we become aware of and understand them. This means that a joke or piece of comedy using these biases will continue to work even with audience members who know and are aware of their own biases. I should say that I am not a scientist, so the connections I am suggesting here are my own.

Anchoring bias. The bias: A piece of information that we already have or is easily available to us becomes the starting place for what we think we know about a topic or situation (even if that situation is entirely unrelated to the original anchor). For example, if I mention that I recently traveled to New York City, and then later in the conversation I ask an unrelated question about cities, you will likely refer first to cities in eastern North America as opposed to those in southern

Africa. You might not go directly to New York, but the research suggest that your brain will tend to start with the initial anchoring detail and then adjust from it rather than reach for wholly new information.

Comedy use: An incidental piece of information can be inserted early into a story, sketch, or joke and the audience will anchor on that information as being important. This sets up an expectation. A comedy creator can choose to fulfill or subvert the expectation.

Salience bias. The bias: We tend to focus on the most obvious or easily recognized features of an object, person, or a concept. For example, a person wearing yellow pants in a crowd of people in jeans is going to be more memorable and important.

Comedy use: Putting something obvious in the foreground of a comedic visual or describing something in detail at the start of a narrative or joke will draw focus and take attention away from a different element that can be brought forward later for comedic effect.

Story coherence bias. The bias: We create narratives to explain or find connections between random events.

Comedy use: Create events and then see what connections your audience makes. When I first started improvising, I did a lot of work in my head trying to create a narrative for my audience. It was a revelation to me that if I walked onto the stage and committed to behaving in a way that was focused and recognizable, I didn't have to do any of that work. The audience was creating the narrative for me, finding the connections on their own.

If you come to see a show at The Second City, most nights you are invited to stay and see the "set," an improvised third act. Sometimes the set consists of improv games or longer scenes created on the spot. When we are creating a new show, we use that time to workshop new material for that show. This allows our writer/performers to make use of the mistakes and assumptions generated by the audience watching as the scene develops. Improvising from a premise can be as simple as making a couple of clear choices, discovering what the audience expects through their response, and then either satisfying or subverting those expectations. It's a kind of superpower, because a narrative that is discovered by your audience and is based in their common biases will usually continue to be effective for most audiences over a long time.

During the break between the show and the set, our actors often change into their street clothes. The performance has a more casual feel that is reflected in the music and lighting as well. We know from experience that those minor changes can have a large impact on how the audience responds to our works in progress.

Context

Physical (Where Are You?)

In 2012, The Second City opened the UP Comedy Club, a new full-size performance venue in the Piper's Alley complex. The two primary resident theaters at Second City are relatively unadorned cabaret rooms with low ceilings, simple tables and chairs, all battered by years of performances and smelling of decades of spilled beer and cigarette smoke. It seems impossible now, but when I started working there in the late 1980s, smoking was allowed inside the theater, and both actors and audience smoked during the shows. The UP Comedy Club was meant to host stand-up performances as well as specialized revues, and physically it was a significant upgrade, with more comfortable seating, cushy booths in the back of the room, and a fancier supper club vibe.

During this time it was common for one of Second City's touring companies to perform matinee or off-night performances of *The Best of Second City* in one or more of the theaters. These are shows that combine material from past Second City revues with improvisation and some more topical original sketches. The shows are designed to tour to colleges and performing arts venues across the United States. After UP opened, the decision was made to add some matinee *Best of* performances there. The touring companies quickly discovered something strange. The exact same show, performed at the exact same time of day with (one would assume) a highly similar audience would get a dramatically different audience response when it was performed in UP than in the other two theaters. It wasn't that the shows were better or worse, necessarily—they were just really different. Sketches that got enormous laughs in the shabbier Mainstage got fewer in UP, and pieces that killed in UP felt much more average in the older theater. What was going on? The physical context of the two spaces created a different audience experience even though the two theaters were only about a floor and a hundred feet away from each other.

Context is important to comedy because it strongly affects two of the three major elements. The physical context in which you are viewing or listening to something will trigger associations and enhance certain kinds of recognition. It's as simple as this: If you are in your house, you will be more likely to able to list objects, events, or activities that might exist or take place in that space. If you are at your job or school, your brain will have readier access to the elements that belong in that environment. Physical context also affects distance in a multitude of ways. Certain environments feel more dangerous or charged than others. Some will feel that way for everyone, and some will feel especially charged for those with certain identities or life experiences.

Just changing the color of the walls of a room can change the emotional tone inside and alter the level of distance we have to whatever happens inside that room. I know this from experience: At some point in the early 2000s someone had the idea that it would be cool to paint the walls of the Chicago classrooms in Second City's signature red. It was not a good idea, either for the comedy created inside those rooms nor for the emotions and energy of the students. Being in a red room for a extended period of time "can make us irritable, less relaxed, more aggressive and even increases your heart rate."[3]

Context creates expectations, the terms by which your work can be understood and assessed. But it also forms the setting for your work: It is a frame through which what you create is viewed.

There are contextual elements that clue us in to the fact that what we are viewing is a comedy: the title of the show, the venue we watch it in, whether drinks are served, the style and colors of the set, and the clothing the performers are wearing. When you enter the Second City theater, you are met with a variety of pictures of famous comedy alumni such as Bill Murray, Amy Poehler, Tim Meadows, and ER Fightmaster. These pictures tell you that you can expect to see comedy, and even a certain type of comedy (all of these performers play characters and have a fairly strong point of view; some have a political take, and some are sillier). The Improv stand-up club in Los Angeles has huge caricatures of famous standups on the wall of the parking lot outside the theater that does the same for their venue.

When Second City began performing on cruise ships in the early 2000s, our performances took place in the grand showrooms that were traditionally host to spectacular musical revues, circus-style acts, etc. We provided posters with pictures of the cast to put up on the marquee but discovered that for many of the cruise ship audiences, that wasn't enough to help them understand the type of show they were coming to see. Without that initial contextual expectation, we had to work doubly hard to help those audiences learn how to watch the performances. Eventually we created a movie-facts-style slide show that included pictures of famous alumni and simple trivia questions that allowed the cruise ship audience to begin the performance with a clearer context for what was to come.

But it isn't only physical context that affects us. World, national, and local events can create context for a performance. Heightened awareness can make certain issues more immediately painful or give audience members less psychological distance. Immediately after 9/11, a throwaway joke about "Afghan rebels" in a silly spy sketch that my touring company was performing suddenly elicited audience gasps instead of laughs. As a comedian, you don't have any control over what is happening on the news or the specific life experience and current emotional state of individual audience members. There are also several other aspects of context that you likely don't have any power over, such as the type, appearance, and temperature of the room you are performing in or the style and content of the act that precedes yours in that venue. If you are creating a project that will be watched remotely on film, video, or online, you have some control over the context provided by your specific medium, but you have no control over the physical or temporal context in which your audience will choose to watch.

All the more reason to consider the aspects of context that you can control when you create your comedy. Think about your show titles or posters for live events. Pay attention to the colors and styles of set pieces and costumes you use in video content. I also encourage you to look at how various contexts affect the comedy you personally like and consume. It's quite eye-opening to experience in a large movie theater a comedy film that you previously have seen only on a laptop screen. This is especially true for films from the early part of the twentieth century—you don't realize how much you miss if you don't see them on a big screen in a dark room with an audience.

Economic (Who Is the Customer?)

Comedy is a popular art form, it's for people. Audiences want to see comedy, and comedy generally wants an audience. While there may be a few not-for-profit theaters or spaces that produce comedy, it has traditionally been an art form that is practically interested in making a profit of some kind. Over the years of teaching history of comedy, I have found that thinking about this aspect of the business is an important part of understanding what kinds of comedy have been produced and why and how financial incentives created certain forms.

For example, the producers of vaudeville at the beginning of the twentieth century were looking to appeal to a very wide audience that was generally middle to lower class and ethnically diverse (although not necessarily racially diverse). They advertised their performances as being for the whole family. For vaudeville performers, the more popular you were with audiences, the farther you moved up the bill and the more money you got paid. So a vaudeville act was designed to catch an audience's attention and hold it. It was presentational, playing directly to the audience, and attempted to get the most applause and responses of all kinds. There was frequently a gimmick that made the act memorable. Even the memorable acts added additional gimmick elements: For example, there was a famous regurgitator whose act consisted of drinking both water and gasoline, lighting something on fire, and then vomiting up first the gasoline to make the blaze bigger and then the water to put it out. Unrelated to the act, he also dressed as an "Arabian sheikh" and went by the name of Hadji Ali.[4]

It's important to note that vaudeville began during a time of tremendous change and opening of travel and immigration across the globe. Working-class audiences were seeing differences in the race and ethnicity of the people they encountered out in the world. There was a significant amount of exoticism of difference, and stereotypes were common in media and performance, especially in popular comedy. Unsurprisingly, those differences were recognizable and painful, and exaggerating them made for some popular comedy—most of which feels deeply inappropriate from our modern perspective on issues of race, gender, ethnicity, and identity.

Creating a comedy act in vaudeville meant that you also included some sort of dancing and singing or extravagant physical comedy to get you audience's attention. You honed your jokes over many performances so that nearly any audience would get and understand them. Timing your jokes to get maximum impact and using familiar material to get as many members of the audience to laugh as possible was much more important (for both the producers and the acts) than quality of material or cultivating a specific audience.

It's worth thinking about the finances of the comedy "system" you want to work in and to ask yourself, "Who is the customer in this system?" and "What kind of comedy is going to be rewarded in this kind of system?" Let's look at the differences between "club comedy" (the dominant type of stand-up from the 1960s to the 1990s, and truly still a force in current comedy) and "alt comedy" (literally an alternative to the stand-up clubs; it made its clearest first appearance in the 1990s).

The financial model for "club comedy" is that the club owners make their money from alcohol sales, hence the two-drink minimum. Clubs like these make more money if they have a full house of people who didn't pay for their tickets (all of whom will have at least two drinks) than with a smaller audience who come and pay for a ticket. As a result, they set up lots of free ticket giveaways, and they may choose a headliner they think will draw people in, but for the most part they aren't "curating" an evening. The audience is likely to be uninhibited and a little bit unruly, and if they don't like a comedian, they aren't invested in that comedian doing well. Which leads to potentially antagonistic relationships between audience members and comedians (can you say "heckling"?).

Who is the real "customer" in this scenario? Whose experience is most important? The drinker. The goal is to get the drinkers to drink expensive drinks (at least two) and to stay and drink more. The comedy experience is then designed to sell drinks and reward the type of audience member who will buy a lot of drinks.

What sorts of material play well in front of an audience that came to see "comedy" without really caring what kind it is? And have been drinking? You get material that is heavy on jokes (a drunk audience will have less ability to focus on and follow a longer story). The recognition and pain will tend to be connected to taboos (foul language, sexual jokes, and stereotypes of gender, race, ethnicity, and sexual preference). This environment favors comedians who can control an audience and play high status. It's also going to favor a confrontational style of performance, especially since that drunk audience will have fewer inhibitions and be more likely to heckle or comment aloud on the show.

I want to be clear: I think good comedy can happen in these sorts of clubs, and many good comedians have come out of the comedy club scene. But the financial model does set up a dynamic that supports the creation of a certain kind of comedy and favors certain comedians. If you want to work within that model, you need to think about how you can shape your style of comedy to have more success in that type of venue.

The long-form improvisation boom of the early 2000s had a financial model that functioned very differently but also created a certain kind of comedy. Long-form improvisation, in which performers create a series of improvised scenes based on a single audience suggestion, is relatively easy to do but not necessarily easy to do well. It's a niche art form, and the more you know about it, the more interesting it is to watch. Most of these improvisation-based theaters began as spaces that provided an (unpaid) opportunity for performers to "play," to get reps and have experience in doing the work. These spaces were supported by offering classes to aspiring improvisers who also wanted to perform. This led to a situation that I used to call the "improv industrial complex"—a kind of pyramid scheme that fed on itself. The audiences for the performances were usually other performers, and the performers themselves had paid for classes that gave them a spot on the stage. In this instance, the customer was often the performer and rarely a ticket buyer or spectator.

What kind of comedy happens in a room in which the performers are focused on their own experience and the bulk of the audience members are students or in some way connected to the performers? Lots of inside jokes and a preference for novel types of actions and formats. There may be lots of commonly understood conventions that are obscure for someone unfamiliar with the "scene." It's no surprise that it was difficult for those who expected to make long-form improvisation into a career that paid them money—unless they created their own improv theaters that created more customers/performers.

Again, long-form improvisation is a valid comedic art form that can be highly entertaining to a general audience. Certainly, the sensibilities honed in doing this type of work can be brought to a different audience, as is demonstrated in films like *Anchorman*—director Adam McKay is a highly skilled long-form improvisor who worked closely with Del Close—or in the television show *Broad City*, whose creators and performers, Ilana Glazer and Abbi Jacobson, started at the Upright Citizens Brigade (UCB) in New York. But it is worthwhile to understand how the original financial model created a certain kind of content. If you want to bring versions of that content into a different space, you are going to need to adjust what you make for a different audience (the duo Middleditch and Schwartz do a pretty good job of making this adjustment for the streaming video audience). Think back to our original definition of comedy. We're looking to generate humor and laughter in a specific audience. There are, of course, all sorts of reasons to create comedy that are not financially motivated, and you can get joy and fulfillment out of making comedy in all kinds of ways. However, if you want your work to have a chance of being financially successful, you'll want to think about whether the audience you are creating for is the customer who will pay you.

Putting the Frog Back Together

The other day I was starting a new semester of my Comedy History class. I reviewed the comedy triad of recognition, pain, and distance and the five components of comedy. We had a lively discussion about how various sorts of modern comedy fit into the various structures, and I smoothly segued into discussing the active assignments that are a core part of the class—the ones where I ask my students to make comedy. I could see one student near the back of the theater we hold class in shifting uncomfortably in her seat. And then she asked the inevitable question.

"I understand all of this, but you keep saying I can use it to make comedy. How do I do *that*?"

My friend, the rest of the book is for you.

PART 2

MAKING IT FUNNY

I imagine that a certain number of readers of this book flipped through the previous chapters on comedy and humor theory wondering, "Where's the good stuff? Didn't this book promise to make me funnier? When does that start?" There's a lot in the first section that will help you be funnier. I encourage anyone who skipped forward to go back later and take a look at that earlier section, but this begins the more practical part of the book.

To start with, we are going to look at how we can use the recognition/pain/distance triad to create comedy. This may or may not be good comedy, but the real secret to creating good comedy is to start by creating comedy that is likely not good at all.

If there is one lesson to take from this entire section of the book it is this: Separate generation from analysis.

Teach your brain to create a lot of things before you worry about doing anything with those things. This has nothing to do with the recognition/pain/distance triad—it is just classic good creative practice. As I have said over and over in this book, I am primarily a comedy teacher, and if you do this one thing, it will make you more successful than 90 percent of the people who want to become comedians. Make a lot of comedy. Over and over and over again. Make things you love, and make things you aren't sure you love. Make things that are terrible and you never want to think about again. Make jokes. Make sketches. Make videos. Create characters. Many of the things you make will not work, but if you make enough of them, some of them will. If you get out of your own way and create without judgment, you will have things you can later revise. Things you can make funnier.

This section of the book is roughly organized by comedy component, but I'm not focused here on keeping the components separate from each other. I'm going to assume you understand how they all work together. Think of this section as including all different kinds of comedy practices, ways you can play with creating comedy. Lots of it is "lore" that doesn't come from any one specific thinker, so there will be less citation here. (Anywhere I am working from a base exercise or practice I learned directly from someone I have worked with or studied, I will try to give them credit—it's just going to be less of an academic credit than in the initial part of this book.)

The practices contained here are designed to provide an interested reader with opportunities to take the elements of recognition, pain, and distance and apply them to various kinds of comedy. Some will be more focused on writing, and others will be connected to movement and performance. This section is in no way designed to cover all of the ways people create comedy or all of the forms comedy can take. Instead, my goal here is to provide concrete ways to practice working with the triad to create comedy across the components.

Throughout this section there are points where I generate material of my own as a demonstration of a process. This is my own original work in first-draft form. I'm not pretending to comedic brilliance here, and I didn't check to see if someone else has written something similar. I'm just holding myself to the same standard that you should hold your own first-draft work to—done.

I've also included tools I have found to be useful in the creation of comedy. Not all of these tools are unique to comedy, but they are all tools I have found especially helpful at one point or another in creating or revising comedy.

So let's get to it, shall we? We're going to start with a ridiculously easy answer to a question every comedian gets all the time: "How do you come up with your ideas?" And we're going to use recognition and pain and distance to do it.

7 GENERATING COMEDY IDEAS

I've worked in comedy and improvisation for a long time, and I know comedians of all kinds (working and not working) really well. Here's what I can tell you. The worst way to come up with a comedic idea is to sit in front of a keyboard, or with a notebook or recording device in front of you (or with a group of collaborators), and "try to think of something funny." First, as Yoda once said, "There is no try. There is only do."[1] The minute you "try to come up with something funny," your brain immediately leaps to all the funny things other people have already made that you enjoy. This is natural—it's how brains work. So the key here is to start by tricking your brain. Tell it that you don't have to come up with something funny—yet. The funny thing can happen later.

If you read the first part of this book, you'll know that my comedy theory is pretty simple. Comedy is the manipulation of three elements: recognition, pain, and distance. A comic idea consists of those three things. So, to get to a comedic idea, start by giving yourself a big chunk of raw material based in one or more of those elements. I recommend that you begin by mining your brain for things you already know, think, feel, and believe. In other words, things you recognize.

Why? Well, it's the easiest one to start with. We all have lives, we all have a whole catalog of specific things that have happened to us, that we have experienced with our five senses, not to mention all of the things we have heard about from other people or learned in school or on the street. Some of those things will be so unique that certain audiences won't understand them, but lots of them will be surprisingly universal.

In my large first-year lecture class on comedy, I require my students to start a regular material generation and observation practice. Even for those who don't primarily see themselves as writers, I encourage any budding comedian to have a practice where they regularly capture thoughts and ideas in some way they can return to for inspiration or material generation. So pick a format, any format. It could be a notebook, it could be the notes app on your phone, it could be a file on your computer, it could be a physical folder or even a box where you stuff random small pieces of paper. Just make it one that you can use consistently and that meshes well with your life.

I recommend that you try some version of all those things over time and then settle on the ones that work best for you. You'll notice that you write differently when you handwrite something in a notebook or on a piece of paper than you do when you type with your thumbs on a phone. But I still encourage you to pick one spot where all the creative stuff is stored so that you can come back to it whenever you want raw material for creating comedy. This just means that if you are playing with putting things in the notes app on your phone, but most of your comedy material is in notebooks, you should eventually print out what's on your phone and stick it into your notebook (this is why I like to use notebooks with little folders in the back). Or you could just write the dates of the digital notes into the notebook with a reminder word or two.

I find it is useful to start thinking about generating material by making lists of things you know or observe. Start with a topic and then write at least ten items. Let's try one together right now. Get out a piece of paper and write a list of at least ten things you can see in the room you are in—this one, right now. You don't need to move to a more interesting place. Just list ten things. *GO.*

Did you hit ten items? Try for at least a couple more. Get to a point where it's just a bit hard.

Here's a list I wrote sitting in my living room in July 2020:

- Chair
- Bookcase
- Pillow
- Drum-like thing that holds sewing materials and also functions as a side table
- Books
- Coffee cup
- Two Kindles on top of each other
- Glass of ice water
- Bernese mountain dog
- Small portable speaker with a piece of broken dog biscuit on top of it
- Pile of *New Yorker* magazines
- Stone carving of a bull and a calf that my son made in high school
- Family pictures
- Scented candle
- Martha Stewart cookbook
- Wooden rocking chair

Let's go back to the experience of writing the list. Did you find that you were editing yourself as you wrote your initial list? That you dismissed a certain item because of some reason (too boring, too personally identifiable)? Did you make up a rule about why it wasn't a good choice? Don't do that. Really. Write it all down. There are no rules for what goes on your list. And stopping yourself from writing because of an arbitrary rule is how you end up sitting for an hour staring at a blank page. My experience is that the way to get material on your list that you can use is to just write down the thing you want to edit out and then keep going.

It can be tempting to get ahead of the game by writing lists of funny things. You certainly can do that. But I don't recommend it, particularly not at first. Why not? Let's do another list first. Write a list of at least ten things that people eat for breakfast. Here's mine:

- Scrambled eggs
- Eggs over easy

- Hardboiled eggs
- Pancakes
- Waffles
- French toast
- Bacon
- Sausage
- Toast
- English muffins

Did you find that as you wrote this list you started to think you were cheating? I did. I started with eggs and then continued with eggs, which felt wrong. So I jumped to pancakes and then other forms of pancakes (waffles, etc.), and then I judged myself for getting on that train. There is nothing wrong with my list. But also there would have been nothing wrong with my list if I had just listed a whole bunch of different kinds of egg dishes. Or if I had just listed breakfast cereals.

You are doing two useful things for your comedy work at the same time by doing this exercise in this way: You are generating a large amount of potential material for comedy *and* you are training your brain to separate different modes of working. You can think of this as separating generation from revision or learning to work with your intuitive fast brain rather than your slow analytical brain. Why is it important to train yourself to do that? Practically, you want to use your fast brain because it's, well, faster. You'll get a lot more material out there much more quickly. It's infinitely easier to create a large amount of potential material if you aren't worrying about whether it's any good. And for comedy it is important to create a lot of potential material. Jon Vorhaus, the comedy writer from whom I first learned about lists of ten, says that a pretty good rule of thumb is that for every ten jokes or ideas, nine will suck. In an interview at SXSW, the late-night comedian Amber Ruffin suggested that the yield might be even worse: "We pitch so many things, we write so many things. The percentage of the stuff we generate that they actually use might be like 2 percent."[2]

It's hard to anticipate what might work for an audience. Sometimes the premise you thought was boring or impossible or too "something" to work will end up being the best part of your show. Sometimes the joke (or character or physical gag) you thought was hysterical doesn't get the laugh you expected. If you have a lot of jokes, then that one joke that doesn't work is easy to get rid of. If you have one "perfect" fussed over, honed-to-an-inch-of-its-life joke and it doesn't work, you will be frustrated and exhausted. And not particularly likely to keep writing jokes. Just as bad, maybe that joke does get a huge response, but then you discover that someone else has written an almost exact version of the same joke (happens all the time). Or maybe right after you perfect your joke, there is a societal change (say a pandemic) that makes something innocent in your joke feel sinister. All of this happens constantly, and it is completely out of your control. But if you have many, many jokes and you know that you can write many more at the drop of a hat, then you aren't bothered by accidental duplication or new contexts. There's way more where that came from. An incredibly useful muscle for a comedian to build is the one that allows you to generate a great deal of material and to do so without worrying about its quality.

Eventually, over time, after doing comedy in front of many audiences, you get a sense of what might hit well without necessarily having to put it up in front of an audience first. This explains why most of the comedians who work in film and television get their start in stand-up, improv, or live sketch comedy. It also explains why some of them lose their sense of what an audience will like as they get further away from live performance or more famous. (If you are famous enough for being funny, it's common to get laughs simply because your audience is already fans of your work and is primed to laugh.)

Here's what I recommend: Set a goal for yourself of doing one generation activity a day. Or set a timer on your phone every day and do ten minutes of lists or any of the prompts I've included in this chapter (you can write a surprisingly large amount of stuff in ten minutes). Try it for a week—I make my students do it for an entire fifteen-week semester, you can do it for a week. Don't worry about making any of what you write into a joke or a story or an anything. I've included a couple of weeks' worth of prompts and suggestions below. If you want to, you can use those.

Then, at the end of that week, set aside some time to read back through what you have created. Make note of what strikes you, what interests you, even what feels like it might be the germ of a comedic idea.

Go back and look at your initial list of things you can see in the room you are sitting in. There are likely things on your list that don't feel like they have any use, and others that appeal to you and spark questions or memories: Do I actually have sewing materials inside that side table we inherited from my husband's mother? I have absolutely no idea. If not, what else is in there? What else could be in there? It's roughly big enough to contain a human head. What other places in my fairly modest Chicago home could contain random body parts? This train of thought is exactly how you find a comic idea that can be expanded and built on. With little effort I could turn these thoughts into a joke or premise (and I do just that in the "Comic Premise" section of the "Creating Comedic Narratives" chapter, if you want to see how it's done).

This is the work of being a comedian. If you spend a week setting aside time regularly to generate without judging, you have begun to build the habits that will serve a career in comedy regardless of what forms your particular comedy will take. Later in this book, we'll do some exercises in writing a joke, creating a comic character, playing with a bit of physical comedy. Your personal trove of raw material will jump-start all these processes by providing specifics that you can borrow from and play with.

Material Generation Prompts

In this section you'll find some of the prompts I give my comedy students to use as part of their required writing practice. Use the ones that work for you. Once you get the hang of this kind of work, you can (and should) create your own prompts.

Lists

The "Tool: List Ideas" box below includes some ideas to get you started, and I also encourage you to create your own list topics or to borrow them from other places. Some of the most useful lists are ones that come directly from your memory, things you have instant or easy access to because you already know them. You personally recognize them. Remember that at this point, you aren't creating comedy—you are just mining your own experience. Be as specific as possible:

Names of people you met at summer camp. Foods carried at your corner grocery store. Things that used to be cool.

You don't have to generate lists by yourself. You can brainstorm lists in pairs or small groups. This generates different lists than the ones you make on your own—other people's contributions can inspire you to think in new and creative ways. You could even use AI to generate lists but I haven't found it useful. AI is predictive, it gives you the most obvious answers. A primary goal of these lists is to move past the obvious answers.

You can crowdsource lists, too. For years at the end of every Second City show, after the "outro" where we remind people to tip their waitstaff and promote other shows and classes in the building, two people would come out on stage with a giant pad of paper divided into quadrants and take suggestions from the audience. What we knew at Second City was that the audience was likely to laugh at something they had suggested if we put it into a sketch. But often the suggestions that were the most useful weren't the ones that were already funny. They were the ones that resonated for some reason, that triggered a feeling or suggested there was more to the story. Creating comedy using those suggestions didn't just please the immediate audience; it also opened potential avenues for comedy that we hadn't considered.

TOOL: List Ideas

Here are some of the prompts I share with my first-year comedy students. These lists move roughly from simple things that will be easy to generate to ideas that have an element of comedy. For the last set, "Opinions," you can write either simple lists or long-form descriptions.

Items

- Bands
- Colors
- Things you shouldn't do on a school night
- Family names
- Kinds of Halloween candy
- High school teacher names
- Things in a bathroom

(continued)

- Rooms in a museum
- Scary things
- Animals
- Things you find at the bottom of your backpack
- Jobs that actual people you know have had
- Lunch foods
- Toys
- Rich people names
- Embarrassing ways to die
- Bad wedding themes
- Things that used to be cool
- Great spots to live if you were five inches tall
- Things that happened on your worst day ever
- Dumb things that make you laugh
- Things that begin with *G. B.* (like Good Beer or Green Beret)
- Things that drunk people say
- New superheroes
- Bad names for a tiny dog
- A movie and its nine sequels (with subtitles)
- Middle school fashion statements
- Laws in your empire
- The worst insult ever
- Imaginary Pokémon

Descriptions

- Your bedroom—can be your current bedroom or any room you have slept in
- The face of someone you know very well
- The face of someone you see regularly but don't know well
- All the things you see on a walk or trip you take regularly (this is a good one to do once from memory and again after taking the trip while paying close attention)
- The exact events of a holiday from your childhood
- How you make a meal, exactly
- How someone you know orders at a restaurant
- Someone you see frequently but don't know much about, like a person who always rides the same train or bus as you do

Opinions

- Plan your perfect vacation. Where would it be? What would the activities be? What food would you eat? Who else would be there?
- If hell existed, what would be your own very specific version of hell? What would you have to do? Who would you have to spend time with? How else would you be tortured?
- What are your deeply held convictions, your own personal "hills to die on"? They can be trivial—"David Tennant is the best Dr. Who." Or serious—"The United States should offer universal childcare."
- Pick a minor controversy—"soda vs. pop," "crunchy vs. smooth peanut butter," "the correct way to put toilet paper on the roll"—and make a case for what you feel is the correct side.

Parts of a Whole

Another list type I find useful is a written version of a Spolin improvisation exercise called "Parts of a Whole." Pick an object and then generate as many elements of that thing as you can. Let's try "Parts of a Car."

- Hood
- Driver's seat
- Passenger seat
- Trunk
- Engine
- Windshield
- Windshield wipers
- Glove compartment
- Gas gauge
- Heater
- Air conditioner
- Odometer
- Speedometer
- Dashboard

If you expand the definition of what a "part" of something is, you can add things or experiences that you remember from specific cars:

- Snow scraper
- Reusable grocery bags
- Crusty stuff under the baby's car seat
- The uncomfortable feeling of sitting next to your significant other in the car when you're mad at each other
- Fighting with your sister over who gets to sit next to the window

You can do "Parts of a Whole" for a location, like a fast-food restaurant. Or an even a bigger location like a city or country. How about doing "Parts of a Whole" for an idea, like "Freedom" or "Poverty"?

Freewriting

Freewriting is taking a topic or idea as a prompt and then writing nonstop in a stream of consciousness fashion. As with lists, the goal here is to just get a whole lot of words down on paper without editing yourself. Generally, for freewriting you want to set some kind of goal in terms of length or writing time. Set a timer for five or ten minutes or decide you will freewrite for a certain number of pages or number of words (only if you can see the word count while you write; you don't want to stop writing every minute to check the word count). In her book *The Artist's Way*, the creativity expert Julia Cameron recommends a form of freewriting that she calls Morning Pages. First thing in the morning, you write longhand in a notebook for three full pages. In her version, there is no topic or prompt—you just write whatever comes to your mind. And if nothing comes to your mind, you write about how you have nothing on your mind.

You can use list prompts as freewriting prompts. Or you can start with one of your lists, pick an item that appeals to you, and then freewrite from that.

Observation

Another way to generate material is to write down things you can actually see or observe. Observation isn't just visual detail. It's all the things you perceive—sounds, smells, mood. The first list we generated in this chapter was observational.

Pick something you do regularly, like grocery shopping, and pay attention to every detail both of how you do it and what you observe while you do it. Make sure to note what draws your attention, as you do it. It can be interesting to do this exercise first from your memory of how the activity normally goes and then do the activity with awareness and write a new version of the same list. Often you discover a slew of new and potentially funny details you completely missed the first time around.

This might immediately suggest to you a certain kind of stand-up joke telling. There's a reason they call it "observational humor." Jerry Seinfeld is the king of this style. His frequently imitated "Airport" routine slowly takes his audience with him through the experience of going through security, walking through the terminal (including using the bathroom), getting on the plane, and preparing for takeoff. All with an obsessive attention to small details.

Yes. You can do that, too. Well, probably not exactly that. But highly specific observations of everyday things can provide you with a wealth of material to work with.

Start by really observing other people, not just what is obvious to you or confirms your biases about them but what the human beings around you *actually do and say*. Remember when we talked about heuristics and biases? One of the great sources of comedy is to point out something recognizably true that everyone tends to ignore due to one of those heuristics. Pay close and deep attention. You don't have to be obvious about it in a way that suggests a stalker, but get used to watching other human beings and noting their specific behavior.

Observe everyday interactions between people. Exactly how do they talk to each other? How do they stand? Move their bodies? Gesture? What do they say and how do they look when they say it? You can take your notebook out with you, or you can spend time paying attention without your notebook and then make your notes later (as with the observing an activity, you get two different kinds of useful material from this).

You can keep track of your observations in any way that makes the most sense to you personally. All you are doing at this point is capturing them in a rough format to be mined for comedy later. So, you could describe what you see using speech-to-text on your phone. You can make a list of what you observed. (Lists are good; have I made that clear?) You can freewrite while you observe. You can make sketches or take pictures or video on your phone. Whatever works for you. Again, the key at this point is to not worry about making anything out of it—just accumulate stuff you can use later.

Research

What I mean by "research" is to search out material that exists in the world that you might choose to use for your comedy. You don't have to go to a library; the topics don't have to be educational. It doesn't have to be particularly academic or even require much work. Just as with lists, you don't have to do this on your own, either. Get a research buddy and try out something new together.

Go to a (noncomedy) news website and write down headlines that spark your interest. Don't look for things that are already funny. Just make note of things that catch your eye. Even better, get an actual newspaper (local or national) and pay attention to what interests you. Why even better? Because these days a lot of what will show up for you, even on a news website, depends on an algorithm designed to show you things you might like based on what you have looked at before. An actual newspaper isn't filtering things for you (well, it is, but not for *just* you, which is a big difference), so you are likely to see things you wouldn't see otherwise. Read the ads, read the obituaries, read the advice column.

You can also give yourself a simple research prompt—for example, to go through a newspaper or magazine and write down interesting names. Or random quotes. Or specific locations.

More research possibilities:

- Combine research and observation—go to a place you have never been, or go for a walk or a drive in an area of your city or town that you don't generally spend time in.
- Try a new thing that you've never done before and pay close attention to what happens and what you experience while you do it.

- Interview a person. Not necessarily someone famous or important. This could be someone you know well or someone whom you don't know but see all the time (like your barista at Starbucks).
- Pick a random topic, say, red wagons, or a skill (pottery or auto repair) and learn about it in detail. You'll get different material learning about it from a book or website than you will from actual experience. Experiment with both.

As I said earlier, how you document any of this is up to you. Just be sure to keep track of your research somewhere you will be able to access it easily on an ongoing basis. You may have already noticed that all of this has been focused on generating material through recognition. The next step is to add the elements of pain and/or distance.

Prompts That Work with Pain and Distance

Start by adding a negative quality to your recognition lists. What do you hate about going out to eat? What do you hate about Christmas? Fear is also a great way to introduce the element of pain. What are your top ten fears? Why are you afraid for your country, your city? What are the tiny things that make you irrationally angry (pet peeves)?

Play with your own fears over time: What were you desperately afraid of as a kid? What about as a teenager? For those of you playing along at home, the prompt "What were you afraid of as a kid?" provides all of the pieces that you need to generate comedy: Something you were genuinely afraid of is likely to be a fear (pain) that others had as well (recognition), and the fact that it's in the past provides distance. No surprise this is a common theme in stand-up, from Kevin Hart's description of how his fear of gnats followed him into adulthood to John Mulaney's discovery that his fear of quicksand did not.

You can generate lists of taboos, make a list of things you would never be allowed to do onstage.[3] This is one of my favorite prompts when I am working with a cast creating a show. I have everyone come in with a sketch idea they believe I would never allow them to do in the show. Not all of these ideas work, but almost every time I have given this prompt, the cast comes in with material that is different from what they have pitched before, and despite the name of the assignment, there are often several ideas that I'm thrilled to give a shot at trying in the show.

Positive emotions help to provide distance. You can make lists of things you love. Or things you love about a specific thing. For example, things you love about Christmas, things you love about your hometown. What about things you love to fight about with your partner? This final one has potential to deliver all three parts of the triad.

Making lists that allow you to play also creates a kind of distance. Take two random letters of the alphabet (say *L* and *G*) and come up with a list of things that begin with those two letters.

- Lord Golden
- Little Goblin
- Lego Globe
- Living Green
- Lady Godiva
- Little Girls
- Laughing Goddess

You can do the quick character creation that I mentioned earlier in this book by writing two lists: occupations and adjectives.

Occupations

- Plumber
- Dentist
- Administrative assistant
- Sex worker
- Barista
- Fisherman
- Librarian
- TV news anchor
- Baker
- Accountant

Adjectives

- Spidery
- Agile
- Exhausted
- Chipper
- Scary
- Apprehensive
- Blustery
- Naive
- Impatient

Now mix and match in ways that enhance the incongruities—“spidery barista” or “agile accountant” (as opposed to “blustery TV news anchor,” which is still a comedic character but has less incongruity).

Here are a few lists of ten that are designed with built-in incongruity:

- Stories that should never be made into Disney full-length cartoon movies
- Terrible names for dogs
- Things you find at an inconvenience store
- Types of children who deserve to be bullied
- Mascot names for retirement home sports teams
- Oprah Winfrey’s least favorite things
- College majors for lazy people
- Best parts about breaking up with someone

You’ll notice that finding ten items for these lists is a little harder than for some of the original lists. That’s because you are using your System 2 brain along with your System 1. You aren’t just remembering something or jumping to a quick conclusion—you have to do a bit of analysis, which makes it harder and slower.

These are fine to do, but I’m going to give you a hint. What you are doing now is starting to write things that work like jokes.

TOOL: Truth

My initial version of my theory of comedy used the term *truth* rather than *recognition*. I've detailed my reasons for that shift already, but when I am working with comedy makers, it's not unusual for me to slip into talking about truth rather than recognition. I think that for most comedy makers a good place to find ideas is indeed truth.

Recognition is important for revision—you want your chosen audience to get the joke, to feel at home in your sketch premise and to believe in your characters. But starting with recognition has a downside. It means that we are beginning by predicting what other people know and believe. Behavioral science has shown that humans are quite bad at predicting what is happening in other people's minds. Straight-up terrible at it. When we try to generate comedy by guessing what other people will recognize, our efforts tend toward obvious generalities and easy targets.

On the other hand, the very fact that humans are so bad at understanding each other means that truthful detail or the revelation of genuine personal thoughts and experiences are fascinating to our audiences. And often recognizable in a way that is much more interesting and useful for comedy than when we try to predict what our audience knows or understands.

When my students in the Comedy Studies semester do their stand-up sets for each other, what always strikes me is that the moments in which the room really laughs are often not the result of crafted jokes but some tiny true detail somewhere in the setup. The description of a very specific and somewhat bizarre childhood game or a unique quote from the performer's father that simultaneously feels like a very "dad" thing to say even though our own father would never say exactly that. The highly specific and true has a universality.

One of my favorite exercises to do with intermediate-level students is to have them improvise a short scene with the directive that they should throw as many personal truthful details into the scene as possible.[4] They are given deniability by being allowed to also include extravagant lies. Inevitably, the classroom feedback is that the truthful details were the funniest, the most surprising, as well as the most relatable and recognizable. The players will note that at a certain point, they were getting so much good response from using their truth that they gave up fabricating and just stuck to the real detail from their lives. Truth is not only stranger than fiction—it is also funnier.

Writers who work in sitcom writers' rooms are constantly mining their own lives for truthful details and events that can be shaped into jokes and situations for the show's comic characters. As Stephen Levitan, the cocreator of the sitcom *Modern Family*, notes, "Chris [Christopher Lloyd] and I, we were working on a couple ideas, and we realized that we'd come in on Monday mornings and tell a funny story about something our kids did or some sort of thing that happened with our wives or whatever it was. And it started to dawn on us that maybe that was more interesting than what we were working on at the time. So we started writing the script."[5]

Your truth is going to be more recognizable to an audience than any guess you might have about what you they might know. It's going to feel more novel as well, because it is unexpected to the audience. It is doubly funny because they recognize it as true, it feels true, and yet (for precisely the same reasons we are terrible at predicting other what others think) it feels very strange that someone else should have had a thought that in some way mirrors our own. Or conversely, we recognize the thought as deeply true but realize it's one we have never thought or experienced. Which, if you are playing spot the comedy theory at home, you'll notice provides a great triple shot of recognition, pain, and distance.

This doesn't just work for creating specific comedy situations and details—it is also important in terms of the premise and point of view or thesis of a piece. If you begin with a thought or belief that is (or was) true for you, the comedy you create will likely feel recognizable throughout even if the details are not. You can get away with highly unrealistic or unrecognizable elements if the central thesis has a truth at its base. One of my favorite sketch shows is the British comedy show *Big Train*. In the titular sketch from the first season a transportation expert is using a model to demonstrate a high-speed rail project to a government official who takes each element of the demonstration literally. When he moves the model train on a map of England to show how quickly the train will allow people to cross the country, she is astonished that it will now take only a second or two to get from London to Edinburgh. Her lack of ability to think in metaphors is absurd, but the experience of explaining something

(continued)

(or having something explained to you) when there genuinely isn't enough information to make sense of what is going on is universal.

Ashley Nicole Black's "Invisible Spy" sketch from *A Black Lady Sketch Show* took a somewhat painful truth from her own life (people who did not see her as important or valuable because of the way she physically presents) and reimagined it as a superpower. The genuine truth of her experience of not being seen anchored the comic conceit in the genre parody.

If you are playing with a premise or situation where you have characters behave in ways that don't feel true or real to you (even if you can make it work logically), it won't feel recognizable to your audience. This is one of the primary difficulties in constructing good farce: The escalating ridiculousness of the actions and behavior of the characters need to continue to at least feel possible, even if it is highly irrational and unlikely to occur in real life.

Some suggestions for how to play with truth in your own comedy:

- Start with elements that are real or truthful for you. Use real first or last names of people you have met, specific parts of experiences you have actually had in your life. Try writing or improvising using as much true detail as possible and see what you discover.
- Base a character on someone you know well. Use as many tiny specifics as you can. A note I frequently give students is to not just play a teacher, but to play a version of their own fifth-grade teacher. Or their high school math teacher. Ultimately, you should change some details or exaggerate others, since our goal here isn't to get sued for libel, but starting with truth will frequently create a character that feels unique. Another way to do this is to base a character on yourself, the truth of yourself at a specific of age. Can you play a character who is an adult but sees the world the same way you did when you were thirteen? Or five?
- Examine your own thoughts and assumptions (both current and past) and base your premises for sketches or stand-up on those things that were or are true for you. Make lists of your current or past beliefs about yourself, your family, your community, or the world and mine those for premises.

8 WRITING A JOKE

"I've been in love with the same woman for twenty-nine years. If my wife finds out, she'll kill me."

—Henny Youngman

"I saw a lady on TV, she was born without arms. Literally. She was born with her hands attached to her shoulders. And that was sad. But then they said, 'Lola does not know the meaning of the word can't. *' And that to me was actually kind of worse, in a way. Not only does she not have arms, but she doesn't understand simple contractions."*

—Mitch Hedberg

"Lots of strip clubs in Florida. Good grief, Florida has so many strip clubs, they need to change their state flag to a brass pole."

—Wanda Sykes

What Is a Joke?

The simplest and most easily defined element of comedy is the joke. A joke is a setup and a punch line. That's it.

Jokes play with the natural human System 1 tendency to look for patterns, to jump to assumptions. The setup of a joke creates an expectation of what is going to come next. For example, a riddle asks a question to be answered. In a knock-knock joke we expect to find out who is at the door. The punch lines to these types of jokes answer the question or tell us who is at the door but do so in a way that subverts or plays with our expectation.

All jokes work like this. Let's look at the three jokes that start this chapter.

Here's the setup of the Henny Youngman joke: "I've been in love with the same woman for twenty-nine years." What is the natural expectation of the audience? If this were not the setup to a joke, we would expect this line to be the prelude to a tribute to the fine and continuing qualities of the woman Youngman has been joined to in a nearly three-decade marriage.

The punch line does indeed reference a wife, but only to suggest that she has been duped for an equivalent length of time.

The Mitch Hedberg joke has a slightly longer setup but works in a similar way. He describes a televised tribute to a woman with a congenital handicap. Anyone in the modern era who has seen a similar "Profile in Courage" has an expectation based on their familiarity with this trope.

This time the punch line is an illustration of how Hedberg misconstrues the description of the woman as "not understanding the meaning of the word *can't*." He takes the description literally—she is multiply handicapped, both in her body and in her mind.

The setup for Wanda Sykes's Florida joke starts with a simple observation about the state. On its own, this might get a recognition laugh from an audience member familiar with the parts of Florida she is describing, but it also provides setup information for the joke that follows. This joke is quicker, so I'm going to diagram it to make the parts clear.

Setup: "They need to change their state flag to . . ."
Expectation: A flag with some sort of picture on it.
Punch line: A brass pole (no flag, but appropriately something that both strip clubs and flags are likely to have).

Oh, my god, there is nothing more boring than explaining a joke. Nothing. This was boring when I wrote it, and I assume it is equally boring for you to read. But bear with me and slog through. We're going to ruin a couple of jokes for ourselves and we're going to get extremely pedantic about joke structure.

Because here's the other thing about jokes. They work like algebra equations. Yes, a lot of comedy is math. It really is. I'm sorry. I know you were hoping for a form of comedy Hogwarts where the chosen get to learn how to cast the joke spells. It turns out that comedy contains very little magic. It's math. (By the way, I have a sneaking suspicion that most of magic is math as well.)

The setup of a joke is one side of the formula—an equation with what appears to our fast brain to have an obvious answer. Anyone with any Western schooling over the age of six will likely see 2 + 2 and involuntarily have the answer of 4 leap to mind. Jokes use that involuntary reflex, but they twist the equation and then show us there is another equally valid answer that is different from the immediate one fed to us by our intuitive brain. Sure, 2 + 2 does equal 4, but what if it is also something else entirely? That something else is the other side of the equation—the punch line. Also, if you Google "two plus two joke," you will discover a whole series of additional answers to that question, many centering on ethically corrupt accountants who ask, "What would you like it to be?"

All jokes contain a duality. Light bulb jokes, and simple riddles (What is black and white and red all over?) show us their duality pretty immediately in their question-and-answer formula. Longer narrative jokes might take us down a long path introducing characters and situations, but they are still setting up a false reality that will be revealed in the punch line.

Here's the formula for your basic knock-knock joke:

A: Knock-knock.
B: Who's there?

A: [*Something that seems like a first name*].
B: [*Something that seems like a first name*] who?
A: [*Some sort of pun that begins with the first name*].

Puns have been called the "lowest form of humor," but it would be more accurate to say they are the thinnest form of humor. For the most part, puns are one of two things: either (1) words that sound alike in our language but are really two different words entirely (the business that specifies "No Checks" but has to make it clear that they are happy to welcome those born in Prague), or (2) words or phrases with multiple meanings depending on their context (another one from Henny Youngman—"My wife will buy anything marked down. One day she brought home an escalator"). A pun-based joke works because of a simple misunderstanding, misspelling, or mishearing.

Metajokes play on our familiarity with how jokes work. We have the expectation that our expectation will in some way be subverted. Metajokes subvert *that* expectation.

Question: Why did the chicken cross the road?
Answer: To get to the other side.

Despite the current popularity of anticomedians like Eric Andre, metajokes are in no way new. That chicken joke can be traced at least as far back as the minstrel shows of the early nineteenth century, and since those shows were notable for their borrowing of traditional folk humor, likely its real origin is much further back in the past.

Traditional riddles of the kind that Bilbo Baggins has to guess in *The Hobbit* or that the Sphinx poses to Oedipus (Question: What walks on four feet in the morning, two feet at noon, and three feet in the evening? Answer: Man) use the same "fast brain / slow brain" equation as these jokes but do it backward. They start with the complicated slow version, and the pleasure is in how long it takes to discover an answer that seems obvious to our fast brains, but only once it appears. These kinds of riddles aren't funny to us exactly because of their backward nature. It's partly because there's no surprise but also because they begin with confusion. Audiences don't laugh when they are confused.

How to Write a Joke

The real key to joke writing is to not worry about whether what you are working on is objectively funny. The trick at the beginning, anyway, is not to try to write a good joke at all. Instead, use a formula for the sort of joke that you want to write and churn out a whole series that fit the formula using the same process you used for the lists. Keep the stakes as low as possible.

Anyone can write a joke if they don't worry about quality. At least to begin with, I encourage you to set the bar as low as possible. Let's say you wanted to write some terrible knock-knock jokes. To use the formula above you might first start by brainstorming a list of first names. In fact, let's do that right now. However many you like, but ten is a pretty good starting place. As we did in the material generation section, don't worry about quality—just get at least ten names down on a piece of paper.

Here's my list:

- Anna
- Bart
- Charles
- David
- Ernest
- Fred
- George
- Harry
- Irene
- James

Set a timer for five minutes or so and use that list of names to write as many knock-knock jokes as you can. Don't let your judging brain get involved. Don't worry at all about whether the jokes are any good. In fact, if possible, revel in how fundamentally terrible they are. Just write as many as you can in five minutes. Or, if you prefer, use all ten names to write ten jokes as fast as you can. You can absolutely cheat, too. If a name that isn't on the list pops up in your head, go ahead and use it. If you come up with two ideas for one name, write them both down. If you get stuck on one, write "stuck" and move on to the next. Also, don't get hung up on writing out the whole joke. Just fill in the blanks.

Here's what resulted from my five minutes:

ANNA: Anna-ther knock-knock joke is done.
BART: Bar the door, it's a full moon. I'm becoming a werewolf.
CHARLES: Stuck.
DAVID: Also stuck.
ERNEST: Earn'rest of your butler salary for this week and open the goddamned door yourself.

Whew, that was five minutes.

And I got out three fairly terrible knock-knock jokes. But I have three more terrible jokes than I had five minutes ago.

I can hear you saying that you don't want to write knock-knock jokes. Of course you don't. No one wants to write or hear knock-knock jokes over the age of five, but you can use the knock-knock joke strategy for any classic joke structure or riddle.

This section is not about how to write a good joke. Or a funny joke. Or a new joke that has never been written. You're doing joke exercises, getting used to the form. The good, the original, the transcendent—all of that comes after the work of learning how to get a bunch of jokes out and down on paper. The more jokes you write, the better off you will be. It's the practice that's important here. I want to encourage you to think of this as an extension of the generation exercises, with an added degree of difficulty.

Let's try another one. First let's deconstruct a classic light bulb joke. It's a riddle in that it starts with a question and ends with an answer.

Question: How many [insert category of people here] does it take to change a light bulb?
Answer: [Number]. [Explanation of number using a commonly understood stereotype or habit related to that group of people].

So, to write a light bulb joke, you start by making a list of at least ten occupations or groups of people and, just as we did before, set a timer and see how many jokes you can get. Light bulb jokes are marginally more difficult than knock-knock jokes, because there's a bit more to the recognition element: You aren't just playing with the sounds of words—you are mining mostly negative beliefs about groups of people.

If you're finding that you are stuck filling in the blanks, try this. Take your list of groups of people. As quickly as you can, write as many things as possible that are true or assumed to be true about each group—in other words, stereotypes, the foundation of all light bulb jokes. For example, let's use video gamers.

Here's my list of gamer stereotypes:

- Male
- Nerdy
- Sleepless
- Overweight
- Obsessive
- Competitive
- Single

Now see if you can use those qualities to come up with punch lines.

This entire exercise may feel somewhat ridiculous to you if you are genuinely interested in working in comedy. After all, no one writes riddles anymore unless perhaps you work for a popsicle stick company. In fact, for the most part, no one really writes or tells these kinds of jokes professionally anymore. There's a reason we now call these contextless jokes "dad jokes."

So let's look at a kind of joke you might write professionally, the mainstay of late-night television talk shows—the news joke. These jokes are a staple for comedy shows from *Saturday Night Live*'s "Weekend Update" to *Late Night with Seth Meyers* and *The Daily Show*. In a slightly different form, they appear as headlines on satiric topical websites such as *The Onion* and *Reductress*.

How to Write a News Joke

News jokes are based on current events and provide a built-in recognition factor. Additionally, many of the shows and sites that play with news jokes are in some way parodying existing television news broadcasts, print, or online journalism. This means they are in existing formats that already create expectations in listeners, viewers, or readers.

We're going to do the same thing here that we did with riddles. Break down the structure (the joke equation) and then practice creating an abundance of jokes that follow the format without worrying about whether any given joke is especially funny.

Start by gathering headlines or news from a newspaper or internet site. It's useful to look at a variety of news stories—national, international, and local. Have both headlines and the actual articles at your disposal, since you never know what might spark an idea. Then reread your material and look for expectations that are already there.

I'll start with one at random. The *New York Times* reports that more multigenerational families are buying and living in homes together. We're going to use that report for the setup of the joke.

Just as in a riddle, a news joke uses our expectations of how news is presented to us. To write the joke, we need to project what those expectations are and then reverse them in a way that feels equally plausible if unexpected.

Here are some expectations I would have of the article after reading that headline:

- That the article would discuss something happening in the modern world that led to people moving in with their families.
- That the article would have members of those families comment on why they do so.
- That the article would connect this trend with other related modern trends.

Now you want to brainstorm some potential reversals of those expectations. For example, the family dog might comment on the trend rather than a person: "American Dog Thrilled That Loss of Job Brings Boy Home." Or we might suggest that the Western model of extended families living apart is both recent and not necessarily a good thing: "Local Woman Moves Home and Finds Parents Are No Longer Annoying." We might also relate it to any one of a number of television dramas and sitcoms that have played with this idea in the past and comment on that.

Another way to think about these sorts of reversals is to use the "two stories" concept popularized by stand-up comedian Greg Dean. Your setup creates a story in the audience's head. It's like a mystery novel—you gave me a bunch of clues, and I assume I know how the murder happened. Then you reveal that there is an equally plausible reason for the murder that had not occurred to me. As a reader, I dismissed a crucial clue: That pool of water was originally the murder weapon—the corpse was stabbed to death with an icicle.

Most late-night-style news jokes will start with some version of the original headline or news story. Then they segue to the punch line / reversal using a connector of some sort. Below are several classic connectors that help create the second part of a news joke, with explanations of how they work logically.

- **Because**—gives a reason for what is being reported that feels true but is unexpected.
- **In Related News**—connects the story to another completely different story that comments on it in some way.
- **That's Like**—describes the story in terms that equate it with something more every day or points out how ridiculous the story might be in a different context.
- **And / And Then**—creates a new (generally untrue and unexpected) ending to a true beginning. It takes the familiar story in a new direction.

There are more. I encourage you to watch an episode or two of your favorite late-night comedy show that use these kinds of jokes and see if you can find other connectors.

Here are some instantly outdated examples—in fact, I'm going to purposely use examples that were outdated at the time I wrote this book. Because nearly any news joke is going to be outdated hours after it is written.

- **Because:** "Catherine Zeta-Jones and Michael Douglas celebrated their wedding recently and singer Tom Jones sang at the wedding. Because like the bride, he is Welsh, and like the groom, he is old and creepy" (from a "Weekend Update" segment in the early 2000s).[1]

- **Which Is Why / I Always Thought:** "Around 150 million Americans are expected to experience temperatures above 90 degrees this week, thanks to what they call a 'heat dome.' I always thought the heat dome was that weird helmet thing my grandma sat under at the hair salon."[2]
- **In Related News:** "Yesterday, officials confirmed that at least six of President Trump's closest advisers used a private email to discuss official White House business. In a related story, Hillary Clinton was hospitalized today after rolling her eyes so hard she threw her back out."[3]
- **That's Like / It's Like:** "Internal strife is tearing the Republican Party apart at the seams. It's like a new Civil War, only this time neither side is trying to help Black people."[4]
- **And / And Then:** "After a US drone was forced down yesterday by a Russian fighter jet, Russia's ambassador to the US denied that the two aircraft collided, and Putin is claiming the drone just fell out a window."[5]

Now take the headlines and news stories you have pulled from today's news, and create a series of headline jokes. Again, the goal here is not to write good jokes. It is to write jokes. I find that sometimes it helps to tell myself or my students that we aren't even writing jokes. We are creating joke-like objects.

As we've done earlier, I encourage you to pay attention to your thought process as you do the exercise. Was there a point at which you got stuck? Why? Were you judging your jokes? Worried that the jokes were too close to a joke you had heard already or someone else had told? Trying to come up with something especially interesting or unusual instead of the obvious joke? Trying to disrupt a pattern? How many did you get out before you started to get stuck? Did you find yourself just staring at a headline trying to make it work rather than moving on to another one that might inspire you more? Did you allow yourself to rewrite or change the original information so that it made it easier to write the punch line you had in mind? Yes, this is allowed. No one cares if you quote the original story exactly.

Once you have a number of joke-like objects, read through what you have. Is there a particular joke you like better than the others or is there one that seems to make more logical sense? Any that feel like they have promise? It may just be one or two. That's great—the yield on this kind of work is really low. If you have one or more than one, take the win.

Creating Original Jokes

The next step is to take the training wheels off and to just play with writing jokes that don't have a hard-and-fast structure. Jokes are an equation, so the fundamental idea of setup and punch line still applies. This is where the work of material generation really comes into its own. Go through your notebooks (or wherever you decided to keep your ideas and generation lists). Look for information or details that create expectation of some kind: observations, personal stories, lists of things that lots of people know about, details from your research.

Once you have material to play with, see if you can use it to create setups. That is, begin to tell a story or create a narrative pattern. I encourage you to just experiment with creating setups without worrying about the punch line. Here are some possibilities to start with:

1. Write the beginning of a one-liner, just one sentence that creates an expectation or suggests an outcome. For example:
   - My high school had this thing where they voted for "Senior Superlatives," who in the graduating class had the "Best Hair" or was "Most Likely to Succeed." I was voted . . .
   - I was a weird kid. When you're a kid everyone asks you, "What do you want to be when you grow up?," I always answered . . .
   - I recently got a dog. You know how when you get home, your dog is waiting for you at the door? My dog . . .
2. Write a short paragraph or two that is the beginning of a story. It could be a true story that actually happened to you or be completely fabricated, but it should create an expectation of what might happen next.
3. Use something from your observation practice to create a setup. What do you see while taking public transportation? What happens on a social media platform? What do people do at a public place or event?

Once you have a group of setups to play with, the next step is to try to find ways of reversing the expectations generated by the setups you have written. I recommend that you continue to use the brainstorming-style methods we have been using thus far. See how many different punch lines you can come up with for each setup without worrying about quality. Or start with a long list of setups and come up with a punch line for each, just moving along to the next one if you get stuck.

When you do an exercise like this, it's common for a new and completely different setup and punch line to pop into your head. Write it down! One of the side benefits of practicing joke writing in this way is that your brain sometimes begins to play with the joke puzzles without you consciously directing it to do so. There's probably some good neuroscience term for this that I'll find out about later. For now, I recommend that you accept these gifts from the joke-writing gods when they come and notice that inspiration often strikes because you already started doing the work.

Joke Filters

There are lots of different ways of getting at that punch line, and just as in the news jokes section where I gave you a number of connectors, it can be helpful to look at some different methods of arriving at punch lines.

In his book *How to Write Funny*, *The Onion* cofounder Scott Dikkers makes a case that there are exactly eleven different "funny" filters that cover all types of comedy: analogy, character, hyperbole, irony, madcap, metahumor, misplaced focus, parody, reference, shock, and wordplay. Because Dikkers is the cofounder of the satiric parody newspaper *The Onion,* his filters are well suited to written comedy and news parody. I'm not quite as definitive as Dikkers about the exact number of filters that exist, but I still find that it can be highly useful to use general tools like these to expand your joke-writing skills. Start with one setup and apply different filters to generate a variety of punch lines or try one filter at a time and run a bunch of setups through that filter.

I've included some of these filters below along with others that I have found useful in teaching comedic joke writing. What all these filters do is provide concrete ways to apply the recognition/pain/distance triad. Some give you just one element. The shock filter generally heightens pain. Exaggeration can create pain or distance depending on the (recognizable) setup or source material. You will notice that some of these suggestions are similar or overlap in some way. They absolutely do. I have found that a slightly different angle or thinking on what might be considered the same filter can open up possibilities and free your brain from a metaphorical rut it may be stuck in.

- **Tell the truth in the bluntest way possible.** Most of the time, in the news and in life, we avoid the most obvious or blunt truth. So just tell the truth. This can result in a metajoke (like the old "Why did the chicken cross the road?"). It can be something uncomfortable: There is a reason that the truth is hidden. Or just surprising because it is rare that certain truths are spoken aloud.
- **Lie extravagantly.** This is especially good when your setup is personal or based in a true story. Let go of what happened and instead make up the craziest possible consequence of the real event.
- **Worst possible response.** What's the worst answer to the question? What is the least likely or least acceptable thing that could be said or done? How about a non sequitur, something that is just weird and makes no sense whatsoever (see Dikkers's "madcap")?
- **Shock.** This is another version of inappropriate response, but take it to the farthest places. Put taboo elements into your punch line—sex, graphic violence, obscenities, gross-out humor, bodily functions.
- **Reframe.** Literally, show us that what we are seeing in the setup of the joke is not the whole story or that the setup has focused on the wrong element. Pull the frame of your metaphorical camera back to show that there is more there, or zero in on a detail that the viewer might have missed because they were distracted by elements in the larger picture.
- **Make a new story.** I mentioned this one earlier. What story do we expect to happen from the setup of your joke? What is another story that makes equally or even better sense that it could lead to?

- **Change the perspective.** Whose eyes are we seeing the situation through? What happens if we shift to a different viewpoint? This is also a character explanation. What would a character inside the joke say about it? What do they see that no one else sees?
- **Build on our expectations of a character.** If a character is in a joke, have them do or say the things we expect from them. What is something your mom or dad says? Put them in the setup and then have them say it. When I started writing this book, Donald Trump was president. He is a huge temptation to comedians exactly because he is such an obvious character. We know what he says and how he speaks (or communicates on social media—SAD, FAKE NEWS! BIG LEAGUE! TREMENDOUS!) So if Trump is in the setup of your joke, have him say or do what we expect of him.
- **Reverse our expectations of a character.** Same thing, just do the opposite. What is the most unlikely thing to come out of Trump's mouth. Establish a character in your setup and have them say or do something unexpected.
- **Exaggeration.** Take your expectation and exaggerate it to the furthest possible extreme. If we expect that the characters in a joke are stupid, make them too dumb to live. If we expect them to be smart, make them super-geniuses. If we expect that something will happen, what is the most extravagant bonkers version of the expected event?
- **Wordplay.** Is there a word in your setup that might have a different meaning? Or that is a homophone (sounds like) another word? Use those to reverse expectations. But also play with the sound of the words in the punch line: What sounds funny in the setup? What are the silliest words, or silliest-sounding words, you can use in your punch line? Can you rhyme them?
- **Analogy.** Compare or relate two things and find surprising or insightful connections between the two. Look at your setup and see if there are other situations you might relate it to. Two of the connectors I offered in the news jokes section earlier ("In related news" and "That's like") suggest analogies.

- **Misplaced focus.** Find an element of your setup that appears minor or unimportant and make it the focus of the punch line. Who or what do you expect the punch line to be focused on? Can you find someone or something else minor in the setup that might be affected and make that the important thing?
- **Antihumor.** What is the most unfunny version of the punch line? What would never be funny in a million years?
- **Metahumor.** What's the obvious punch line? Take that obvious punch line and comment on the fact that it is the obvious punch line. Step away from the joke and, rather than write the joke with the idea of telling it to someone, think about what would be interesting to observe if you described someone else telling the joke *to* someone else? Make fun of the idea of telling a joke. Much of Steve Martin's early comedy was this—he wrote things that sounded like jokes but purposely took the "funny parts" out. So, it sounded like a joke but wasn't—which, of course made it a joke.

You can see that some metahumor can also be described as completely inappropriate response. Or that sometimes when you "make a new story," you are also reframing. Yes. That is true. All of these are in some way, shape, or form doing the same thing. This is why, to a greater or lesser extent, jokes are the simplest unit of comedy. They are what they are—a setup and a punch line. The setup creates an expectation and the punch line upsets or reverses that expectation. Everything above is an example of a way to reverse or upset the initial expectation.

Writing jokes is hard but simple. Rewriting jokes is easy but complicated.

How to Rewrite a Joke

If I haven't already made it abundantly clear, I believe that the most important step in rewriting jokes is to have written them in the first place. Lots of them. Many many many many jokes or, even better, "joke-like objects." Then just as you did with the material generation exercises, once you have a long list, go back and look at what you created. Scan it and make note of what catches your eye. Are there any ideas that feel like they have potential? Any that particularly please you? Are there jokes that already work? That feel like a joke you might have read or heard in a stand-up set? Start by rewriting those jokes. Don't be tempted to rewrite everything.

My experience has been that the pieces that already work continue to work and get better. The pieces that don't work mostly will continue not to work. Even the ones that feel like they "should." RIP Glengarry Glen Ross / Girl Scout Cookie parody sketch that I forced a cast of mine to try over and over again. It's a good premise. It should work. It likely has worked for someone else in another sketch show. It did not work in mine, and by hanging on to the possibility that it might, I wasted an enormous amount of time and energy that could have better been spent improving the sketches that did work.

Still, there might be things you wrote that delight or tickle you in some way but aren't necessarily functioning jokes. Don't ignore those. Make sure to keep track of those half ideas or flights of fancy. Put them in the place where you keep your generation work and come back to them later. Often fresh eyes on an idea will spark something down the road.

Rewriting a Joke, Part I: The Quick Edit

Take a joke you already like, read it out loud, and ask yourself the following questions:

1. Is the idea you had when writing it clear? If not, play with several different ways to write the joke so that it makes more sense. Often the best way to clarify is to rewrite the setup rather than the punch line. For example, a light bulb joke may work better if you revise the name of the "group" that is doing the light bulb changing, making it more specific and aligned with the reasoning in the punch line—say, changing handymen to carpenters. Why? I have no idea. Maybe the joke is funnier if it isn't gendered or if it relates to something connected to the more specific occupation.
2. Can you rearrange your punch line so that the reveal of the twist or incongruity is at the end of the joke? If the reversal of expectations is made clear in the final word or phrase of the

punch line, you should get a stronger laugh. In performance, if you keep talking after the reveal, the audience may stop themselves from laughing in order to make sure they don't miss information.

3. Now read the joke through out loud again. Are there any extraneous words you can cut from either the setup or the punch line? Are there any words you can make more specific without losing the logic of the joke?

Once you have made your changes, read it aloud again.

Now go try it out in front of a friendly audience (say, your roommate, spouse, or sibling) and see if they laugh. If not laugh, do they nod or smile? Or are they confused? If so, don't explain the joke to them—see if you can find out what they thought was happening or going to happen that didn't.

Rewriting a Joke, Part II: Revising Based on Feedback

Based on the information you get and what it felt like to tell the joke to someone else, look at what needs to be added or altered to make the joke less confusing or feel better in the telling. The truth/pain/distance triad can help here.

- **Recognition:** Do you need to set up the expectations more clearly? Can you make the joke thicker by adding more recognizable details? Does the math or logic of the joke work? What can you do to make the two sides of the "joke equation" more equal?
- **Pain:** Is the joke too obvious? Can you alter the setup or the punch line so that it's more surprising? Can you use exaggeration to give the joke more punch?
- **Distance:** Is the joke too dark, or does it include taboo elements that you need to frame differently so they feel safer?

Then, if you like, go back and tell the joke again to the person you told it to the first time. Or try this new version of the joke out on someone new.

Congratulations! You have successfully written and then revised a joke. If this was just for practice, you can stop here. If you want to do more, I encourage you to check out the chapter on variety narratives for how to put together a simple stand-up set and my suggestions for finding audiences and testing material in the chapter on revising comedy.

Jokes That Use Other Comedy Components

Gag Cartoons

If you like, you can start to play with thicker jokes that utilize additional comedy components. The classic visual comedy joke is the one-panel cartoon.

At base a one-panel or gag cartoon is a joke in which the setup and punch line aren't told in a linear fashion. They are both available at the same time. So while you could think of the photo as the setup for the joke and the caption as the punch line, you may experience the joke in the opposite direction, beginning with the caption and then looking at the picture. Even more often, because these kinds of jokes tend to be thicker, you may go back and forth between the caption and the drawing more than once to capture the various incongruities and connections.

The *New Yorker* is the traditional home of the one-panel cartoon and is so well-known for them that they created a cartoon contest. Every week they take a captionless cartoon and post it online and on the last page of the magazine, and then invite submissions for possible captions. The top three are voted on, and the winner gets some form of prize.

If you are not a visual artist (and I am *so* not a visual artist), one way to try your hand at gag cartooning is just by playing with the *New Yorker* caption contest. Look at the *New Yorker* website and search "caption contest." The picture that shows up on May 3, 2021, looks like two firemen who are staring at two different entrances to two fire poles (one with a circular shape around the pole and one with a square shape).[6] My suggestion is to simply follow the exact same plan as we have with our other joke structures.

Set a timer and try to get as many captions as you can in a minute. Here are mine:

- Our new captain is a square peg.
- It's called inclusive design.
- SpongeBob sure has changed things around here since he moved from Bikini Bottom.
- What's interesting is that neither of us is shaped like either of the holes.
- We're getting a triangle next week.
- What do you think they were smoking?
- If they were really trying to be useful, they would just make one the shape of a rhombus.
- Steve, I think you were confused when they asked for a square deal.
- What's the worst that could happen?

I'd like to point out that my attempts at captions for this one are terrible. Really genuinely terrible. Especially the sixth, which feels like a copout to me because there is no real comedy logic—the people who created the square peg and round hole were just on drugs. But I can look at these and start to see some promise: The idea of square peg and round hole seems to be valuable here. Also, I kind of like the idea of there being someone the square hole was created for (à la the SpongeBob joke), but it doesn't logically work for SpongeBob, because he's not square, he's rectangular.

The eventual winner, from Andy McDonald of London, England, was "Since when did the pizza delivery guy get his own hole?," which does indeed play with the idea that the hole was created intentionally.

If you are interested in creating your own original one-panel gag cartoons with original artwork, here are three suggestions to play with.

1. **Start simple, with an existing joke.** It could be one you have already written or a classic riddle. Draw the punch line and write down the setup as the caption. For example, draw a chicken getting to the other side of a road and then title it "Why did the chicken cross the road?" Now play with both sides of the joke equation to see if you can make the joke make

sense no matter whether you start with the caption or the picture. Perhaps the drawing is fairly spare, just a chicken and a couple of lines that denote the road. The chicken is looking back at the road he just crossed and seeing no difference on either side. Then the caption becomes "Why *did* the chicken cross the road?" (implying that there's no difference between sides).[7]

2. **Start with recognition and add a bit of pain.** Draw a picture of a common, recognizable scene (family birthday party or someone with their pet) and then add a simple pain element. Incongruity and/or exaggeration are good ones to start with here—the cake could have a bonfire on top of it; a tiny child is holding a giant hamster. You may or may not want to caption these, but for this sort of cartoon you might want to play with describing the craziness reasonably or comment on it. ("Let's see Tommy blow out all *these* candles in one breath!" Or "Living near a nuclear test site provided Tommy with a variety of unusual pets.")
3. **Start with pain and then add recognition and distance.** Cartoons in particular provide automatic distance; the style of the drawing adds an element of unreality. In the 1950s and '60s the great *New Yorker* cartoonist Charles Addams created a family who did horrific things but drew and captioned them as if his characters were an adorable nuclear family of the type then seen frequently on comics pages and in sitcoms. For example, in a Christmas series the family's two children happily play with their new gifts of a doll and a tiny guillotine, or carolers stand outside the front door while the whole family gathers on the roof to pour boiling-hot oil onto them.

Blackouts

A blackout is a scenic joke but one that also includes elements of physical comedy, narrative, and/or character. It's called a blackout because when it is performed in a theater, the lights traditionally go quickly to black right after the punch line, thus signaling to the audience that the scene is over and they can laugh. But a blackout can also be used in a screen medium, ending with a quick cut.

Blackouts are still jokes in that they have a setup that sets up an expectation and then some form of reversal of that expectation. In a blackout, the audience should start by believing they are watching the beginning of a longer scene of some kind. A couple is walking along holding hands and discussing how happy they are. The assumption is that the two are in love, perhaps at the end of a romantic date, and the audience subconsciously begins to predict what might happen next—perhaps the couple will discover some minor flaw in each other, or an old flame will appear. Instead one of them turns to the other and says, "We should have gotten divorced years ago."

This may or may not be a particularly good blackout. I just made it up on the spot right now. But it is a blackout. A scene sets up expectations using physical (a visual of a couple strolling and holding hands) and narrative (a story that begins with happiness but suggests there will be more to happen) elements. Then a punch line (in this case verbal/narrative, but probably also physically embodied) provides the audience with a joke-style reversal of these expectations.

Writing a blackout is similar to writing a traditional setup and punch line joke. To write one, start with a long list of visual images and scenic setups that create immediate expectations. Sketch comedy utilizes the components of physical comedy, narrative, and character, so you have a larger palette of options to play with for your setup than you do in a traditional verbal joke or a gag cartoon. Think of cliché images and opening lines of dialogue from plays and films or the types of obvious initiations that a beginning improviser might use. For example:

- Someone on one knee proposing
- Someone waiting at a bus stop or train platform
- "I suppose you are wondering why I called you all here today."
- "Jenkins, would you step into my office, please?"
- The reading of a will
- A group of people cheering at a sports event
- A group telling scary stories around a campfire
- "Storm's a-comin'."
- A student meeting with a guidance counselor
- Two people run into each other and drop something (as in a romantic comedy meet-cute)
- A man regales a friend with a story about a wild night of sex

Most blackouts rely on one of two primary joke filters. In the first we have a worst possible response. Here's an example of how this filter might work using the setup of a person waiting at a bus stop. They look at their watch or their phone, step out into the street to see if the bus is coming, look back at their watch. And then a bus comes from the opposite direction and runs them over (this blackout would probably work best on film). Or a person is on one knee in front of someone proposing: "Will you marry me?" There is a pause, and then the person being proposed to turns out to the audience and says loudly, "Line!" In a classic Second City blackout, Richard Kind came onstage singing loudly and dancing to the tune of "Broadway Baby"—"I'm a morning person, / I wake up with the dew. / I'm a morning person"—and then Bonnie Hunt entered in a bathrobe and sleeping mask with a cup of coffee in one hand and a gun in the other and shot him.

Here's another from a student show I directed.[8] We hear a man offstage vulgarly insulting a woman, then she comes running onstage barefoot and dressed in a robe, and shouts to him, "Scott, I hate it when you talk to me that way." He enters, also in a robe, and says, "I'm sorry, but I warned you that when I wear a condom, I'm less sensitive."

The other kind of reversal is "reframing." In a reframe, the audience is looking at a picture or event from a specific vantage point and then the (metaphorical) camera pulls back and they discover that they have jumped to an incorrect conclusion based on limited information. This reframing can be literal: For example, the proposal blackout above could also be said to be a reframing: We are looking only at the couple, and when the camera "pulls back" we understand that the event is happening onstage in a theater. In this case, it's still a "worst possible response," since it is highly unlikely that an actor would forget their response at this moment in a play. It's a slightly thicker joke because it uses two mechanisms.

In a stage production that uses minimal props and costumes, a blackout often supplies clues that trick an audience into assuming one context when another is correct. For example, in a blackout written by a student of mine a few years ago,[9] lights come up on two chairs next to each other, and a man seated on one of those chairs is writing suggestive graffiti on the imaginary "walls" around him. "For a good time, call Mary Kathleen O'Malley," he says aloud as he writes. Someone enters the stage and goes into the "imaginary" cubicle next to him. The man turns in his seat to face the person who just entered, who says, "Bless me, Father, for I have sinned." The original audience assumption is that the scene takes place in a bathroom. The discovery is that it is a confessional.

Revising Jokes That Use More Than One Component

As much as possible, the goal in revising these sorts of thicker jokes is to make certain that all of the different components of the setup and the punch line are in alignment with each other. Is there an element in the cartoon that doesn't make new sense when viewed through the lens of the caption? Or, vice versa, is there an element in the caption that doesn't explain the entire cartoon picture?

Most of my favorite gag cartoons invite a bit of looking back and forth between cartoon and caption, as in Robert Mankoff's cartoon with the caption "What lemmings believe." At first glance the picture of a line of pairs of small creatures rising off a cliff and into the sky appears whimsical and nonsensical. The tagline is at the top of the drawing and not only contextualizes the drawing but also rewards a second look—some of the minor oddities (why are they in pairs?) now feel more appropriate without being wholly explained.

When we revised and staged the confessional blackout discussed above, it became clear how much care we needed to take with the components of visual, character, and narrative in order for the joke to work best for an audience. The two chairs onstage needed to be at a specific distance from each other (farther apart than we initially assumed), and they needed to be set with seats facing the audience. When lights came up, the man onstage had to be sitting facing toward the audience and "writing" on the imaginary wall on the side away from the other chair. The person entering had to sit down sideways on their chair, and the first man—the "priest"—then pivoted to face them.

It also works much better if the initial person on stage is someone who presents as male. This reinforces the type of misogynistic graffiti being written on the wall of his stall. Not to mention the fact that the reveal is of a Catholic priest and (at least as of this writing) that is strictly the province of those whose birth gender and identity are male. Using a more traditional Irish American name in the graffiti is a detail that doesn't take away from the audience's initial expectation, and it makes the payoff more pleasurable. It made OK sense when we thought he was in a bathroom, but the specificity of the name (and the fact that it's just a little bit old-fashioned) feels even more apt once we know the true situation, which might, after all, be a moment in the past, since traditional confession is not as common as it once was. The blackout works just a bit better if the person entering presents as female. It provides a brief moment of extra pain (incongruity or taboo of a woman entering a men's room) that is then explained and made safe fairly quickly.

TOOL: Novelty and Surprise

Novelty and surprise represent an interesting combination of all three of the primary elements of my theory of comedy. This is one reason so many people have suggested that the key to comedy is surprise. If I have assumptions and norms about how the world works and they are upended in an unexpected way, there is an automatic combination of recognition (those norms) and error (pain). The concept of surprise also implies a kind of distance. We didn't expect or anticipate an unusual outcome, but it is not necessarily unwelcome or negative—just unexpected. This suggests a level of psychological distance or safety. Similarly, novelty implies a sense of discovering or learning something unfamiliar that is interesting rather than uncomfortable.

These two concepts also have an underlying sense of playfulness and pleasure that reinforce their use in comedy. A surprise is usually pleasurable and mostly welcome. A surprise that is not pleasurable is generally coded as such—an "unwelcome" surprise. In horror films, we call moments of sudden surprise "jump scares," focusing on the fact that the startling sensation of surprise is combined with something unwelcome and uncomfortable.

For the comedy practitioner, thinking about surprise and novelty is part of both the creation and the revision processes. When we are creating comedy, the ideas or concepts behind our work require a certain sort of divergent thinking. We start with something known and recognizable, and then we look at it from an odd angle and create a new version of reality—we discover an unusual element and build on that element. Normal moves to not normal. Comedians put two things that shouldn't go together in the same place and then find a way to make sense of what shouldn't make sense. We look at something deeply familiar, notice something odd about it, and then put intensity of focus on that oddness. When we revise, we pay attention to when and where the joke occurs, and we adjust language and behavior so that we don't give the surprise away too early. We adjust and readjust the recognizable elements so they feel simultaneously familiar but not too familiar.

With old-school one-liner stand-up comedians, the jokes themselves aren't necessarily new, but the delivery creates a sensation of surprise. The setup is rattled off so quickly that the audience can't quite piece together the elements of the joke before the punch line is revealed. Then there is a pause after the punch line, to allow the audience's brains to catch up with the comedian's mouth. The solution to the puzzle is revealed just a second or two before the audience would have figured it out themselves, and partly it is that space of surprise and discovery that triggers a laugh.

As comedians we obsess about whether jokes or premises have been done before, and the answer to that question is usually yes—it's all been done before, there are no truly new jokes or premises. Characters in the ancient Greek comedies of Menander and Aristophanes are confronting many of the same essential family dynamics and human failures that (with minor changes in detail) exist in our modern era. At the same time, there is so very much that individual people don't see or know. Our brains filter out so much information in order for us to continue to function every day that there is always a new way to see the world or a new viewpoint to take in. Each new person has a unique perspective, a unique set of experiences, beliefs, and understandings that are delightful to explore. This is connected to what behavioral scientists call perspective taking, trying to see the world through another person's eyes. And what science shows is that while we assume we are really good at understanding what others are thinking, we are actually terrible at it.

(continued)

The gap between what we assume we know and what we actually know is the space where the surprise lives. The novelty exists in the opportunity to see our world through someone else's eyes—discovering that they see something we have seen a thousand times or had a thought that is as deeply familiar to us as our own thumbs and then discovering that they have also seen, felt, or understood something that we have completely missed. Something minor, or maybe so deeply bizarre that our busy brain filtered it out as unimportant. Someone else's brain didn't do that. It not only noticed—it also spent some time there in that moment and then revealed it to us.

Suggestions for thinking about surprise and novelty in your own work:

- Don't worry about finding brand-new ideas that no one has ever thought of before. Just concentrate on your own take on the idea even if the general concept has been done. The more specific to you and your experience your observations are, the more likely they are to feel new to others.
- In material generation exercises, push past the point at which you feel stuck, the point at which there seems to be no more examples in that space or category. See if you can find three or four more elements or details. Pushing past those initial ideas can help you find something that will be novel to others.
- Another material generation exercise under the umbrella of "research" is to put yourself in a position of experiencing or learning about something that is unfamiliar to you: Go to a part of town you never spend time in or give yourself a miniquest that forces you to be in new versions of the spaces and places you normally go to. My son and husband have done two of these, the first for the best fried chicken in Chicago and the second for the best Italian beef. They solicited suggestions from all sorts of people and then got more suggestions as they shared their favorites on social media. These challenges weren't just about the food, they required going to new neighborhoods in the city or visiting unfamiliar parts of familiar neighborhoods. There is something especially useful in honing your sense of novelty by

looking at multiple versions of the same thing—it allows you to see the familiar in the strange and the strange in the familiar.

- When you watch comedy (especially live comedy) pay attention to your own responses. What surprises you? What feels old to you and what feels novel? As comedians we get jaded really quickly—everything can feel done and old to us. I remember a comedian in the late 1990s announcing that breaking the fourth wall and talking to the audience was "hack" and overdone. But I still can't imagine a comedy show in which we wouldn't ever talk to the audience. There is an interesting challenge there: If something feels overdone it contains an opportunity. Dig into the reasons something feels "done" and also the reasons why it works, and then find three to five twists on the original bit that avoid or subvert the most commonly used parts.
- Conversely, when you watch someone else's comedy, pay attention to when the rest of the audience seems to "get" the joke. When exactly do they have that moment of surprise? Which specific pieces of comedy appear to be novel to the audience? A very common device in observational comedy is to introduce a new way of looking at something very familiar and then to use that lens on a number of other familiar things.

9 PERFORMING COMEDY

We're going to switch gears now from generating jokes and writing to generating and performing comedy with an emphasis on what academics call "embodiment." Mostly, this just means getting up and doing something either by yourself or with other people.

As I have noted already, comedy is not just one thing. When you are working with the comedy triad, you can have pain elements that come from character while the recognition elements are in the narrative structure. The distance elements may be connected to point of view. You can use timing and delivery to enhance the pain elements of surprise. It is the combination of all of those pieces that creates comedy which works for a specific audience. It's important that comedians consider both the writing and performance aspects of comedy even if there is one arena they prefer or specialize in.

If you are a performer, this next section should be especially useful for you. There are tools you can use both in generating comedy and when working with someone else's written comedic material.

If you identify mostly as a writer, I strongly encourage you to play with creating comedy using embodied tools. It's a great way to make your written comedy work better, since a primary mode for comedy in our culture is performance of some sort or another. My experience is that different approaches solve different comedy problems: They create different kinds of comedic material, and as a result they provide your comedy with layers that make it funnier.

Discovery

As I've already established, a great deal of comedy is math. My comedy theory itself is at base a formula. Playing with and practicing the formulas is a useful way of getting yourself to create comedy—especially with jokes, where the formula of setup and reversal can be clearly used and manipulated.

I came to comedy through improvisation rather than stand-up, however—particularly the kind of improvisation based in the work of Viola Spolin. One of the central tenets of Spolin improvisation is that when we improvise, either by ourselves or with others, we don't decide in advance what we are going to do. When a performer with this mindset enters a space or a relationship or a moment, they don't use a formula—they just use their creativity and their sense of play. Viola Spolin was working with using traditional children's games as a path to creativity long before Daniel Kahneman was theorizing about systems in the brain, but her methods give comedians and improvisors practical tools to access their intuition. The Spolin games occupy the part of our brain that judges and analyzes, with a simple problem of some sort. This point of concentration (or focus) is simple and achievable. You have to keep an imaginary ball the same size and weight as you throw it around a circle. Or make your body into an exact mirror of the person standing in front of you. The work created using these techniques is qualitatively different from something created using a formula.

When you use discovery or improvisational methods, you don't start from nothing. You generally begin with something simple and recognizable. In a common Spolin exercise, a player walks into a room and discovers an object that might be in that location. They explore the object, maybe have a little difficulty with it in ways that can make it more real to the player and to their audience. Not infrequently they discover some small moment of comedy in this simple interaction. If you are playing the comedy theory game, that bit of difficulty adds some pain. But they are not entering with a comic idea. They are not "combining two things that might be incongruous"—they are making a discovery.

When you are using a discovery approach, it's important that you not try to decide in advance what is going to be funny. You don't plan the comic idea. Instead, you set yourself up with a couple of comedy variables and see where they lead you. You purposely remain open to being led in unexpected directions. You behave, you play, you check out the possibilities. You may collaborate with one or more other people who are also doing these things. What you don't do is go into the exercise with a fixed idea of what the comedy thing you are making should look or feel like.

I find working from a discovery mindset particularly beneficial when I am collaborating. My focus is to discover something different from what I would make on my own—or what I might make on my own and then force my partner to execute with me. One of the brilliant things about creating material in this mode in front of an audience is that they will often make the discovery for you. You may not have had any idea that something highly specific to yourself and your experience is shared by a large number of people, but their laughter of pain or recognition will open up the discovery of a previous unforeseen source of comedy to be explored. That's not to say that you can't or shouldn't use a discovery-based approach when you are writing or working alone—you can and should. And one of the most useful discovery concepts I use in my work is called "Explore and Heighten."

TOOL: Explore and Heighten

You may know "Explore and Heighten" by its catchier improv bumper-sticker name "Yes, And." I prefer "Explore and Heighten" because it more clearly describes the tool. "Yes, And" suggests a conversation in which you say yes and then talk more about and expand on what you said yes to. "Explore and Heighten" includes the potential for action. You can explore and heighten movement, sound, emotion, and ideas. "Explore and Heighten" doesn't have to be positive. Frequently it isn't. It is just as easy to explore and heighten a no as it is to explore and heighten a yes. This technique is used to brilliant effect in Monty Python's Michael Palin and John Cleese sketches about the cheese shop that has no cheese or the "Dead Parrot" sketch, in which the pet shop owner refuses to acknowledge the bird's demise.

(continued)

Here's how I introduce this concept in my improv classes. If I wanted to verbally explore a topic like cheese, I could list types of cheeses. I could discuss the ingredients of cheese, I could describe how cheese is made, I could describe the various uses of cheese in cooking or how to make a cheese board. How could I heighten cheese? I could literally make it bigger—talk about giant, important, or award-winning cheeses. I could make the topic more emotional and personal, tell a story about my mother making grilled cheese sandwiches or describe my late-night obsession with cheese and heighten it further by writing a song about it. This is how you get to something funny and ridiculous like Tina Fey as Liz Lemon in a Snuggie singing "Working on my night cheese."

You can explore and heighten movement. Move your arm. Explore the movement. Is it awkward and stiff or smooth and flowing? Heighten that—do what you are already doing but do it more, faster, bigger. Eventually you won't just be moving your arm anymore. If you explore and heighten enough, the rest of your body will get involved. You are no longer just moving your arm—the action has transformed. This is a moment of discovery.

Once that happens, you can explore and heighten the new thing. It may transform into you not having enough arm strength to continue to move. That's fine. Explore and heighten that. Not having the strength to move your arm. Do *that* more. You may end up in a heap on the floor which is yet another transformation. If you explore and heighten being a heap on the floor, even that can transform. Having the impulse that it is ridiculous for a grown human being to be in a heap on the floor is a kind of a transformation—you can explore and heighten that impulse. There is always something available in your life or your world to explore and to heighten. This means that you never have to worry about being stuck as a writer or performer with nothing to do or say. Just explore and heighten what is already there and discover where it leads you.

In my improv classes I lead an "Explore and Heighten" exercise in which I have three students get up and start by miming a simple activity (like painting a wall). I tell them that they don't have to do anything other than listen to my voice and explore and heighten what I tell them to do from the sidelines. Very quickly they are running around the room, dancing or chasing each other. It is ridiculous, very funny to watch, a kind of clown game. They almost always tell me afterward that the exercise was very easy and enjoyable. They didn't have to come up with new ideas for their performance—I did it for them. The irony here (often noticed by members of the class watching) is that when I side-coach this exercise, I don't "come up with" anything. I simply watch what is happening and point out the moments of transformation as they take place and encourage the group to explore and heighten the new action they have already created.

A good exercise for physical comedy is to explore and heighten all of the ways you might do a seemingly simple activity, like putting together an artificial Christmas tree. If you watch early silent films, you'll see that much of the comedy is derived from this kind of simple "Explore and Heighten" interaction between a character and an environment or activity. You can explore and heighten tightening bolts on an assembly line, as Charlie Chaplin does in *Modern Times*, or spend an entire film exploring and heightening how *not* to deliver a piano, as Laurel and Hardy do in *The Music Box*. Generally, when you work in this way the moments of transformation lead to interesting comedic discoveries. There will likely be objects that don't behave as you or your audience expect them to. Or you will find that certain objects create pleasing or unusual effects when you use them in a way you might not normally use them.

"Explore and Heighten" is at the core of comic narrative. Pretty much every kind of comedic narrative from stand-up to sketch to sitcom starts with a simple topic, situation, or game of some sort that is then explored and heightened to a natural end point or until it transforms into a new topic, issue, or game. For example, let's say you have a premise for a scene in which a group of friends all go out for dinner together and everyone is served their meal except one person at the table. There are a number of things you can explore here: What did everyone order? Why did only one person's food not arrive? Is it the fault of the kitchen or the waiter? Should the rest of the table start eating? How does the person who was not served feel? Once you get started, you realize how much there is to explore and heighten in a relatively simple premise. The emotions of the people at the table, the progressively weirder excuses of the waiter or the incongruous elements issuing from the offstage kitchen that suggest some kind of

(continued)

unseen calamity. You could explore and heighten everyone trying to be polite about not eating but being very hungry. You could have the food-less friend make a big show of not having anyone wait for them and then explore and heighten how much everyone is enjoying their food while the one person has nothing to do and can't contribute to the food conversation.

Film and stage farces and television sitcoms create longer narratives by allowing the characters to find a solution to the initial problem which is then explored and heightened until that solution itself transforms into a new problem. I encourage you to watch one of your favorites and see if you can identify the initial problem, how it is explored and heightened, and then what it transforms into. By the way, transformation doesn't always occur organically. When the hijinks have reached their peak and the cops come in and arrest everyone involved, that's a transformation too.

What Is Physical Comedy?

When we think of physical comedy, the first thing that comes to mind for most people is slapstick. Slapstick is comedy that involves some level of exaggerated physical pain. The origin of the term *slapstick* is quite literal: a stick you slap someone with. It has been used in physical comedy for centuries. The commedia dell'arte is credited with its invention, but some version of a slapstick was likely in existence much earlier. The slapstick itself is simply two sticks connected by a strap of material or a spring. When you hit someone with a slapstick, you don't have to hit them particularly hard to make a loud and satisfying smacking noise, just as the Three Stooges do in their films. An actual slapstick makes the comedy funnier by adding extra and unusual sound to a (perceived) painful interaction and thus providing distance.

This kind of simple physical comedy contains automatic elements of recognition and pain that we don't really get to play with elsewhere. A pie in the face is both deeply recognizable and deeply wrong. We know what it feels like to get hit with something. We know we are not supposed to make a mess. This is early training, received from our parents. Distance is provided through character. Does the person who gets hit with the pie deserve it? What about the person who thinks the hose has been turned off and lifts it up to look at it and suddenly gets a face full of water?

Physical comedy provides audiences with the opportunity to have an experience of the recognition/pain/distance triad that is visceral instead of logical. Physical comedy is traditionally categorized as "low"—it's comedy of the body and not comedy of the mind and as a result has traditionally been seen as less valuable than the "high" comedy of wit or manners. Yet physical comedy, like comedy of character, is infinitely more universal than comedy based in jokes, narrative, or point of view. You don't have to understand references, speak the same language, or even speak language at all. Babies across the world laugh at funny faces or a simple activity done incorrectly. Put a piece of clothing on the wrong body part? Hilarious!

There is a sense of event in physical comedy. A real thing is happening. Someone is getting hit with something. Someone is falling. Real whipped cream is on someone's real face. An audience watches this kind of comedy in a different way. This may seem obvious until you think about how much of modern entertainment is virtual. When I teach silent film to my students, a common observation is that there is a perceptual difference between how they feel when they watch the kind of physical gags that silent film comedians do and more modern CGI-based physicality. When the front of the house falls over Buster Keaton and leaves him standing in the center of the tiny window, it isn't just funny due to the surprise of his narrow escape. We have a kinesthetic understanding of the events. Our bodies seem to respond differently to something that happened and has affected another body rather than to something that just appeared to happen.

Making Physical Comedy

Physical comedy is comedy of the senses, but it is also comedy of action and movement. In this section I want to encourage you to move off of your couch or away from your computer and to start working with your body and your physical environment. Turn off your logic brain a bit and instead allow yourself to play and get messy.

You can do this on your own, but working with a couple of other people is helpful here. Take turns being an observer. What do you see that surprises or delights you? What were your expectations of how an object or body was going to behave, and how did the actual properties of the object or body part reverse your expectations? By doing this, you can find a physical joke in real time, and it's likely to be all the more powerful because it was discovered actively.

Recognizable behavior. Often it is enough for us to laugh at behavior because we see it and understand it without being told. We feel that we see a person's mind through their behavior. We can tell who they are and what they are doing or what they want through their movements and actions.

Start by doing something recognizable. Closely observe yourself as you perform an everyday activity. Make a peanut butter and jelly sandwich and really take the activity apart step by step. How do you open your fridge when you take out the peanut butter? How many items do you have to remove from the middle shelf before you can get the peanut butter from the back where it got pushed to? Does the jar stick to the shelf a bit because someone spilled something, never wiped it up, and then put the jar of peanut butter on top? I am, of course, describing my own fridge. Yours may be perfectly clean. But if that's the case there may be something else specific about how you interact with your food. What do you do with the knife after you spread the jelly? Do you wipe off the jelly with your fingers and put them in your mouth?

Now perform the action again as exactly as possible, putting the focus on these specific details. A version of this on its own using real objects and made a little thicker by adding a persona or character could be a short video. For the live stage you could take the same specific recognizable details and mime them as exactly as possible. There are several Second City scenes played to music in which a clothed actor mimes the details of taking a shower. While there is some gross-out humor involved (washing your butt) the most telling moments are the ones where the audience laughs at the regular behaviors that most of us do in private: feeling the water coming out of the faucet and adjusting the hot and cold water, picking a hair off of the soap,[1] the moment of leaning back your head letting the shower spray pour down your back. The mime version not only contains the recognition; there is also just a bit of extra pain for the audience, who might need an extra second to identify the specific actions, as well as distance provided both by the skill of the performer and the "doing / not doing" represented by a clothed performer behaving as naked.

Recognizable behavior plus exaggeration. The double take, a classic trope of comedy, exaggerates a behavior that in real life is barely noticeable to an outside observer, a situation where we see something and think of it as normal, and then a moment or two later realize that we passed by and accepted something that is decidedly *not* normal.

To get comfortable with double takes, start with the first part of the "take." It helps if you break it down into little tiny increments.

1. Walk past something.
2. Have the thought "What was that?"
3. Look back to check.
4. Think to yourself, "It's OK" and continue on your way.
   Do each step slowly a couple of times and then gradually speed it up. For a "double take," you are going to add two additional steps.
5. As you start to continue on your way, have the thought "Wait, what the hell was that?"
6. Look back yet again.

Once you are comfortable doing a natural version of a double take, play around with it. Do slow-motion double takes or try a faster than natural version. Exaggerate and escalate, making the takes bigger or more important. Play with exaggerating the movement until it is just at the edge or a tiny bit over what someone might really do. Try adding more "takes," maybe even four or more.

You don't have to limit yourself to these old-school bits. Spend some time observing real people and look for other common behaviors. Break them down, re-create them, and then explore and heighten what happens.

Recognizable behavior plus incongruity. Take your observations further, and do something completely normal but include one element that doesn't belong. In Monty Python's "Ministry of Silly Walks" sketch, a set of high-status government employees walk to work in a way that is familiar except for the bizarreness of their gait. John

Cleese appears to be a normal uptight bureaucrat from the waist up and an out-of-control stork from the waist down.

Do your own silly walk challenge. Try to maintain as normal a movement as possible from the waist up while exploring and heightening the movements of your hips, legs, knees, and feet. Try switching it up so that your lower body is normal and your upper body is the silly part.

Pick an activity that you normally do all of the time (texting on your phone, making coffee, putting on makeup) and play with adding a movement or doing one thing very differently from the way you or most people do it. Even better, see if you can execute the activity perfectly well while maintaining some movement or shift that is the direct opposite of the normal behavior.

Tension and release. Physical comedy is where the theory of tension and release mentioned in the earlier chapter on humor theory is especially useful. Any time a comedian creates the appearance of action and reaction or forward movement and then withholds it, there is automatic tension for an audience. The silent comedian Harold Lloyd was known for creating tension in the audience for films like the classic *Safety Last* by using real (or at least perceived) danger and fear of heights. Often in this case, the audience will laugh to release their tension and fear on their own without the presence of an actual release from the performer.

Playing with tension. In the classes I teach, I use a classic improv-based entrance and exit exercise called "Info Booth." We establish a center stage information booth with someone giving direction or help at a location like a mall or amusement park. One at a time students enter in character, take focus, ask a question of the info booth person, and then leave, throwing the focus back to the booth.

Inevitably, one of my students will enter and as slowly and as painstakingly as possible make their way onstage to ask a question. Then it begins to feel (to the performer) that the slow choice they made at the beginning is boring or wrong, and they will speed up on their exit in an effort to get offstage in a timely manner. When this happens, I have them redo the entrance and force them to do the entire exit as slowly as they did the initial entrance. The whole way across the stage. Slowly and deliberately. Usually what happens is that the class laughs early on and then the laughter dies down. But if the performer continues to commit to slowly working their way across the stage, the laughter will begin to build again and get much louder and longer.

By the way, the students' choice is often an elderly character with a walker, a character type that can feel ageist and ableist in a way that it didn't in the past. But this bit can work even better if the character isn't disabled but just naturally exceptionally slow. We have even more distance when the pain of incongruous speed is voluntary as opposed to involuntary.

Another great way to create tension is to start an action and then hold off on completing it. For example, lift a bite of food toward your mouth, but don't ever actually allow yourself to eat. Explore and heighten all of the different ways you can almost eat it—have it nearly get to your mouth without ever going in and being chewed and swallowed. My intuition is that real food is going to be funnier here than mimed food and that certain foods will yield more comedic potential, but play with it and see for yourself. You can build the tension by setting up a situation in which there is someone very hungry watching the eater but can't eat themselves until the eater takes the first bite. Or is hungry and not allowed to eat for some reason and is frustrated by the other person not doing what they themselves crave. There are elements of play and game here—we're waiting for the moment of release, but we are also enjoying all of the tricks and traps of the game along the way.

Try to take something away from someone else without their noticing it. Play with how blatantly obvious you can be for an audience while not letting the object of your thievery see what you are doing.

Props

The comedian Steve Martin's early stand-up act was full of props, from balloon animals to a ridiculous hat that looked like an arrow through his head. He notes that "the minute you pick up a prop, the audience is attentive."[2] Early silent film comedians would get their props together or go to a location where they planned to film and just play with what was there. Take advantage of the inherent tension in bringing something real into your comedy. You can start by manipulating simple objects and materials and see what discoveries you make. Don't assume that you know how cooked spaghetti is going to behave if it is dumped on someone's head. It may slither down your face, but if it's cold, it is just as likely clump up and land on top of their head like a bizarro-world hat.

Have difficulty with a small prop. What are all the ways that you can use a comb that aren't the way you're supposed to use it? Explore everyday objects as if you are an alien from another planet and have never seen them before, trying to figure out what they "might" be used for. The more wrong you can be, the better. Really let yourself make discoveries and play.

While we are mostly talking about real objects in this section, when you do this with mime or object work you can get extra mileage out of the license you get to alter the properties of the object once you create it for an audience. For example, establish an imaginary baby, cradle it, and hold it. Then sit it up on your lap, twist its head off, and throw the "head" at an imaginary basketball hoop.

Build on this exercise by doing an activity. Using real objects for this exercise allows for different kinds of discoveries. Try spending an hour or so playing with the materials you need to wrap a present. You have tape, wrapping paper, a pair of scissors, and a box. The key here is to find as many ways of doing it wrong as you can. Don't be afraid to waste tape or paper—for some reason when we do this exercise our inner grandmother who used to save the wrapping paper can come to the fore. Just revel in wasting it—the stranger and more out there your choices are, the better. Explore and heighten. Allow the activity to transform. Maybe you are no longer wrapping the box and instead are wrapping yourself.

Don't be tempted to just imagine what the qualities of a particular object or activity will create. The best of this kind of physical comedy comes from surprise and the insight that elements of our everyday physical world that we take for granted have qualities we have never explored because we have always used them in the way we have been told to use them. I suggest that you work like a silent film performer, spend a lot of time playing and making discoveries with the actual substance. Allow the objects and activities to surprise you, and they will likely surprise your audience.

Get messy. I have a particular fondness for comedy that gets genuinely messy. I've argued many times for a room at The Second City or Columbia College Chicago where we could all spit water at each other or throw pies and then just hose it all down some central drain. I highly recommend finding a place that you can practice spit takes that's easy to clean up later—we used to do it late at night in our college kitchen, and I have to share that it is not necessarily fun to wake up hungover to a floor covered in water and saliva—so go outside, wear your old clothes or a bathing suit, and have at it.

A spit take is like a regular take, but instead of moving forward physically, you have the response while you are just about to eat or drink. Something happens and you take a drink of water or a bite of food before the event registers in your brain. When it does register, the surprise causes you to spit out the food or water. There's really no way to practice a spit take without having something to spit out. Water is your best bet to start with. It's easy to clean up and unlikely to injure a bystander.

It's especially helpful to work with a partner when doing spit takes. Watch or film each other as you do so. Make shapes with the water using your mouth. Add a spit take to a double take and spray water as you jerk your head around like a human sprinkler system. Spit on or at each other. There is something particularly satisfying and comedic about this kind of slapstick both for the performer and for the audience. There are so many related taboos or rules about not making a mess and not getting other people messy, but as long as everyone involved is in on the game, it's also completely benign.

When my son was twelve or so, he worked briefly as a birthday party clown for smaller children. As his big finale he would hand a whipped cream pie to the birthday child and instruct them to push it into his face. What I loved about this bit is that every time I saw my son do it, the birthday child never just hit him with the pie. Instead there was a long pause as they registered the fact that they were being asked to do something wrong and messy. And it was really going to happen, and no one was going to get mad at them. Not to mention, the combined fear and glee of the assembled children at the party when the pie made contact.

As long as we are on the topic, a couple of quick thoughts on cream pies and pie throwing. I love pie gags. They have a similar quality to a spit take but even more so because there is an added kinesthetic response in your audience—watching someone get a pie in the face is a cliché, but like the children at the birthday party, we rarely get to see it in real life. And as with spit takes, an in-person pie gag provokes a kinesthetic response in our own face—we feel it as well as see it. Plus, the person getting hit is really getting hit, there's a moment of recognizable human behavior that you can't fake when your face is suddenly hit with a great deal of a soft and sticky substance. And finally, once that cream pie hits someone's face, it's an instant comic mask—it transforms them into something or someone different than they were before.

Having said that, a couple of words of warning. Don't use real pies with crusts and hard pie tins—that's a lot of unnecessary stuff that will just hurt your face. Also, whipped cream in a canister needs to be kept really cold to whip up well, and it can't sit around for long without melting, so if you want to use real whipped cream (or an artificial version), know that and test it out ahead of time. Second, be prepared for mess: No matter how much tarp you put down on the ground, the trajectory of where that cream flies will surprise you. There is often a second and unintentional physical comedy act that happens after my students do their silent-film-style performance pieces, one where people covered in mess attempt to clean up the mess they made while inadvertently making new and worse messes. Speaking of which, if you don't do a particularly good job of cleaning up, old whipped cream goes sour and smells like you wouldn't believe. My general recommendation is to use a nonmentholated shaving cream instead. It doesn't melt as easily (which can make for fun shapes left on people's faces after the pie hits), and it's much easier to clean up.

Slapstick

During the Second City show *Southside of Heaven*, Tim Mason and Tim Robinson played a carriage driver and a horse, giving a not-so-romantic ride through downtown Chicago to a young couple. In the sketch, a foam pool noodle stood in for a whip. Like a slapstick, it didn't particularly hurt the person who was hit, but it made a terrific noise every time it made contact. It allowed the players to create what seemed like an enormous beating while simultaneously maintaining safety (and distance).

Slaps, pies in the face, falls, slipping on a banana peel, much of what you see in the work of the Three Stooges or Laurel and Hardy all contain this essential element of pain or taboo combined with exaggeration that creates a distance that will allow us to laugh at it.

How do we make physical pain funny?

- We can exaggerate it. As in the work of the Three Stooges, we can add huge sound effects that create an air of unreality.
- We can exaggerate or change the response to the pain. A slap doesn't just knock someone over—it causes them to literally go stiff as a board and fall backward flat onto their back. Or a knock with a hand spins them around so hard that they fly into the air. My colleague David Woolley at Columbia College, a stage combat expert who runs the school's minor in stage combat, suggests that another (and quite safe way) to do this is for the vocal response to be the opposite of what we expect—a high-pitched squeal as opposed to a low grunt.[3]
- We can turn it into a machine of some sort, as Henri Bergson might have suggested. An initial hit creates some form of chain reaction with a whole series of surprising but logical consequences.
- We create distance by removing the human element. Punch and Judy shows are funny because puppets can beat the hell out of each other and not get hurt. Cartoons are similar. Even the intentionally horrific violence of *Itchy and Scratchy*, the parody of the cartoon *Tom and Jerry* on *The Simpsons*, is funny (in a dark twisted way) because the extreme violence is happening to characters that are not only not human but also further removed by the distance of happening in a cartoon world inside another cartoon world. Silent films with human beings in them could get away with a much greater degree of physical violence and pain than later sound films could, because the lack of sound creates its own distance—we don't hear the hit of object to flesh, which generates an aura of unreality. Ironically, physical comedians on screen during this era were more likely to do their own stunts and to actually take the punch or the fall rather than using stuntmen or stage combat. The combination of really doing something with the

distancing of lack of direct sound is a really effective (although genuinely dangerous) comedy device.

But as Robinson and Mason did, it is possible to use real objects to create slapstick in simple ways that are relatively safe for performers and audience. Try dueling using pool noodle weapons. Or scarves. Have a war with marshmallows as grenades.

Skill

Over the centuries, comedians have regularly included skillful performance into their acts. Clowns dance, do acrobatics, balance things. Vaudeville comedians sang and danced and took difficult pratfalls that were both funny in their subject but also objectively skillful. Andy Kaufman used expert lip syncing in his "Mighty Mouse" routine. Modern musical comedy acts like Garfunkel and Oates, Lonely Island, and Rachel Bloom combine highly skilled musical performances and video production with comedic premise and lyrics.

Take the challenge I give to my students during the vaudeville assignment in my comedy history class and ask yourself what you can personally execute really well physically and make it the center of a sketch or stand-up bit. It can be singing or dancing or juggling, but it doesn't have to be particularly difficult if you execute it well. A favorite piece from a recent student show involved a full-cast re-creation of a synchronized swimming routine. The actual choreography was simple but impeccably executed, and combined with the incongruity of "swimming" onstage below and above a fabric wave, it was both delightfully novel and funny to the audience.

TOOL: Status

Somewhere between physical comedy and character lie behaviors that Keith Johnstone describes in his book *Impro* as "status." Using status helps improvisors create recognizable human behavior and dialogue, but understanding status behaviors does much more than that for comedians. It's a powerful tool that works across components of physical comedy, character, and narrative.

Status is a set of verbal and physical traits and behaviors that provide cues to indicate relative social precedence or importance. For example, someone who holds their head still and holds eye contact is generally perceived to have higher status and someone who frequently nods their head or breaks eye contact and immediately looks back is generally perceived to have lower status. When I introduce status in my classes, I ask the students at my downtown urban college to go to a restaurant during a lunch hour and seeing if they can tell which tables consist of colleagues or friends and which have bosses dining with employees. I suggest using whether they hold their heads still and how they make eye contact with each other. It's surprisingly easy to discern relationships based on just this short list of status behaviors.

When thinking about status it is important to note that, on their own, these are just behaviors. They are morally neutral. It is the context in which they are displayed that makes us see certain status behaviors as "polite" or "nice" and others as "annoying," "rude," or even "evil." When we see these behaviors as "inappropriate," it is generally because in a particular situation or interaction someone is using a behavior that appears incongruous and not appropriate to the context. For example, pushing ahead of someone walking in front of you and cutting across their path is a high-status behavior, but how you judge that behavior will depend on the circumstances. You might see it as distinctly less rude if you are in an airport and the person is clearly running to catch a flight. It might bother you to see someone with a first-class ticket or TSA PreCheck jump a line, but it's likely to bother you a great deal less than when someone ducks under a rope to get ahead of you in the security line without the official sanction.

The status I am describing here is connected to but not directly related to money or power. It is not unusual for those with money and power to use high-status behaviors—they pay for the right to do so when they purchase a first-class airplane ticket; they get to skip certain lines and board first—or to expect those who serve them to use low-status behaviors, but the two are not intrinsically linked. Whenever I teach status, the conversation begins to devolve the minute someone brings up working in the food service industry, possibly because a large percentage of future comedy students have spent some time or another working these sorts of jobs. The power

(continued)

dynamic in food service creates very specific status interactions—there are those who serve (low status) and are served (high status).

We get restaurant customers who assume the highest of status behaviors like snapping their fingers to get a server's attention, or expect very low-status behaviors, as when a server is expected to remain standing next to a table for an indefinite period of time while the served considers the taste of a sip of wine or ponders a menu. When I worked for a cruise company, a member of the management took a group of us out to dinner several times on one of the ships. He would order wine for the table and perform the "wine tasting" ritual as slowly as I have ever seen it performed. The waiter would pour a sip of wine into a glass, and this man would tell a long story holding the stem of the wine goblet between his pointer and ring fingers, creating slow circles on the tablecloth. The waiter had to stand at attention next to the table, as the swirling and the monologuing continued for five or more minutes.

While most status behaviors are used across cultures and times, how they are read is highly variable from era to era and from culture to culture. Many actions that a modern American perceives as comfortable and friendly would likely be seen as deeply insolent among the seventeenth-century French aristocracy (who would have been quite comfortable with the behavior of my wine ritual friend). In our current era, Person A, a descendant of West African enslaved persons and raised in the US Southeast, might view certain status behaviors at a party as sociable, while Person B, whose family of origin has Scandinavian roots and settled in the Upper Midwest, might see the exact same behaviors as impolite. And vice versa.

In public, most of us have a status level that makes us comfortable, and we display a fairly consistent set of behaviors that signal the relative status we prefer to play. Most public social status "games" consist of minor status movements—for example, I say, "Please pass me the salt" (raising my status just the tiniest bit with the request to be served). You do so (lowering your status a hair by serving me), and I thank you (lowering myself and bringing us back to whatever status relationship we had to begin with). But in private, especially with our most intimate partners, we comfortably play with much greater range and variety. Think of the baby talk between lovers or easy put-down teasing between close friends.

Comedy and Status

The most classic comedy duo is that of the very high-status player and the very low-status player. It seems to be common across many cultures and eras to enjoy the master-servant relationship, in which the master bosses the servant around and the servant grovels. This dynamic goes all the way back to the Athenian comedies of Menander and appears in sitcoms like *30 Rock* with relationships like the one between Jack Donaghy and Kenneth the Page, where Kenneth refers to his boss as Mr. Donaghy and in turn is referred to, at best, only by his first name.

There is a tradition in many cultures of enjoying the antics of low-status characters. The clowns of commedia dell'arte that most fully translated to the modern era are the servants. This is the primary comedy of Jerry Lewis, the Three Stooges, and pretty much the entire cast of *It's Always Sunny in Philadelphia*. Low-status people doing low-status things appears to be a hallmark of comedy from the all the way back to ancient Greece and Rome.

Laurel and Hardy were both low-status characters. Still, as Michael McKean in the documentary series *Make 'Em Laugh* describes them, "Hardy is the dumbest guy in the room, and Stan Laurel is his stooge." In their Oscar-winning short film *The Music Box*, they continually lower their own and each other's status physically and verbally, but some of the funniest bits are where they behave in a high-status manner toward a policeman and a wealthy aristocrat type (who turns out to be the person to whom they are delivering the piano). John Cho and Kai Penn in *Harold and Kumar Go to White Castle* start out as a classic high-status/low-status pair. In the opening moments of the film, Harold is taken advantage of at work by a white "bro" colleague, while Kumar intentionally blows a med school interview, humiliating the head of the program and dumping coffee on his lap. When they get stoned, the status gap between them remains, but the addition of being high exaggerates the status games between them and with others.

The second is the classic status reversal. In this kind of comedy, we see someone of a certain social class take on the status behaviors connected to the opposite class. Human beings seem to find status "mixes" particularly funny—the low-status king who apologizes continuously to his jester for interrupting the jokes, or the high-status servant in the employ of a buffoonish millionaire or lord. The principal in *Abbott Elementary*, Ava Coleman, as played by Janelle James, has the highest-status job at the school, one for which she is thoroughly unqualified. Her absolute confidence and assumption of privilege is thus doubly funny. In P. G. Wodehouse's Jeeves and Wooster books, Bertie Wooster is an upper-class idiot full of low-status behaviors and ridiculous language, and his butler, Jeeves, is all smooth intelligence and complete reserve. The lead in a comedic film is often someone who begins without cultural status and then suddenly finds that status raised while still displaying many low-status behaviors, as Melissa McCarthy does in *Spy* or Eddie Murphy does in *Trading Places.*

Finally, there is the swift reversal of status—in particular someone who is high status suddenly dropping in status through internal or external means. The funniest characters to get a pie in the face are the high-status ones, whether through position or behavior. Buster Keaton's stoicism (a classic high-status character trait is to display little or no movement in the face) makes the enormous physical dangers he faces seem funny rather than tragic.

A classic sitcom premise is to put lower-status characters into a higher-status environment (for example, *The Beverly Hillbillies*). *The Fresh Prince of Bel-Air* used the juxtaposition of a young Will Smith's high-status (but ostensibly low-class) behaviors with the class and status expectations of his wealthy Beverly Hills family. *Schitt's Creek* does the opposite, forcing high-status characters to handle the loss of their wealth and prestige among the lower-status inhabitants of a small Canadian town.

Comedy narrative frequently hinges on status shifts. A classic comedic sketch formula is to start with two characters of vastly unequal status (both social and behavioral). Over the course of the sketch, the two switch status. This may occur fairly naturally through gradual shifts in character interaction, quickly through a surprising discovery or action, or through a somewhat unnatural mechanism—quite literally, "Let's switch places so I can show you something." By the end of the sketch the power dynamic has shifted: The high-status character has been brought low, the low-status character made high. This is not infrequently followed by a joke or event that quickly switches the status back to where it was at the outset. Another formula used in sketch has someone with a small bit of status gradually being brought lower and lower through a series of trials or negative interactions and then pulling themselves back to their previous status place with an angry rant.

Most ensemble sitcoms begin with a set status dynamic. We know exactly what the "normal" status relationships are between the characters on *Friends* (Monica is the highest status, Joey is the lowest), and a common sitcom plot device is that some external force shifts the status relationships between the characters (Joey gets a highly prestigious job, for example) and then the group must deal with the repercussions of the status change. By the end of the episode (at least in traditional sitcom) whatever status upset has occurred is resolved and the characters return to their original status relationships. In comedic film a common trope is the character who suffers indignity after indignity lowering their status by progressive steps, as happens to Ben Stiller in *There's Something About Mary*, or they may begin the film with some status but then dramatically lose it, like Jason Segal in *Losing Sarah Marshall*.

Additional Strategies

I've discussed aspects of performance here in terms of physical comedy and we'll look at character more closely in the next chapters. But comedy performance is more than just the inclusion of those components. A dramatic performer certainly intends to affect their audience, but the clues about whether and how any given audience is responding as intended are subtle at best. There's no true requirement that the audience all have the same experience, let alone have the exact same response at the same time.

Comedic performance is different in terms of its intention and relationship to the audience, live or virtual. By my definition, performing comedy requires the intention of evoking a specific response and whether and how an audience laughs provides actual evidence of whether a comedic performance is working or not—especially in the case of a hard laugh, one where the whole audience laughs loudly and at the same time.

A comic performer must be more aware of the audience than a dramatic actor. At its simplest, this means that timing is adjusted for laughter. When an audience laughs, comic performers "hold for the laughter": They wait until the laughter begins to die down before saying their next line. Otherwise, the audience won't hear what happens next. The "hold" also indicates to the audience that laughing is the right and appropriate thing to do in that moment. If it doesn't happen, the laughter will be a lot shorter and taper off quickly.

Because Second City creates its scenes in front of an audience and the physical scripts are shaped by audience responses, they have a rhythm that is based on when the audiences laughed night after night. When we rehearse certain sketches, we will literally stop and say out loud "laughter, laughter, laughter," or we will make a sound like the roar of the audience before continuing with the next line in order to account for the way the audience response affects the timing of the scene. As a director, I've been spoiled by the opportunities that Second City affords to test material out in front of an audience. My personal preference is to roughly block a sketch, put it into a protected spot in an existing revue, and then let us all get a feeling for where the laughs and responses are going to be for a couple of performances before bringing the scene back into rehearsal to "tighten down the bolts." When I have directed comedic plays outside this process, there's a moment in later rehearsals where the play and the actors' performances feel unfinished. A good live comedic performance doesn't feel complete without live laughter.

Timing is not just holding for laughs—it's connected to the comedy triad, especially the element of recognition. In a joke where the punch line is easily predictable, the delivery of that setup needs to be just a little bit faster. Speed adds a tiny element of pain, but it mostly keeps the audience from guessing the (recognizable) punch line before it happens. On the other hand, a more absurd one-liner of the kind told by standups like Steven Wright might need to be delivered much more slowly so that the audience has time to understand the logic of the information completely before it is reversed. Additionally, the rhythm and cadence of speech creates patterns that the audience recognizes subconsciously and allows for other sorts of expectations that can be subverted or played with for comedic effect.

This connection between performer and audience extends far beyond simple issues of timing and rhythm, I would argue that it's an essential piece of what makes a comedic performance fundamentally different from dramatic performance. In a comedy, the performer is aware of the audience, and the audience is aware that the performer knows they are there. There is a connection and a complicity between audience and performer. One job of what was traditionally termed the "straight man" is to give the audience a cue for when to laugh, frequently through a take to the house making a visual connection with the audience. This breaks the fourth wall and announces (subtly or not so subtly) "Here's what I'm thinking." But this doesn't just happen in the presence of a live audience. The comic power of semi-mockumentary formats in television shows like *Abbott Elementary* is in the presence of an unseen camera operator. This allows the characters to maintain a naturalistic presence with recognizable human behavior but to also have complicit responses to the events of the show by connecting with the audience through the imaginary documentary camera operator.

Mutual acknowledgment of the artificiality of the moment is one way the audience knows they are watching a comedy. This provides a crucial amount of distance. If the audience has a clear sense of the performer underneath the character, then the action of the play (however tragic) has the potential to be absurd, to be a "funny story." Comedic stories are somehow always told in some version of first person. There is a sense of an "I" who is sharing this with a definite "you"—the look that says, "Can you believe this is happening to me?" or another that says to the audience, "This is fun! Watch what happens next!" Or, "Can you believe I have to put up with this garbage?"

Part of a comedic performance (whether on stage or on film) is literally playing a game with the audience. In drama, the audience is swept up in the story, in comedy, they are aware of the game behind the scene, of the performer inside the character, of the human being who is telling the joke. This sense of complicity can be created technically (and it is commonly how traditional theater programs teach "comic acting"). You can alter your speaking pattern so your voice goes up at the end of a line, emphasizing the joke and sending it out to your audience. You can do a genuine "take"—say your line to a fellow performer and then hold for a beat and look directly at the audience. You can make a face to indicate that a joke was just told (the pejorative term for this is "mugging").

This sense of being in the moment and simultaneously being aware of being watched and in connection to the watchers isn't just a set of mannerisms. Yes, there are bound to be useful techniques that "play" more cleanly. The musicality, rhythm, and skill of physical comedy are an integral part of comedic performance. As are the nuances and exaggerations of creating and playing a comic character. For what it's worth, I find that I think of this complicity with the audience as a part of the component of point of view.

I have a couple of additional recommendations for ways to play and practice when you are acting in scripted comedy.

Have a comic secret. Do you know someone who seems always be thinking funny things to themselves and somehow that makes everything they do or say funnier? I recommend this to former students and friends who are auditioning for comedy shows or ensembles. Think of something silly, maybe something that brings you joy or a deeply weird inside joke you share with your friends. Or you could actually carry or wear something that pleases you (underwear or socks with something ridiculous printed on them). Before you walk onstage, into the room (or even the building), take a moment to bring awareness of the secret into your mind: Let it affect your attitude; bring it into your eyes, your mouth; let it transform your posture. Hold on to that comic secret lightly, as a point of concentration, throughout your audition. Try bringing this sort of comic secret into a rehearsal or performance and see how it changes what you do or how the audience responds to you.

Play a game. Adding the element of "game" to scripted work almost always provides a lift to the comedy. In some ways this is an extension of the comic secret, but one you can share with other players. The minute you are actually playing, trying to win or affect your partner in a tangible way, you begin to exhibit behaviors your audience will recognize and find funny. I have had good success with having actors play "tag" or "keep away" with a small object as they rehearse a scripted comedy scene. Once we have made some discoveries with this, I like to experiment with using these games in scripted performances in front of an audience. The key point of concentration is to play the game to win, while also not allowing the audience to "catch" you playing. I like to use the Spolin exercise "Eye Contact to Speak" while working on scripted comedic material: The point of concentration here is that you can't speak unless you make eye contact with your partner, and if you or they look away, you have to stop talking. This game forces the performers to really pay attention to their partner. If you want to know more about using game as a writing tool, I go into it in more depth in the chapter on writing sketch.

Start with strong simple choices. Most comic characters and stories (especially in shorter forms like sketch) are defined by one primary simple comic driver or game. If you can execute that, you have the key to unlocking the whole. From my experience, the best comic actors will start with by making one or at most two strong simple choices and often what works best in the very first read through of the script is the essence of the final performance. When you are starting work with an existing comedy script, I encourage you to pick a simple physical, vocal, or character filter and commit to it. If it doesn't work, you'll know quickly, and often the way it doesn't work will give you strong clues about what you need to change to fix it.

Share your experience with your audience. Think of the audience as a friend who is hidden nearby or watching you on a hidden camera. You can't actively make eye contact with them except secretly, when no one is watching, but you know they are there, and they know you know. There are a lot of situations in which comedians treat the audience as the enemy (we killed tonight, that crowd was dead). I encourage you to go onstage and actively play with the sense of "You and I are in this together and it's going to be fun." Allow yourself to include the audience in your enjoyment of the show. Play with them, see if they like the same bits you like or if they don't laugh at your favorite joke, show them you are surprised. Be wide open to the fact that this performance is gong to be completely different from the last because this particular group of people is different, and fully embrace what you discover together.

Play with tempo, rhythm, and musicality. Comic characters and comic dialogue both tend to move in ways that are just slightly off from the way normal humans move and speak.

Comedy performances are often more effective when sped up just a touch. There's an underlying truth to the cliché of the comedy director shouting "Louder! Faster! Funnier!" See what happens if you speed through your lines. Conversely, find breaks in your rhythms, move fast and then suddenly slow. Even if you aren't delivering a classic one-liner, it can be helpful to give the setup for a joke just a bit more quickly and then briefly pause before the punch line. Or as I described in the discussion of tension in physical comedy, test how long you can hold an audience's attention by moving and speaking as slowly and deliberately as you can.

Variations in tone can be more than just speed. Try singing your lines to find a natural way to get that lift at the end of a line or play with using speed and tone to help create either distance or pain. When comedian Chelsea Devantez was on the Second City Mainstage, she created a dating sketch in which every time her character mentioned that she was a feminist, the word came out slowly and monstrously (effectively presenting what the man in the scene was hearing in his mind).

If you are working with plays that fall into the category known as "high comedy" (comedies of wit and manners, like those written by Noël Coward, George Bernard Shaw, or Oscar Wilde), it is especially important to take time to understand, enjoy, and play with the sound and musicality of the language you are given in the script. One way to provide the needed element of recognition in this slightly artificial world that includes a great deal of heightened language is to allow your character to acknowledge and enjoy their own verbal facility, just as two competitive rappers might do in a more modern setting.

10 CREATING COMIC CHARACTERS

Comedic characters function in several dimensions that dramatic characters do not. Dramatic characters are created and written into a narrative to be read or performed by actors who take on the character for the space of time that the narrative is performed. Those dramatic actors may choose to live method deep within their character, but the character itself is a separate entity. Comedic characters live in a space that is always a bit outside the frame of the work of art. They are aware (to varying degrees) of the audience, they are not just behaving within a narrative, they are commenting on the narrative. In prose writing it is not unusual for a comedic story to be told in first person or for certain comedic characters to break from the story and to address the reader directly as they do in cartoons and comic strips. The mockumentary style of television shows like *Parks and Rec* or *Abbott Elementary* provides natural opportunities for their more realistic comedic characters to comment on the action through connection to an unseen camera crew.

As I mentioned earlier, there are roughly three dimensions of comedic characters: (1) persona, which is a stage manifestation of a person; (2) two-dimensional characters, generally stock types with one clear and simple comedic perspective and action; and (3) fully realized characters with a level of complexity that exists outside the realm of the individual comic piece. It's probably more accurate to suggest that these exist along a spectrum of dimensionality.

We can also think about characters as existing on a spectrum in terms of the level at which we are aware of the performer. On one end is a character that appears to be directly aligned with the person who is inhabiting them. This is the persona character of a stand-up like Wanda Sykes. You might assume that if you met her in real life, she would be roughly the same as how she appears on stage. In the middle are characters like those played by Carol Burnett on her sketch show or Kristen Wiig and Maya Rudolph on *SNL*: They have strong comedic perspectives that create expectations; we know who they are supposed to be pretty much immediately, whether they are playing a stock type or doing an impersonation or impression. They take full advantage of elaborate costumes and makeup to make themselves look very different from who they actually are. But at the same time, we are very much aware of the performer inside the character. They are clearly commenting on the type of person or actual person they are portraying. Then we have the sorts of characters created by Maria Bamford or Whoopi Goldberg in their one-woman shows. We know the performer is there, but it is almost as if the character has possessed the performer's body in some way. In the case of Goldberg in the film *Ghost*, we get three layers: Goldberg herself inside a character that is possessed by yet another character. Then we have characters like Borat (created and performed by Sasha Baron Cohen) or Pee-wee Herman (Paul Reubens), who are so far from impersonation that they appear to exist entirely outside the performers who play them. The audience has a sense of complicity but feels the connection is with the character themselves and may forget entirely that there is an actor inside the character.

Comedy writers and performers often work collaboratively, basing the comedy on the strengths and persona of the performer (as in the long-term on- and offscreen partnership between Lily Tomlin and Jane Wagner). Many sitcoms are created around the point of view or the persona of the performer who stars as the main character. The piece is designed to showcase what they do, who they are onstage and how their innate "comedic persona" interacts with the given circumstances of the character in the script.

Classic radio comedians like Jack Benny or Gracie Allen honed highly specific comedic personas over a long period of time starting in vaudeville. These personas were dramatically different from who they were in real life. Benny played a vain, miserly, and selfish man, while being notably generous and self-effacing in private, and Gracie used her unique voice, timing, and native intelligence to play a character who looked at the world quite differently from the woman who embodied her. Conversely, sitcoms like *Black-ish* and *Everybody Loves Raymond* featured protagonists based on their creators and are slight exaggerations of what you would expect to encounter if you met them in real life.

Impressions or imitations of real people and parodies of fictional characters comment on the original from the perspective of the performer at least as much and usually more than that of the writer. Tina Fey as Sarah Palin frequently used verbatim quotes from Palin's interviews and speeches. She took the real person and turned her into a comedic character through exaggeration and complicity with the viewing audience. This allowed the audience to view the Palin character from a distance that revealed and emphasized incongruities they had perceived while watching the real Palin. Classic imitation has the quality of skill based in physical comedy. It also contains a level of distortion, heightening aspects of what we see when we look at the person imitated. The laughter of the audience is connected to how closely the performance resembles memory—literally the impression that is left on the brain—as opposed to an exact copy. I'll say that another way: The difference between a comedic impression of Elvis Presley of the kind that Andy Kaufman did in his stand-up act and a costumed Elvis imitator is that Kaufman isn't doing a direct copy of the man himself; rather, he is re-creating the effect or the idea of Elvis that we have in our head.

The legendary comedian Moms Mabley, whose career straddled the tail end of vaudeville all the way to the modern era of stand-up in the 1970s, played an old woman character throughout her career (eventually reaching the age and infirmity of the persona she had adopted as a young woman). The real woman behind the character, Jackie Mabley, dressed in dapper suits and came out as a lesbian in 1921, one of the first openly gay comedians. Her character "Moms," who wore flowered dresses and worn scuffed shoes, was knowing and opinionated. She wasn't afraid to tell the truth about how women's lives were defined by men, or how women had sexual needs and desires just as strong as men's.

Most of my personal character creation work as a performer has involved some level of improvisation. Sometimes starting with some internal character details provided by a writer or from my own experience. Other times I have started working from the outside in, finding a physicality and then discovering the internal piece of the character by bringing that physical choice into a workshop of some kind.

When I created a character for a sitcom pilot I worked on for Second City called *Homeschooled*, I started by using a specific persona of my own—the me I was when I knew I was going to be late to pick up my daughter from daycare and all of the excuses and outright lies I would rehearse in the car on the way there. As I improvised in this persona, I discovered that she was someone who never wanted to be wrong or in the wrong. That enabled me to build the persona into a character by drawing on various people I have met over the years who are performative about their "goodness" but not actually particularly thoughtful—the sort of women who bring elaborate homemade treats to a meeting that no one requested while showing up late to the event or, vice versa, arriving hours early to the house of the couple who were hosting the neighborhood home school and then criticizing the lack of healthy organic food options for breakfast and presenting her lack of consideration as "having high standards."

I did the complete opposite when I participated in a fully improvised show *The Quest*, based on the work of Joseph Campbell, in which I had to play several different characters, I made a strong physical choice for each of my characters—one of them gestured with both hands while holding her elbows close to her body, and another stood very straight and barely moved her head. Using this physicality when I improvised these characters allowed me to discover their primary points of view (talkative busybody and cold judgmental aristocrat) while I was performing over many improvised iterations. If you have read the section on status, you might note that the second of these characters has an automatic high-status element. My memory of creating the character is that I just grabbed a choice and went with it, but my previous knowledge of status behaviors most likely had an impact on my choice. It doesn't really matter whether it was conscious or unconscious. Embodied character creation is frequently a dance between physical discovery and intellectual choice.

The ultimate goal of creating comedic characters is the same regardless of process: to create a character with a strong comedic point of view and then to find ways to demonstrate that point of view actively through language and behavior. Let's look at some ways we can use the recognition/pain/distance triad to create original comedic characters. Some of these exercises lend themselves more strongly to embodied discovery and some more strongly to a written or analytic approach. I encourage you to try working both ways and get a sense of what is right for you and what works best for certain kinds and types of characters you want to build.

Starting with Recognition

Start with an archetype. An archetype is a pattern or model of a type of person. I love building characters in this way because they are so resonant—they are the kinds of characters that appear across a variety of times, spaces, and often across lines of identity. One benefit of using this tool is that you can create an archetypal character and then make them more specific depending on who you elect to cast in the role.

Start by looking at the general qualities and actions of the archetype. For our purposes, we're going to use the modern archetype of "Nerd."

What are some of the qualities of a nerd?

- Socially awkward
- Obsessive
- Technologically savvy
- Intelligent
- Poorly dressed

What do they do?

- Speak frequently about the object of their obsession
- Interrupt
- Respond inappropriately to social cues

You can add more based on what you know or enjoy about nerds. But I want to point something out here. This is an archetype—we haven't added anything to this list that would directly connect this character to a particular race, ethnicity, or identity. Some aspects of "nerd" can suggest a level of neurodivergence. We'll discuss the difference between archetypes and stereotypes later, but for now, we want to stay away from character traits that suggest identity too strongly.

An archetype is general, but we want to create a character, so we're going to get specific. If we are creating a nerd, the first thing we want to do is to find their fandom. What are they obsessive about? It could be a video game or tabletop role-playing game. Or it might be fun to play with a nerd who is technologically savvy and nerdy about something a touch more unusual. What about a romance novel nerd? Or a weather nerd?

Let's play with the idea of weather nerd. I feel like this has comedic potential. I'm going to start by creating a short character outline.

- **Character:** Weather Nerd
- **Comic Point of View:** Obsessed with all kinds of weather
- **Comic Game:** Constantly monitors a weather app, carry a variety of meteorological equipment with them at any given time, predict future weather, describe people, places, and events in connection to extreme weather events. Favorite song is "The Wreck of the Edmund Fitzgerald."

Because this is a comedic character, I am looking to bring elements of pain to this rough outline. Here are three ways I've added pain to this character: (1) I've exaggerated their comic point of view in terms of what they do. They aren't just obsessed with the weather—they carry equipment with them. (2) A weather nerd feels incongruous (although not impossible). (3) There are flaws implicit in my character description: This character is obsessive and rigid (they carry equipment with them constantly).

For this sort of character, the most important thing is what they do, their actions, how they demonstrate who they are out in the world. You'll notice that I haven't provided any details such as name, age, or occupation. This weather nerd could be an old white man who teaches in a high school or a young Black woman who runs a tech company. Those details might become important as you build a narrative of some kind around this character. But just as with the archetypal characters of the commedia dell'arte, this character could show up in many different narratives in different roles.

Start with an object. Pick a physical object like a pencil. As with the archetype exercise, start by listing the qualities of a pencil and what a pencil is, does, or is meant to do. A pencil

- Writes
- Is rigid
- Can erase mistakes it makes
- Can be harder or softer depending on its number
- Is required for a standardized test
- Is generally painted yellow/orange with a pink top

The next step is to take these qualities and apply them to a person. You can do another character outline, but I love starting with an embodied exercise for object-based characters. Try taking on a point of view and be physically inspired by all or part of this list. I don't know whether or not the color or standardized testing pieces are going to be useful to you, but they might be. I kind of love the idea of a character who proctors written tests and *is* a pencil on some fundamental level down to a bright yellow shirt and a pink baseball cap, but that's only one potential version. Explore an object-based character using one of the embodied exercises later in this chapter. Make discoveries and then look at the discoveries you have made and decide which work and which don't support building a character you could easily play. There is a definite element of trial and error here: You might find something you like but then realize it is in conflict with a stronger quality that works better for a particular context or situation.

Start with a physicality. Hold tension or put your focus strongly on a specific part of your body. Explore and heighten that physicality through movement. Focusing on or tightening the sphincter muscle almost always creates an immediate shift into a character that feels comedic (probably no surprise, we're adding an element that is taboo or may actually be painful for a variety of physical reasons). Putting focus or tension on any body part yields a shift that can be built and exaggerated into a character element.

Another approach is having a certain part of your body lead your movement. What do you discover when you walk while leading with your pelvis? How does that change when you lead with your forehead or chin?

Play with a random physical gesture or body stance, as I described myself doing earlier. As in all these exercises, as you experiment with a physical choice, pay attention to how it changes your point of view. What do you see and perceive in the world while using this physicality? How does your frame and filtering change?

Start with costume pieces or props. Go to a resale shop or Salvation Army and look through the racks and pick out any pieces that interest you or strike your fancy. Most classic silent film comedians wore outfits that didn't fit them in one way or another. See what happens if you pick items that aren't in your size, either much too large and much too small or a combination of the two. Experiment with random wigs, glasses, or hats. Create a full outfit or see how just one costume piece affects or alters the ways you move or behave.

Pick a real object or hand prop to carry with you as you build your character. Some objects will immediately spark specific types of people in the way that a long cigarette holder covered in rhinestones will suggest someone who is retro and glamorous or at least aspiring to be. The prop doesn't have to be too obvious. Something as simple as holding or handling a variety of cups or mugs (giant pottery mug, delicate bone china teacup) can inspire something that can be built out into a full character point of view.

Start with an observation. Go people watching or pay attention in a group setting. Allow yourself to notice other people from an objective place, one where you don't make judgments about them but just pay close attention to the details of their bodies, clothing, and movements.

Pay attention to physicality. Look for the shapes in the ways people hold their bodies or their gestures. You can sketch these shapes in a notebook. It can be helpful to mirror or subtly take on a physicality that you observe and then pay attention to how living in that physicality makes you feel or affects your thoughts. Then play with the shapes or gestures you observed—exaggerate them, allow a certain gesture or movement to transform the way you move or hold your entire body. Look at the world from that perspective and make discoveries.

Look for your own version of stock or archetypal characters. What is a kind of person you always see in a store, or meet at a party? Once during a long afternoon of auditions for the Second City Training Center, I looked up and saw that Tina Fey—who was a teacher while she was acting in the Mainstage company—was amusing herself by creating a cartoon on the back of her audition form labeled with types of improvisers you would find in an improv class or team (this was the mid-1900s; the list would be likely be different today). I remember it being something like: white guy who always wears a hat, funniest guy in his fraternity, girl who talks about her high-level corporate job and does all the scheduling, other white guy who wears a hat, dude who smokes a lot of pot, guy whom everyone loves but who isn't very funny.

Play with making your own list of generic types that show up in your life. Feel free to base them on real people, but be sure to allow yourself to turn them into characters who have the qualities of people you know without being strongly tied to the actual people. What are the three types of people that everyone you know has in their friend group? Or what do you notice about the differences between the graphic artists and the members of the HR department at your job? What are the unifying qualities of the students in specific majors at your college? What's a common type you notice in a group you belong to?

My children went to Waldorf schools. These are the Germanic equivalent of Montessori schools—lots of knitting, wooden toys, and beeswax crayons. No media for small children. It was a great school for both of my kids, but it was also the source of a lot of comedic material for me. There was a certain type of mother I met there who shared many of the qualities I built into my *Homeschooled* character. These were women who had been high achievers in their careers, had left work to be primary caretakers of their children, and had then applied their goal-oriented processes from work to parenting.

Starting with Pain

Start with incongruity. Mixed-status characters are an easy way to create a comic character using the pain of incongruity. Pick a role, occupation, or position in society that normally assumes a certain set of status behaviors, and have the character use the opposite-status behaviors: high-status assistant, low-status CEO, etc.

Or go back to the "Mix and Match" character exercise I suggest in the idea generation chapter. The game of this sort of character is similar to Steve Kaplan's definition of a character in a comic film as someone who tries to accomplish a task without having the required skills to do so. The key is to these sorts of characters is to balance the two elements so that we're constantly seeing the two parts of their personality at play in their actions. How extreme the incongruity is will depend on the format you are working in. Sketch characters can have high incongruity, like the waiters played by Stephen Colbert and Steve Carrell on *The Dana Carvey Show* who are disgusted by food. For characters who appear in longer-form stories such as sitcom or film, like Janelle James's self-centered and egotistical principal in *Abbott Elementary* or Jason Sudeikis's warm positive football coach in *Ted Lasso* the incongruity can still be strong but should have a logic that allows the character to continue to maintain their comic perspective over time.

Start with flaws or vice. Make a list of common human flaws or weaknesses and make them the primary filter for a character. You can start classically with the seven deadly sins (lust, gluttony, greed, sloth, envy, pride, anger), or you can start closer to home with your own faults or the flaws that annoy you the most in other people. You can use a process similar to the one I recommend for archetypal characters. When you start with flaws, it can be useful—especially for a character you want to use in a longer narrative—to add some positive incongruity as balance. An angry idiot who really like puppies. Or a control freak who just wants everyone to be happy.

TOOL: Character Spacewalk

I teach a version of this in my classes. I use the Spolin technique of "spacewalk," in which players walk around a room (the space) while taking in and responding to prompts from a facilitator. If you are creating with a group, you could have one person read the prompts below while everyone else moves. If you want to do this exercise by yourself, you could record this script (or your own version of this script) on your phone. I generally speak slowly with long pauses between each sentence or two. I've broken the script into paragraphs at the places where you should take an even longer pause to allow for more exploration.

Doing this exercise in motion while just taking in and responding to the prompts is key. My experience is that participants are more likely to make discoveries they would not otherwise make. Note that this version has you create a new character by imagining their shoes and working upward. It works just as well if you bring a preexisting character idea into the exercise. Feel free to use my version as a base and add or delete elements to create a spacewalk that works best for you or the group you are working with.

Character Spacewalk script. Start walking around the space. Let yourself get used to your body in motion. Take a moment to be aware of any tightness or tension in your body and consciously choose to relax and let that tension or tightness go. If you need to move or stretch anything in order to get yourself into a neutral and open space, feel free to do so now. Let your vision be soft—just take in the details of the room you are in without landing on or focusing on any one object or person around you.

Now as you walk I want you to pay attention to your feet. Begin to imagine a different kind of shoe on your feet as you walk. These are the shoes that belong to your character. They might be boots or sandals or athletic shoes, or high heels. You don't need to show that you are wearing a different shoe, like by walking on your toes if you are wearing a high heel. Just let the fact of having these shoes on your feet to affect the way you hold your body and move. Feel something essential change in yourself change as you walk in these shoes. Really adjust to the sensation these shoes create in your body.

(continued)

Begin to pay attention to what is on your legs. Are you wearing pants, shorts, or a skirt? Do you have on leggings or tights? Is what you are wearing on your legs, tight or loose? What color is it? What fabric is it? How does it feel on your body? Allow this clothing to affect the way you move and walk. Start paying attention to what you are wearing on your torso and your arms. Allow yourself to discover what it is based on what you are already wearing. Let whatever it is, be. Are you wearing a shirt or a sweater? Do you have a jacket on? What color is it? What fabric is it? Is it tight or loose? Is it high on your neck, or is there an open collar? Continue to walk just letting yourself feel the clothing on your body, paying attention to how your body moves while wearing this particular set of clothing.

Become aware of your hands. Are they large or small? Are you wearing a watch or a bracelet? Do you have rings on your fingers? Pay attention to your fingernails. Are they short or long? Are they clean and manicured or is there dirt under the nails? Do you bite them? As you walk with this awareness of your hands, allow yourself to really sense that this body may be different from the body you started this exercise with. Let yourself discover this body as you walk and move, it may carry weight in a place that feels different to you, or your limbs may be longer or shorter than you are used to. Without judging any of these choices, let yourself explore how these new elements change your walk or how you hold yourself.

Now pay attention to your neck. Are you wearing anything around your neck? Necklaces, a scarf, a tie of some sort? Is your collar tight around your neck or loose? Start to have a sense of how tall you are. Still using soft focus, check out the world from this new height. How do you feel at this height? What do you notice that is different?

Become aware of your head. What sort of hair do you have? Is it long or short? Curly or straight? What color is it? Are you wearing something on your head, a hat or a cap or a scarf?

Become aware of your face. What sort of nose do you have? What kind of mouth? What kind of forehead? Do you have any facial hair? Allow yourself to look at the world from the perspective of this face. Allow yourself to see through these particular eyes. You may have a sense of what gender, race, or ethnicity you are, or you may not. If you do, just let yourself acknowledge it. If not, that's fine too—we don't always walk in the world aware of our gender or ethnicity.

As you continue walking around the space, look at the world through these eyes, and if something draws your attention, take a moment to look at it a bit longer. What is interesting about it to you as this person? What do you see that is different or new? Continue walking and let your gaze be drawn by another object and allow yourself to pay attention to this new thing through this lens.

Continue walking and as you do begin to play with the actual sound of your voice in this new body. Make some sounds—just see what comes out. Try reciting the alphabet. Play with different vocal qualities as you do so. Once you feel like you have found one that feels right, keep saying the alphabet, but now add emotions. Use this voice to be angry. Sad. Happy. Scared.

If you are in a group, begin to notice others in this group from this perspective. Start to make casual eye contact as you walk past someone, then let that eye contact go. Allow yourself to have some kind of emotional response as you do so; allow yourself to have a brief feeling as you come across each new person. If you like, nod or say "Hey" when you make eye contact.

Now find a spot by yourself with some space around you. I'd like you to pick up an imaginary object. Don't try to name it yet. Just explore the object. What color is it? How much does it weigh? What is its shape? Is it rough or smooth? What material is it made from? As you explore the object, you can begin to know what it is and what it does. Once you know what it is, take some time to continue to explore the object, look at it from all angles, look at it closely. Make a discovery about the object, something you haven't seen before.

Put the object down and pick up a second object. This object is important to you in some way. As before, don't try to name the object. Just explore it, color, size, weight, smell, texture. Once you discover what the object is, get a sense for why it is important to you. Do you need it? Do you like it? Does it evoke a feeling?

Put this object down and notice that behind you on an imaginary table is a vessel containing your favorite drink. To start with, just look at the vessel itself. You can pick it up if you like. Is it a cup or a glass? Is it an aluminum can? Is it a fancy cocktail glass or a heavy coffee mug? Before you take a sip from this vessel, you may want to take a moment to smell the liquid. And then go ahead and take a sip. Is it hot or cold? Is it fizzy or still? Is it alcoholic? Does it warm you or refresh you?

(continued)

Put the vessel down on the table and turn around. You are in your bedroom. Right in front of you is where you sleep at night. Start by just looking at the bed. Is it large or small? Is it on a bed frame, or is it a mattress on the floor? Does it have a blanket or comforter? One pillow or many pillows? What color is the bed itself, and what color are the covers on the bed?

On a wall next to the bed is a picture of some sort. Go ahead and walk up to it. Is the picture itself large or small? Is it a photo or a painting or a poster or a print of some kind? What colors are in it, or is it black-and-white? What is the subject of the picture? How does it make you feel? Do you have a sense of why it is in your bedroom?

There are some things next to your bed. Go over to them. They may be on a nightstand or on the floor. One of those objects is a book. Pick it up and just look at it as an object. Is it a hardcover or a paperback? What color is it? Is there an image on the cover? Take a moment and read the title of the book to yourself. It may be a book that exists in this world, or it may be a book the people in this room have never heard of. Open the book and read to yourself one random sentence. Close the book and set it back down. There is one other object next to the bed that has meaning for you. Pick it up and explore it, allow yourself to see it before you name what it is if you can. Now let yourself feel why it is next to your bed. How it important to you? Is it there for a reason of any kind? What is that reason?

Turn around and on the wall opposite you is a window. Before you look out the window, take a moment to look at the window itself. Does it have curtains or a shade or slatted blinds? Is it large or is it small? Move toward the window and look outside. What do you see outside your window? What objects are there? What light comes in through the window. Do you have a sense of what time it is? Go ahead and open in the window. Feel the weather outside. Is it cold or hot? Is there a breeze or is it still. Listen to any sounds you can hear from the window. Go ahead and have an emotion based on what you see and hear and feel.

Turn away from the window. There is a closet in your room. You are going on a trip. If you want to, you may pick out a different outfit and change your clothing so that what you are wearing is appropriate for travel. Inside your closet is a suitcase or bag of some kind. Take that bag and prepare to leave your room. Wait!—you forgot something very important. Come back into the room and grab it from on top of your bed. What is it? Why is it important to you? Now take your suitcase or bag and exit your room.

Taking Embodied Characters into Relationship with Others

If I'm working with an ensemble that is creating characters to use as a group, I follow the spacewalk by having the players remain in character and congregate in a neutral space such as an airport waiting area. It could also be a party of some sort, in which case I'd lose the suitcase prompt. Giving their character an opportunity to change clothes in order to go on a trip turns out to be an important step if their original choice was that their character was wearing, say, scuba gear. Which happens surprisingly frequently.

I side-coach that their plane has been delayed and they will thus be in the waiting area for some time. I have them find someone in the room to talk to. They should feel free to just ask the sorts of questions you ask when you are chatting with a stranger at a shared location. After a couple of minutes, I encourage them to switch partners until everyone has had an interaction with all the other characters. At this point, I will instruct the students to find a way to physically take off the character they have been embodying and come back to themselves (it can feel silly, but there is value in literally taking off the character as if it were a costume and intentionally "putting it somewhere" so you can come back to it later). Then we will debrief the exercise, discussing what they discovered, what they liked and what they didn't.

Among other things, this exercise helps to pinpoint which elements are most valuable to each individual player when creating character. Some people find the clothing most useful, some find that paying attention to the objects is most useful, and some find that the character didn't come into focus for them until they added the voice. Later on they may use one or two of these elements rather than doing the entire exercise in depth.

I also encourage the players to take a moment to make choices about which discoveries they want to keep from the exercise and which they can jettison. Sometimes there are decisions that make sense at the beginning of the exercise that are no longer useful by the end when the character is more fully fleshed out. Or that are difficult to maintain when they are in interaction with others. That's part of the process of creating a character you can work with in depth.

More Ways to Create or Practice with Embodied Characters

Character "painting." In this version, two players face each other and take turns describing the other physically as a new character, starting with the shoes on their feet and ending with their head. Each player being described takes on the physical qualities of the description. These characters could be interviewed alone or together and put in an improvised scene together.

Character interviews. One performer starts by embodying a character, and someone else interviews the character from a neutral perspective. Depending on the character and situation, it can be useful to start with specific details like name, age, and occupation, but I have often found it more useful to go the opposite way and ask the character to describe their secrets or their dreams before we nail them down to specifics. This is a discovery-style exercise. The person being interviewed should fully inhabit the character before being interviewed but shouldn't plan any answers to potential questions. They should feel comfortable answering as fully as they wish. Allowing yourself to be surprised by your answers helps to make real discoveries about the character.

After the interview, think about your answers to the questions (it can be helpful to record these interviews for later reference). Ask which answers feel most useful and which distract from the essence of the character being created.

Remember that after you do any of these exploration exercises, you can analyze the discoveries you have made and make adjustments over time. Just because in one improvisational moment you provided your character with a hundred-pound Rottweiler named Juicy and a stay-at-home wife named Lucy, it's not required that those specifics are set in stone for every iteration of your character going forward.

It's your character, there may be aspects of them that you create in the moment that feel essential and necessary, and those will be a part of this character in every version going forward. There will also be details that are useful in one iteration and then disappear when you put them into another location, time, or occupation.

Sketch premises with embodied characters. If you are working with a class or ensemble and are building characters together as a group, the next step after using any of these exercises could be generating simple sketch premises using the new characters that everyone is familiar with. Do the characters know each other or have history with each other? What would raise the stakes of this specific interaction?

This is another great moment to consider which character details are essential and which are not. You can and should play with altering specific elements such as age, occupations, or relationship (say, making two unrelated characters family members) in order to make the connection between the characters more interesting or to heighten comedic potential.

Playing with Character Point of View for Writers

Characters have their own frames and filters and hence their own points of view. Without getting too complex about it, when we write a comedic character's dialogue or play a comic character onstage, we are sharing our point of view on that character's point of view—don't think about it too hard, just know that it works.

Another way to play with character is to focus on their frames and filters. A simple exercise I do with my students is to start by writing a three-sentence story based on a fairy tale like "Goldilocks and the Three Bears." You can write your own story, but here's mine as an example:

> Three bears left their house to go for a walk while their porridge cooled. When they got home, their house was a mess—porridge, chairs, beds. A girl was asleep in one of the beds and they chased her out of the house.

This version of the story is roughly from the point of view of the bears. If you wrote a three-sentence story just from the point of view of Goldilocks, the framing would be different, the start of the story would happen after the bears had left and the filtering would focus on how Goldilocks saw and experienced the house, porridge, and furniture. If you wanted either version of this story to be comedic, you'd expand and exaggerate the characters' point of view. You could also use a different character point of view entirely—say, that of the police detective who is investigating the break-in or the lawyer who is suing the bears on behalf of Goldilocks for mental cruelty.

As you may have noticed, I'm adding elements of incongruity (pain and distance) to the recognizable story by using characters with strong points of view who would not normally show up in a children's story.

Below are some exercises for playing with character point of view using some simple narrative structures. Almost all of them can be used as writing prompts or in an embodied improvisation. They can be used both to generate material or to make discoveries about an existing character. Most of these include a simple incongruity that heightens the comedic aspect.

Tell a traditional story or fairy tale from the point of view of a character who normally isn't centered in the story, as I did above with "Goldilocks." For example, tell the story of Cinderella from the point of view of the wicked stepmother. Or from the perspective of one of the mice that was turned into a horse. This is similar to the mapping exercises from the section on parody, but the focus here is on using a strong character point of view or perspective.

Use style or genre as a filter. There is a classic improvisation game called "Panel of Experts" in which each player is given a specific filter to use (an occupation or a magazine) and then they are positioned as experts on an incongruous topic. For example, they could be political commentators from magazines such as *Cat Fancy*, *Popular Mechanics*, and *Bon Appetit*. A version of this game that I've used with students is to pick a magazine or website that would be unlikely to give personal or relationship advice and offer advice from a character who has that highly specific point of view of their publication. I've enjoyed making up the requests for advice as well as using existing questions from newspaper or online advice columns.

Take a character from a classic story or novel and have them rant about an aspect of the story that doesn't normally get focused on—for example, the guy whose train trip was delayed when Anna Karenina threw herself in front of the train.

Once you have created a character, you can make additional discoveries by putting that character into a variety of situations. Some of these can be used to create comic monologues or other content to be shared. You could

- Tell the first-person story of the worst day of their lives.
- Describe in detail their favorite thing in the whole world.
- Have them confess a deep, dark secret.
- Make a fake social media account for them and have them post about local or national events.
- Make an Instagram or TikTok account for them, then make and post "day in the life" pictures or videos from their POV.

Good Comedy Hygiene for Character

When I first started taking improvisation classes at The Second City, there was a "rule" that we shouldn't play old people or children and that we should always play our own gender. There was some value to this rule: Beginning comedians tend to play very obvious and over-the-top stereotypes when they play outside their personal general age range or to parody gender rather than portray it. I find it fascinating that when my students play older people, their characters reminisce about World War II when currently the baby boomers are in their sixties and seventies. But many performers chafed at these restrictions, wanting to allow themselves the full range of possible choices in their character work. Simultaneously, the previously common use of ethnic dialects to denote character felt less and less appropriate (especially in the case of students playing outside their race or ethnicity).

It can be complex (especially when you are transforming yourself without the benefit of costumes and makeup) to portray someone whose body, gender, or identity is different from the way you present in life. You need to work hard to set up clear expectations in your audience. You are fighting their deep-seated inherent biases. We teach the audience what they should be paying attention to and what they should ignore. I once directed a student show with a performer who wore a hijab in life and chose to continue to do so onstage. I found it was easy to establish that the hijab was merely a part of the actor and that it would transform along with her when she played a pirate or a cat. However, once we had established this convention, we had to be especially intentional in signaling when the audience was supposed to see the hijab in a scene in which it was important to the identity of the character.

As I noted in the archetype-character-building exercise, I think it can be valuable to be intentional when you begin creating characters with details that establish what might be called "identity"—gender, race, ethnicity, age, as well as starting with class and social elements such as names and occupations. You should make strong choices for characters in terms of point of view and comic game and be aware that those aspects of the character don't need to be defined solely by identity. Comedy thrives on expectations. We can elect to use the expectations of identity such as race, ethnicity, and gender, but if we eschew those, then we must replace those surface expectations with strong choices that can be played across identities. If we don't, we will confuse our audiences, and confusion is the kiss of death for comedy.

One of the difficulties of using archetypes is that some archetypes can be read as stereotypes when partnered with certain races and ethnicities. There is an archetypal version of the Trickster character. This character is traditionally a low-status servant who tries to pretend to be smarter and better than they are, they often have big get-rich-quick schemes and use complicated language that they don't really understand. In the tradition of the commedia, this character is sometimes known as Scapino. But if you cast a Black actor or identify this character as Black, you need to be aware that you might be unintentionally referencing a character from blackface minstrelsy known as Zip Coon (who has similar qualities to the original archetype but is a derogatory stereotype).

Two things can help you when you find yourself questioning whether you are in the realm of stereotype versus archetype.

Remember that a stereotype is fixed: This character is a member of this identifiable group, therefore they are and will always behave "this way." In stereotype world, blonds are dumb, Jewish people are stingy, and so on. Check to see if you are centering the specific qualities of the character as opposed to relying on a type. You want to create characters who see the world in a specific interesting manner that causes them to behave in a certain way. And that isn't directly tied to their outward appearance or background. Practically, that may not always be enough, and it's important to keep that in mind in casting or as you choose specific identity details for the characters you create.

Additionally, if you are writing comedy, pay attention to providing unique character qualities of some sort for all of the people who appear in your comedic work. If you are a comedic performer, pay attention to adding specific details rather than playing to a generic "type." Lazy comedy puts a one-dimensional sexy female in the role of secretary. There are very few classic secretaries out there in the modern era; most white-collar workers do their own typing on a computer and carry mobile phones in their pockets instead of having someone at a desk outside their office screening calls. There are all sorts of functional roles that still exist in modern comedy narratives—restaurant servers, store clerks, family members, bosses—that can and should be made more dimensional, and this opens up opportunities for added comedic value.

USEFUL DEFINITIONS: Archetypes, Stereotypes, Iconic Representations, Roles

A character is a representation of a specific person (generally imaginary). In addition to qualities and actions, a character may have specific preferences and tendencies. They may be tied to a specific name or identity but also may not be.

An *archetype* is a pattern or a model of a kind of person (or thing, for that matter, but right now we are talking about characters). Archetypes tend to recur across cultures and eras in a wide range of stories and genres. An example of some traditional archetypes that show up in comedy include the Trickster, the Braggart Soldier, and the

(continued)

Absent-Minded Professor. But there are some modern archetypes as well—for example, the Instagram Influencer. Archetypes are generally defined by the qualities they have and the kinds of actions they take.

A *stereotype* attaches qualities and actions of character to a specific category or group of people. Stereotypes are fixed—a stereotypical character cannot grow or change, and even relatively "positive" stereotypical qualities, such as the stereotype of Asians as good students, are problematic, because the qualities and actions are assumed based on external characteristics that cannot be changed or altered.

An *iconic representation* is a usually visual representation that most people in a certain culture understand as representing a larger thing. A stop sign is an iconic representation. Want to quickly get a sense of how iconic representations work? Go to Google, type a job or ethnicity in the search bar, and look at the images that come up. If you Google "secretary," you will see a series of images of women with phones but also lots of sexual or semisexual imagery. If you Google "CEO," you will see a series of pictures that are primarily of white men (although not exclusively) and almost entirely posed in front of windows. An iconic representation is the image that our brain comes up with when we think of an idea of a person. It's shorthand. It's useful for comedy because it creates expectations.

A *role* is a job or a function. It may include actions: For example, a restaurant server waits on customers at a restaurant, or a bus driver drives a bus. Many different characters or archetypes could fill this role.

11 PERSONA

Persona is ultimately a kind of character, but it sits at the intersection of character and point of view, the living embodiment of or frame for an individual comedian's point of view. In comedy, you use your persona to teach your audience how to watch you.

In stand-up, a comedian's persona does a lot of the work of setting up expectations for their act. From the moment a stand-up walks onstage, their physical appearance and clothing set and confirm audience assumptions about the type of comedy they are likely to see. Most comedians will usually start with a joke that confirms those audience expectations and frames them in some way. Go to Netflix or YouTube and watch the first couple of minutes or so of the acts of five different stand-up comedians, and you'll notice that after they acknowledge the crowd, even the best-known ones will start by calling attention to something specific about their physicality, life experience, or point of view. When I did this exercise myself recently, Gabriel Iglesias began by making a joke about his weight, Dave Chappelle referenced his race, and Tiffany Haddish talked about her clothes. Others confirmed different expectations. Both Wanda Sykes and Joe Rogan began by calling out their political leanings, and Taylor Tomlinson, whose work is less political, began by announcing, "I'm an introvert."

Persona is somewhat less pronounced in sketch comedy or comedic film than in stand-up, but here as well, the audience's awareness of the character behind the character is an essential part of what makes the comedy function. The presence of Tyler Perry, Jim Carrey, Leslie Jones, or Melissa McCarthy in a comedic film evokes certain kinds of recognition, priming an audience to expect and enjoy the comedy to come. When comedians play outside their most recognizable and workable personas—especially when they are trying to make the transition from comedy to drama—they are frequently greeted with significantly less success, both critical and financial. This is not to say that a comedian can't ever transition to dramatic work. Bill Murray is a good example, but it's notable that his most successful dramatic work seems to incorporate or play off of his comedic persona in some fashion.

Audiences bring their own preconceptions of race, gender, ethnicity, body type, class, and a myriad of other variables to the comedy they watch. It would be disingenuous to suggest otherwise. Most skilled comedic performers acknowledge these preconceptions and make intentional use of them. Look at Ali Wong's physicality in her first two stand-up specials. While she is very funny at all times, her physical presence here is especially effective: a tiny woman easily six months pregnant and dressed in tight colorful clothing (in the first special she wears a sparkly horizontally striped miniskirt that emphasizes her shape). This immediately creates expectations for both congruence (we're going to be hearing some comedy about childbirth) and incongruity (it's not going to be the sort of comedy normally expected from "moms"). Her height, gender, ethnicity, and impending motherhood evoke images of sexlessness and purity while she simultaneously plays directly against those impressions with her dress, her physicality, and her language. For an audience, it can be doubly funny to hear a pregnant woman talk about sex because it is unexpected and culturally inappropriate even though her state is a natural consequence of the sex act, as Wong makes ample mention of throughout her act.

A comedic persona can seem to be so close to self that it appears to be authentic, as if you are watching exactly the same version of the person that you might meet if you were introduced at a party. The comedian Louis C.K. traded on this impression of authenticity for years in his work. In his special *Shameless*, he reinforced this appearance of authenticity by acknowledging the ways comedians artificially create a setup for a specific punch line, saying, "I was at a bar the other night. It doesn't matter where, because I'm lying."[1] His public face as a deeply thoughtful truth teller who interrogated the darkest parts of himself out loud made his comedy much less enjoyable after his private inappropriate behavior became general knowledge. The pain was still there in the work, but the carefully crafted persona that gave his audience distance on the dark impulses that C.K. considered in his comedy and made it safe to laugh in recognition no longer worked in the same way.

It's instructive to watch early television appearances or initial stand-up specials by comedians who went on to or currently have successful careers. John Mulaney spends a large part of his initial special (titled, appropriately, *New Kid on the Block*) referring to himself in terms of childhood, telling stories of his family, even wearing a suit that is just the slightest bit on the small side, as if he recently had a growth spurt. His later specials don't need to spend as much time or energy to establish his wise sarcastic kid persona, but the material is nevertheless framed by the shape he has created throughout his career. Bowen Yang, appearing on an HBO *Two Dope Queens* special, dresses in a rainbow-striped sequined sweater and begins by making specific references to both his Asian heritage and sexual preferences. He is claiming the focus and attention of his audience by highlighting aspects of his race and identity and then confirming the initial impression he has set.

A comedian's persona consists of how they appear as well as how they want to be perceived. Persona plays with the delicate differences between how a comedian appears and how they choose to be perceived. If a comedian appears "different" onstage, unusual in terms of their body type, their ethnicity, their gender, their sexuality, their abilities, or even just their choices in hairstyle or facial hair, the audience will notice. All these elements will be recognized in some fashion either consciously or unconsciously and trigger a variety of biases. These biases will always create context for the comedy a comedian presents. The challenge is to take those biases and use them intentionally to frame the comedy you personally create to achieve the results you want.

As a comedian you may try out many different personas before you find the one that you are most comfortable with and that suits your material best. Your persona may also evolve with your material: Tig Notaro, whose original comedic persona was slightly space-alienish, opaque but playful, had to evolve it as her material shifted from absurdist one-liners to personal confession. Richard Pryor based an early version of his persona on the casual approachable everyman used by Bill Cosby—another comedian whose real-life actions make it difficult to continue to enjoy his comedy—before shedding it and embracing a more deeply confessional and kinetic style of performance.

The line between the persona character version of your essential self and an actual character is maybe best illustrated by Stephen Colbert's work over the years. I went to college with Stephen, and we are good friends to this day. I introduced him to Second City and got him a job in the box office. I directed him in a one-person show called *Describing a Circle*, based on a series of short stories, monologues, and dialogues he had written. In that piece he played both a persona version of himself and a variety of characters.

The "Stephen Colbert" character that he first built on *The Daily Show* appears to me to be an extension of a character he liked to play when I knew him in college. This character was partially based on the NPR announcer Noah Adams, who seemed to be, as Stephen put it, "the most credulous interviewer in the world," just completely willing to take even the wackiest claim at absolute face value and treat it seriously. The final *Colbert Report* version of the character combined that credulity with the self-importance of Fox News interviewer Bill O'Reilly to create what Stephen has described as a "well-intentioned, poorly informed, high-status idiot."[2]

The ways these various characters and personas intersect with Stephen's essential point of view on the world appears quite consistent to me. Stephen is fascinated by language, by how it works in both directions: We use language to say what we mean, and the language we use also shapes our reality. That point of view was central to the "Stephen Colbert" character who coined "truthiness"—a word that reflects a very real and specific observation about the belief structure of a certain set of people. Stephen's love of language and the language we use to define ourselves remains central to his stage persona now that "Stephen Colbert" of *The Colbert Report* has become the persona Stephen Colbert of *The Late Show*—the persona is lighter and closer to his authentic self, but the awareness of how reality is shaped by language is still an abiding aspect of his comedic take.

Creating Your Comic Persona

When you start out as a comedian, your awareness of your own comedic persona and your ability to introduce it quickly and simply will make your comedy funnier. Your audience will feel a closer connection if you use that persona to show them how to watch your comedy. It will be easier to generate laughs because there are immediate expectations for your material. More established comedians whose personas are well-known need to do considerably less work to bring an audience on board. The trust and connection with the audience created through an understood persona also provides space for a little bit of experimentation and discovery between creator and audience. Once the audience feels like they know you and what you do well, they will be willing and interested to see what else you can do.

It's tempting here to start talking about "branding"—thinking of your comedy persona as being in some way, shape, or form a commercial entity. Since comedy is a popular art form that many people would like to be paid to create, there is undoubtedly a commercial element. But creating your persona isn't about what will sell or what someone will buy. It requires being aware of what you personally bring to your comedy. What is in your writing or your performance that is unique and particular to you? Exploring that can help create a version of yourself that supports and frames the comedy you want to make.

We all use a variety of personas in our daily lives—we are different people with our parents than we are with our lover or with our manager at the restaurant where we wait tables. The difference here is that your stage persona is an intentional conscious choice that supports the material you create for an audience and ultimately the point of view you want to project in your work. You may find that the best persona for the material you choose to create is quite different from the personas you use in your everyday life. However, beginning with the versions of yourself that you play in real life is a good starting place for discovering the persona you would like to use in your comedy.

Here are two quick ways to get to a potential persona:

1. List several adjectives describing the part of yourself that you want to use in your stage persona, perhaps based on material you have written or the kinds of comedic roles you have successfully played or improvised. The adjectives don't necessarily have to be congruent with each other, although they certainly can be. Here are some examples I came up with based on comedians I know personally: "sweet, southern, passive-aggressive"; "nonbinary, obsessive, awkward"; "angry flamboyant dancer"; "nerdy, precise, Californian"; "childlike, high energy, absurd."
2. Make a short list of topics or areas of interest that you could talk about for an extended period of time. Think about things you are an expert in (a particular video game, the geography of your home town, the best Italian beef sandwiches in the city of Chicago—as I've noted earlier, my son and husband had an ongoing top ten list of these, long before the advent of *The Bear*), but don't stress too much about what expertise means in this instance. If you have opinions and information about something you are an expert for the purposes of this exercise. Now give that persona a name—like "Italian beef guy" or "tea-drinking human," "proud resident of Grand Forks, North Dakota," "expert Disney World guest." Allow yourself to really let that name be the filter for this version of yourself.

I've included a much longer persona worksheet later that I use in my first-year comedy class. Feel free to use that worksheet to create different or more in-depth potential personas for yourself.

Once you have settled on a persona you'd like to work with, I suggest that you spend some time using it and see how it works for you. The goal is to be yourself but use the persona as your first and most primary filter. You could

- Go for a walk and just view the world through that persona's eyes. Take note of what draws your interest and why.
- Have a conversation with someone else—ideally with their permission—using this persona. I find that this works best with

both parties playing persona characters, but another option is using an interview format similar to the one in the character section, taking turns asking questions of the persona characters.

- Freewrite a short monologue from the point of view of this persona. I encourage you to pick a neutral(ish) topic, one unrelated or only tangentially related to the essence of the persona, like what to have for lunch or an opinion on a recent news event. Just write about that topic through the filter of the persona. Allow yourself to see the topic through their eyes and to connect to it through their interest/obsession.
- Play with various levels of your persona. Imagine that the persona you have picked exists along an axis from 1 to 10. For this scale, think of "1" as being very close to you as you normally present in the world; someone who doesn't know you very well would not notice that you were using a persona. Think of "10" as very removed from you in real life, not really you at all. You have explored and heightened this persona until it has transformed into a full-blown exaggerated character. Experiment with playing the persona at various points along this spectrum until you find the level that feels right for your comedy. I have found when working with my students that the most useful personas for them are often around level 3 or level 7.

Once you are comfortable with a persona you want to use, test it out in your work. If you are an improviser, use the persona as a close-to-self character in scene work onstage or in rehearsal. Try out jokes or stories that you use in your stand-up, but filter them through this particular persona and see what you discover. Try writing an introduction for your persona to use at the start of a standup set. Don't be afraid to be obvious about it. You can literally begin by stating, "I am an obsessive reader of YA fiction" or "I'm the most Minnesotan of all of the people from Minnesota that you are likely to meet." Write a couple of introductory jokes or observations that support this introduction and use them at the top of a stand-up set.

Persona needs to include or in some way address your outward physical appearance. If you have a giant handlebar mustache that you wax into curlicues at the ends, it will be the first thing about you that the audience sees. They will assume the mustache says something important about who you are. If it doesn't, why do you spend the time to maintain such conspicuous facial hair in the first place? Call it out, dig into it, and incorporate it into your act. The good news is that audiences love it when a comedian references something obvious that they have already seen. It's a quick and easy recognition laugh, and when done well, with good timing and wit, it can feel like a mini–magic trick to your audience. It appears as if you read their minds.

The same thing is true about other elements of your physical presence that are less under your control, such as your height or the size and type of nose on your face. It's very common for comedians to reference these things to get a laugh. But it isn't required for you to comment on your appearance if you don't feel comfortable doing so. Comedy is hard enough; if there's trauma or you have significant discomfort about an aspect of your appearance or identity, it's not going to be great for your mental health to joke about it before you deal with it in therapy. I encourage you to be intentional and aware that the existence of these things will inform how your audience sees you. You get to choose how you want to address your physical body or use your appearance in your jokes.

If your onstage persona is substantially different from how you choose to present in your everyday life, it is even more vital that you define that persona visually through how you dress onstage. Think about how your clothing, hair, and makeup define the identity you want your audiences to see when they first look at you. We all, of course, contain multitudes, and in other venues or other areas of your life, you likely want to be seen as multifaceted (because of course you are), but in this kind of comedy you want to quickly create an expectation that will support whatever follows.

At the beginning of her career, Joan Rivers dressed in a black cocktail dress with a string of pearls. It presented her as a "nice girl" from Larchmont. What was so useful about this presentation is that (not unlike Ali Wong's) it was incongruous with some of her material and made it infinitely funnier when she made jokes about sex. Phyllis Diller wore outrageous costumes, including boots that she had specially made so that they hit her legs at the skinniest part.[3] This clownish persona was meant to be less sexual and less attractive and gave her an opportunity to be more aggressive in her comedy because she had already styled herself as a figure of fun.

Most importantly, your persona frames the comedy you want to make. The whole point of persona is that it creates a bridge between the minds of the audience and the mind of the comedian. Don't force yourself or allow someone to bully you into using a particular persona because it seems obvious or commercial. On the other hand, if you find a disconnect between a persona that feels good and comfortable to you and the work you have been creating, I encourage you to pay attention to that discomfort. See what happens if you work backward and write material that fits the persona you enjoy. You may find a completely new area of comedy that you hadn't thought you could create.

TOOL: Persona Worksheet

If you are at the beginning of playing with your persona in your stand-up or thinking about the persona version of yourself as a writer, one way to start is by exploring the different ways that you view yourself and that others view you. I developed this worksheet for my first-year students.

If you want to get the most out of this worksheet, don't just answer the questions in your head—get them physically down on a piece of paper. (I suppose, if you like, you could complete it on a computer and then print it out.)

1. What are three adjectives that describe you physically?
2. What are three adjectives that describe your outer personality, the person someone would know if they knew you superficially or met you at a party or class?
3. What are three adjectives that describe your deeper personality, the person your close friends and family know?
4. What is your best quality?
5. What is your worst quality?
6. What do you want people to know about you?
7. What is something you don't want people to know about you?
8. What are your identities? (List at least three, but as many as you want to: for example, Minnesotan, bisexual, Latinx, male, Cubs fan.)

(continued)

9. How do you describe your family of origin? What is your family's "story"?
10. What are your obsessions? (List at least three.)
11. What are your areas of expertise? (List at least three.)
12. What is your secret talent?
13. What kind of clothing are you most comfortable in? If you had to wear the same thing every day, what would it be?
14. What is your signature "thing" (item of clothing, catchphrase, etc.)?
15. How do you think people see you?
16. How do you wish people saw you?
17. How are you afraid people see you?
18. What kind of comedy makes you laugh the hardest?
19. What is your secret talent?
20. Who are three characters from movies, books, TV, or plays that taken together describe you?
21. What is something about you that is true but sounds made up?
22. What are three of your favorite things that haven't come up in this worksheet yet?
23. If you could spend your days doing one thing, what would it be?
24. What are three things you love?
25. What are three things you detest?
26. What are three things you fear?
27. What were you like when you were seven?
28. What were you like when you were fourteen?
29. What do you predict that you will be like in thirty years?

Have someone who hasn't known you for a long time answer the following about you:

30. What are three adjectives that describe you physically?
31. What are three adjectives that describe your outer personality, the person someone would know if they know you superficially or met you at a party or class?
32. What are three adjectives that describe your deeper personality, the person your close friends and family know?
33. What is your best quality?
34. What is your worst quality?

Have someone who knows you really well answer the following about you:

35. What are three adjectives that describe you physically?

36. What are three adjectives that describe your outer personality, the person someone would know if they know you superficially or met you at a party or class?

37. What are three adjectives that describe your deeper personality, the person your close friends and family know?

38. What is your best quality?

39. What is your worst quality?

Read through the answers on the worksheet. Pay attention to anything that evokes strong emotions—either positive or negative. You can use a highlighter or circle those things as you go.

Based on this, see if you can create at least three potential personas for yourself. Write a sentence or two describing each one.

12 POINT OF VIEW

I'm going to start out by defining point of view as consisting of two things: framing and filtering. Framing is what we see—what is in our field of vision—and filtering is how we see what we see. If you think of this from the perspective of a camera, the framing is literally what is available to be seen when you look through the finder. It could be a close-up of a face or a wide shot of a landscape. My personal point of view is both literal—my messy attic office, my bare feet on a footstool, the computer on my lap—and metaphoric. What I "see" is what I have access to in my personal world: my neighborhood in the city of Chicago, the information I get from the various media I consume regularly, what I am aware of based on my personal history, which includes my race, gender, ethnicity, class, relative wealth or poverty, sexual identity, etc. Filtering for a person is defined by what we see as important and less important. Experiences, knowledge, and various contexts (religion, family, political, social, occupational) color our perceptions of what we see.

Imagine several different people experiencing the events unfolding at the Capitol building in Washington, DC, on January 6, 2021. What they see will depend on where they are—a congressperson inside the building might be under a desk waiting and see very little. Someone on one side of the building might see a great deal of violence—protesters hitting cops with barricades. A third person on a different side of the building might see people waving flags and chanting but very little in the way of violence. Already, just by virtue of their framing, each of these three people is going to have a deeply different experience and understanding of what is occurring in the city at this point in time.

Now let's add filtering to the equation. That congressperson has been told that they are in danger by Capitol security, and because of that, any noise they hear is going to feel dangerous and scary. The person on the barricade side might have come to Washington with the intention of being a part of what they consider to be a glorious revolution to take back America, and that filter makes the confrontation feel exhilarating and exciting. The third person, the one who doesn't see any cops at all, might have taken part in the Black Lives Matter protests the previous summer and wonder at the number of white people being allowed to gather in this way with no real police interference.

Three different points of view, three completely different perspectives. I've chosen to present points of view that are not immediately comedic, but if the third person has a bit more psychological distance (the people they see are dressed in ridiculous costumes, whereas they themselves have a personal perspective on the world and politics that tends to be more detached and less emotional), their recounting of the story to an audience could have strong comedic value.

The concept of point of view in comedy is far from new. The Greek satirist and playwright Aristophanes shared his negative perspective on the sophistry of Socrates in his comedy *The Clouds*, first performed in 423 BCE, in a style that was echoed thousands of years later by Jon Stewart taking on the hyperbole of Sean Hannity and Tucker Carlson. But beginning roughly in the late 1950s, there was a notable shift in comedy (especially in the West) that has expanded over the past seventy years. Before that time, most popular comedy focused on broad characters with setup and punch line jokes that weren't intended to reflect in any way on the teller. For example, Henny Youngman could do an entire set of jokes about a hypothetical "wife" while his own wife sat smiling in the front row of the audience. The jokes weren't meant to reveal something authentic about Youngman himself or his relationship with his particular spouse. They were "just jokes." Which is not to say that these "jokes" didn't reveal something about the misogyny of the society in which they both lived. Much like the pervasive ethnic comedy of the late nineteenth- and early twentieth-century United States or the class-based humor of Great Britain during the same era—or nearly every country on the planet at some point or another. Making fun of those with less power seems to be a constant over the course of human experience regardless of point of origin; Youngman's jokes demonstrated recognizable attitudes of the society at large but weren't meant to be attributed to him directly.

Mid-twentieth-century standups like Mort Sahl, Redd Foxx, and Dick Gregory pioneered a new kind of comedy that felt unique to its creators. This was not just a phenomenon only in stand-up or exclusive to men—I would include Jean Carroll and Lily Tomlin as well as the sketch comedy of Nichols and May and Ernie Kovacs. The jokes were still there, but laughs were generated less by the mechanism of surprise inherent in a setup and punch line than by a sense of being let into the mind of the joke teller. Modern comedy is now regularly evaluated and enjoyed as much for its point of view as for its jokes or characters, and often that point of view is valued above all other components.

There is research in behavioral science that focuses on the idea of perspective taking—and perspective, in this case, can be thought of as equivalent to point of view. When I engage in perspective taking, I am trying to see the world through someone else's eyes, attempting to understand what they might be thinking and feeling based on what I know about their frames and filters. You've probably done this casually thousands of times. You try to predict what someone you work with will think about a project you have proposed, or you spend time with a friend discussing how someone else in your immediate friend group might or might not feel about you. But as I mentioned earlier, science has shown that humans are, on the whole, particularly terrible at perspective taking. Which is even more interesting, because most of us believe we are brilliant at it.[1] We tend to believe that our predictions of how other people feel and think are accurate, but when scientists test these predictions, they find that we are pretty much totally wrong.

Certain kinds of modern comedy appear designed to provide an experience of what we might call perspective giving. I am clearly defining for you my framing and filtering. I'm adjusting what I personally recognize and find painful, and the distance I have on it, so that you and I (and ideally an entire audience) have the exact same response at the same time. I am giving you my perspective and assisting you in understanding it. For most of us, our favorite comedians are our favorites because we feel as if we see the world through their eyes and in some way it connects us to them.

Audiences tend to see a comedian's perspective giving as authentic to that comedian—to see their acts, characters and persona as being close to and revealing of who they really are. But human beings are complex. I would suggest that for most modern comedians their point of view *is* rooted in some way shape or form in their lived experience. But it's not necessarily their entire perspective as a human, and it might be leaving out an entire giant part of who they actually are. We can often feel as if we "really" know our favorite comedians, and then are shocked to find out that they have entire other lives that we completely disapprove of morally or politically.

Developing your own point of view as a comedian doesn't mean that you are telling the entire truth of your life; you may end up just highlighting one small aspect of who you are. That will depend on the comedy you want to make. But the first step is identifying your own frames and filters.

POV 101: You Already Have a Point of View

When I teach, I often have short meetings with my students at the end of each session to provide a bit of personal feedback, especially when I have directed them in a student show where we focused on material creation and performance. A common question during these sessions is how the individual can better develop their point of view. What's ironic is that it's not unusual for me to then find out a piece of surprising or unique information: that the student in question served several tours of duty in the military, that they have a family business making giant balloon animals for parades, or that they have an advanced degree in genetics. And despite this wealth of personal experience, much of the work they generated in class was about bad dates or arguments with roommates over who does the dishes. Their actual point of view was entirely missing from their work because they didn't think an audience would recognize it.

We all have stories, unique human experiences that define what we see and how we see it. What we don't realize is that it is exactly the things that are specific to us that are fascinating and funny to other people. We don't have to give much context for them to "get it," especially since human brains are primed to pay attention to elements that are novel. I teach an improv exercise where the point of concentration is for students to sneak as much real personal detail about themselves into a short scene as possible.[2] They are also instructed to deliberately include some things that aren't true so that they can feel less vulnerable about what they may be revealing. These scenes are usually riveting. Specific detail of any kind makes for better comedy, but the improvisers also note how easy it was to do—that it had never occurred to them that just using real events and elements from their own lives was going to be so useful or create so much genuine laughter.

I developed an extension of this exercise for a workshop on diversity and inclusion that I created with my team on the Second Science Project. We put people into pairs and had one person describe to their partner for about a minute how "people" grocery shop and then to take another minute or two and describe in detail how they themselves grocery shop. As we were testing the beta version of this exercise, inevitably during the second round there was a great deal of laughter from the listeners. And when we talked about it afterward, many participants shared that they were surprised how such a simple exercise could generate so much humor and laughter.

Let's take a quick moment to look at this exercise through the lens of the recognition/pain/distance triad. Our workshop participants weren't making jokes, and they weren't intentionally creating comedy, but by sharing their actual habits and experiences (recognition) in a way that was slightly vulnerable or surprising (pain), about something pretty everyday (distance), they had made connections with their partners in a way that generated laughter and humor. It's easy to see how this kind of POV sharing could translate into comedy creation.

If you are curious, the point of the exercise in the workshop was to help participants see that sharing small, nonvulnerable details creates connection because it helps others understand you as a human being with a mind. It's a powerful thing to do in your real life as well as in your comedy.

Exercises to Hone Your Point of View for Comedy

I want to point out again that you already have a point of view. You don't have to go out and find one. Your point of view is what you see and how you see it. But if you want to use point of view in the comedy you create, you need to spend some time with your point of view and pay close attention to it. Look to really identify the core of it, cultivate it, and then intentionally pick and experiment with elements of it to see how it can create new comedy or enhance the comedy you want to make.

This is a process, and just like all of the other creation exercises in this section, I encourage you to play, create, and generate POV-based material without judgment. It's going to take a while to identify the parts of your own point of view; heck, it isn't easy to identify the point of view of a well-established comedian. It's a common practice in television to create sitcoms based around a stand-up comedian's act. The most successful of these shows—*The Bob Newhart Show*, *Roseanne*, *Ellen*—have one thing in common: The show in some way represented the comedian's point of view. The ones that weren't (I'm going to leave it to you to fill in the blanks here) tended to be based on the comedian's act rather than their point of view: "Oh, in his act this comedian talks about cars. He'll be a guy in a sitcom who talks about cars." The producers didn't dig into the car comedy to realize that while the comedian's *topic* was cars, their point of view was about how men hide their passions behind material obsession. I'm not calling out any particular comedian with this example. This is an imaginary stand-up with a failed imaginary sitcom.

I've already encouraged you to start by mining your own life in the generating material section. If you have done some of that generation, I would encourage you to go back through that material and start looking for personal specifics that you can use in your work to give it a clearer point of view. If you have been doing observations, take note of what you have observed and what was important to you about it, what feelings it elicited in you because of who you are. You don't have to nail it down exactly and forever; your point of view is going to change throughout your life as you see new things and have new experiences. Or as we do in the "Persona" section, you could start thinking about your point of view with one small aspect or element of your life experience (say your childhood obsession with Pokémon) and create a personal frame and filter based on that.

Here's a quick exercise to get a sense of your point of view. We're going to start with your framing. Let's do a quick list. Right now, without thinking about it too much, write down as many things as possible that you can see from wherever you are sitting or standing. We did a version of this exercise earlier in the book, but this time I'm in my attic office, which used to be my kids' playroom.

- Dolls
- Treehouse
- Tape measure
- Comedy and improv books
- The thing that you can use to clean the computer screen
- Weights
- Computer charging strips

Got your list?

I want you to take as much time as you like to look around the space and find the objects you missed—things you dismissed as "not belonging on the list" or things you see so often that you don't see them anymore. Or things you didn't list because you don't know what they are.

Compare your lists. What's different about what you "see" when you look around and what you don't see? My husband has pointed out on a number of occasions that I have a habit of leaving pens everywhere, not unlike the way our Bernese mountain dog sheds hair. When I look around my office, I genuinely don't see the pens (although now that I do, I can count at least four in my direct line of vision). Another way to do this exercise is to look at a room or outside area, make a list of what you notice, and then take a photo of it and do the same thing. I'm frequently surprised by the prominence of our outdoor grill or how much you can see of the neighbor's backyard when I look at photos I have taken of plants or flowers in my garden. Our brains are constantly filtering for what is important or valuable to us. We *never* see everything; it would make our brains explode. I don't focus on the grill or the neighbors when I look at my garden—I have trained myself to *not look*. The opposite is also true. Have you had the experience of learning a new word or buying something, and suddenly that word or that object is everywhere? There's a behavioral science concept that describes this: frequency bias, or the Baader-Meinhof phenomenon. We tend not to see things if we don't know what they are.

Your first task is just to get a sense of what *you* see. What is in your frame, and what isn't? It's not important to see everything—you can't, you won't, and you don't need to. The piece that is useful here for you as a comedian is to have a nice solid awareness of what you personally see in the world and how you see it.

Framing and filtering exercises. You can do most, if not all, of these as verbal or written exercises. They can be recorded as you talk out loud to yourself or to someone else. In fact, I would encourage you to try them both ways if you can. Frequently you get different results, and that difference can be useful to you.

Framing and filtering 1. Describe a room, a location or an object.

Reread your description, paying close attention to the specific details you noted. What was most important in your personal "frame," and what did you ignore? What was completely outside your frame? For example, if you described the street outside your house or apartment, you may have described the cars and completely ignored the people or vice versa. You may not even have been aware that there was someone behind you while you did so.

Now, describe the same thing again and strongly exaggerate your frame. For example, can you describe your street as if it were *only* about cars?

Those of you who have been paying attention will note that you're already starting to use the elements of comedy in a couple of ways in this short exercise: two kinds of recognition (real things and also a real person's way of framing information); the pain of a kind of an error (the fact that the real person's framing is skewed from reality), as well as exaggeration. The exaggeration and the specificity of the framing also provide a kind of distance.

Framing and filtering 2. Go somewhere and experience something and then recount what you remember. As earlier, pay attention to what you remember in detail and what you left out. This is a fun exercise to do with a friend. Experience the same thing, and then compare your descriptions of the experience.

Now describe it again and strongly exaggerate your filtering: How did you see it? What did it make you feel?

Framing and filtering 3. Do a version of the exercise I created for the Second Science Project: Describe in detail something that you do regularly, the exact way you personally do it. You can write about how you go grocery shopping or what you do to get ready for your day from the time you get up until you walk out the door.

Name your frames and filters. It can be helpful to name the frames and filters that represent your point of view. We all have many of these, and part of honing your point of view is being aware of the possible versions of you that exist within your larger life experience. What are all your different areas of expertise or obsessions? Mine include Picky Gourmet Cook, but also Magazine Hoarder and YA Book Nerd. What are the filters you use regularly? The persona worksheet tool in the "Persona" chapter can help with this process. Make the long list and then go through it and circle the things that feel good and resonant to you.

Comedic Opinion

Once you have a version of your comedic point of view that feels good to you, take it out into the world and see how it operates when you intentionally turn it on something. This is the essence of observational comedy (which, by the way, seems much easier to do well than it actually is). Then expand on your point of view by adding feeling and emotion: Here's what I see, here's how I see it, and here's what it makes me feel.

John Mulaney's now-classic bit from 2016 in which he describes the experience of observing Donald Trump as president as being similar to a horse getting loose in a hospital, is a great example of comedic opinion. He's describing contemporary politics, but the focus is on what he sees, how he sees it, and how it makes him feel. He also found a terrific and insightful metaphor for this particular point of view that (as it turns out) felt very recognizable to a lot of people.

Here are some exercises to help get at comedic opinions.

Rants and Raves. A simple way to play with your comedic opinion is to do a rant.[3] Pick a pet peeve you have, something simple that makes you irrationally angry. And then rant, either on paper or aloud for a couple of minutes. Use the explore and heighten tool to really wring all of the juice out of the topic. Once you have done so, go back over your rant and pay attention to the details. What do you see and respond to specifically? How does who you are and what you know color your particular point of view in this instance? Put the rant into your "file" of in-progress material, including the notes of what you noticed.

Or do the opposite: Pick something minor that you genuinely take pleasure in and go all out praising it to the skies. Pay attention to how the positive creates a different dynamic for you. It's very common for comedians to skew their work negative, but there are interesting discoveries to be made on the opposite end, and this may be a nice direction for your particular point of view.

You may already be familiar with the improv game "Conducted Rant." The difference here is that the comic mechanism of the improv game is ranting about a random suggestion, which creates incongruity. Here the point is to dig more closely into the things you genuinely feel strongly about, however minor.

Comedic Explanation 1. Describe something you know how to do particularly well or understand clearly, but foreground your comedic point of view. Don't just explain it: Make sure to reveal how you feel about it, what specific experiences you've had with it, what is messed up about it, what parts of the subject you know and care about that most people wouldn't.

Comedic Explanation 2. Do some research on a topic or issue of the day and explain it in detail from your comedic point of view (this is essentially the premise of John Oliver's HBO show using his POV/ persona of a somewhat nerdy obsessive outsider of the British variety). Again, the key here is in how you experience the topic, what interests you specifically? How does the topic or issue relate to what you see or what affects you? Explore and heighten those aspects.

Another version of this that has spawned a thousand one-person shows is to go out and do something that might be unusual or uncomfortable for you. Go door to door canvassing for a political candidate, try eating some unusual food you have never had before, go skydiving, or learn how to waterski for the first time. Create an unusual project for yourself. The British comedian Dave Gorman decided to try to meet as many other people named Dave Gorman as he could, which resulted in a one-person show called *Are You Dave Gorman?* that he brought to the Edinburgh Fringe Festival and was later broadcast on the BBC.

Pay close attention while you do whatever you choose to do and then describe the experience from the comedic version of your point of view. Notice that this just a heightened comedic version of the framing and filtering exercises we did earlier—we're adding an element of pain by making the experience difficult or complicated.

Metaphors. Take a leaf from Mulaney's book and play with metaphor. It doesn't have to be as complex or complete as a horse in a hospital. Describe something you have done or experienced in terms of something else. Think about your process of getting up in the morning: What is it like? It might be useful to make a list of ten possibilities first and then pick one or two to try. Keep your focus on what you personally see and what you actually do in this process just use the metaphor to describe or exaggerate the things that are notable and specific to you and how they feel to you.

USEFUL DEFINITIONS: Irony, Sarcasm, and Wit

Irony is a POV filter. At base it is connected to an awareness of two seemingly opposite things existing in the same place at the same time. You say one thing while also meaning its opposite. *Sarcasm* uses a similar mechanism but is differentiated from irony by being more direct and mostly conveyed through tone. A positive is meant negatively and is indicated by a mocking or sneering tone of voice.

True irony is deeper than simple opposition. It is opposition mixed with justice of a sort. Irony suggests that these opposites have a common source or a central connection—they are not just black and white, but two sides of the same coin. It was ironic when several of my first-year comedy students copied each other word for word when answering the prompt "Describe your personal comedy ethics" on a take-home final exam.

Dramatic irony is when the viewer or reader can see or are aware of something that the characters cannot see, and again there is a sort of inevitability in this double seeing. It is not dramatic irony if we see that a tree root is about to trip the protagonist. It is dramatic irony if we see the tree root at the moment that the protagonist proclaims that they are "the least accident-prone human on the planet."

In the context of comedy, *wit* is the way a comment, joke, or story is told. Wit is often a combination of speed, artistry, and musicality in terms of the sounds of the language being used and the intentional choice of language whose meaning conveys the concept in an artful and novel way.

Wit is a synonym for *intelligence*, and you can see how the term *wit* is recognition of a specific point of view rather than a joke, although a joke may have elements of wit within it. Wit is in the specific choices made in conveying information as much as in the information itself. Wit is not exclusive to language, although it does tend to be thought of in written or verbal forms. You could argue that some expressions of wit are a form of physical comedy. You can have music with intentional choices of certain evocative sounds, or the use of instrument conveys an element of wit. A dinner menu might contain witty combinations of ingredients or flavors. While not required, speed is often deemed an aspect of wit—a "quick wit" is someone who comes up with an artful framing off the cuff.

Parody and Satire

In parody you are taking your point of view and turning it on a form or genre to point out its flaws and ridiculousness. *The Carol Burnett Show* was famous for its parodies, which exaggerated and mocked the plot devices, performances, and visual effects of classic films and television shows. In "Went with the Wind," Burnett's Scarlett O'Hara tries to seduce Rhett Butler (Harvey Korman) in a dress made out of velvet curtains with the curtain rod sticking out from her shoulders. Key and Peele did a parody of the songwriting style in the musical *Les Miz* in which Keegan's character begs everyone to sing "One at a Time." A mockumentary such as *This Is Spinal Tap* parodies the entire genre of rock music documentaries rather than taking on just one specific film as the target of its parody.

My students frequently get parody and satire confused. It's helpful to remember that parody is making fun of the form (a film or book or kind of film or book) and satire makes fun of an idea or belief about the world. This is complicated by the fact that it is not unusual to use elements of parody in order to satirize a belief. For example, the *SNL* sketch "Celebrity Jeopardy" parodies the TV game show, and specifically the editions starring celebrities, who appear imbecilic compared to the regular contestants. There is no belief being made fun of here; it is merely exaggerating an element of the real program for comedic effect. On the other hand, the *SNL* sketch "Black Jeopardy" uses a parody of the game show in order to make a satiric point about the ways that racism undercuts the common interests shared by those of the same socioeconomic class. *The Colbert Report* used a parody of *The O'Reilly Factor* to satirize the belief systems behind conservative media and politics. Ashley Nicole Black's sketch "Invisible Spy" from *A Black Lady Sketch Show* is a parody of spy thrillers but also a social satire of the widespread beliefs that women who have a certain type of body are not competent or important. The online parody site *The Onion* parodies traditional journalism, but its content is a mix of news parody with a large amount of satire.

Creating Parody

Mapping. One of the classic tools of parody uses incongruity by taking two wildly different genres or styles and mapping one on top of the other. Think of the book series *Pride and Prejudice and Zombies.* I recently directed a student-created show called *Are You There God? It's Me, Katniss Everdeen* that parodied children's and YA literature. One of our sketches was set at Historical Fiction High and mapped the lunchroom scene from the film *Mean Girls* onto the specific details of characters from the Little House books, *Little Women*, and *Anne of Green Gables.*[4]

In my first-year comedy class, I have my students do a quick group exercise that uses mapping to parody classic Disney animated films. We start by talking about the tropes of those movies: spunky female heroine, talking animal companions, queer coded villains, big musical numbers, generic prince heroes, etc. Then I put the students in groups and have them come up with an existing story that should never be adapted into a Disney animated movie and create the elements of a parody by mapping the story onto the Disney tropes: Who is the heroine? Who is the animal companion? What is the title of the big musical number?

You can play with mapping by using simple incongruities. Put characters from an animated children's cartoon into a police procedural. Make a serious drama into a broad 1950s-style sitcom.

Finding the logical flaw. Almost every story has some gaping plot hole or unanswered question that is glossed over. Why is Dorothy going to miss the Scarecrow most of all, and how do the Cowardly Lion and the Tin Man feel about that?[5] Why does no one in the Pacific Northwest town in *Twilight* notice that the vampires don't age? Why does everyone sit in the room and allow the detective to point out that he has discovered their vast murder conspiracy? Why don't they just kill him too? You can parody any one of these stories by allowing one or more characters to become aware of the plot hole and then play out what happens next.

These types of specific or genre parody can take any number of forms. They could be live or filmed sketch, character monologue, or comedic short story.

Creating Satire

The difference between satire and comic opinion as mentioned earlier is that with satire you aren't just describing or complaining—you are turning your point of view onto the world and its systems (political satire) or its behaviors (social satire) and pointing out things that are wrong and need to be changed. You are saying, "This is something happening in the world and it is a genuine problem." The pain in satire is real, which may be why it's possible for satire to make use of the tools of comedy but not necessarily create actual comedy. The satirist wants to make other people think and may not care about whether or not they laugh or have the sensation of humor.

There is a common tendency in mass media to assume that any comedy featuring politics or making fun of what politicians do is satire. It can sometimes be difficult to parse the distinction. Generally, satire of either sort (social or political) does not simply showcase the behavior that requires changing. Rather, it takes the belief behind the behavior and demonstrates how the belief itself is dangerous and requires action to prevent further harm.

Saturday Night Live has done both comedy using political figures and political satire. Chevy Chase playing Gerald Ford as clumsy is comedy about a political figure; so was most of Alec Baldwin repeating the gaffes of Donald Trump. Tina Fey repeating verbatim the words of aspiring VP Sarah Palin was political satire. Fey's performance demonstrated the dangers of a cynical belief within the Republican Party that choosing to nominate someone so poorly qualified for the position would be missed by the public because Palin was such an attractive and outspoken character.

In the classic piece of satire *A Modest Proposal*, Jonathan Swift takes on a belief that was underneath much of the British government's most heinous policies toward the Irish—the doctrine of utilitarianism, which suggested that only things that were useful should be supported by the government. Using a classic satirical tool of taking the belief to its furthest possible (and darkest) implication, he suggests making Irish babies "useful" by turning them into food. I'm assuming that you are familiar with this one, because it seems to be the only example of satire used in high schools.

Satire practice. Make a list of things that you think need to be changed in your community, city, or country. Remember that satire doesn't have to be about policy or politics—it can be about the way people behave. For example, I have strong feelings about people who deliberately park in two parking spaces so that their car doesn't get dinged. The underlying belief is "My car being perfect is more important than your inconvenience." Pick one or two things from your list to satirize. Identify two or three beliefs that underlie each of your choices (they can be beliefs of your own, beliefs of people you know personally, or beliefs you think other people have).

Write or improvise an argument for the most extreme version of one of those beliefs. You can build on that argument by further filtering it through a specific character.

Create a premise that's set in a world where those beliefs are taken to their furthest possible conclusion. A commonly useful device is to take belief structures of large institutions (political, economic, or religious) and translate those same beliefs someplace more domestic, like a family or grade school. Less strongly satiric (but often more comedic) is to do the reverse: to take the characters from these large institutions and map their behavior onto minor situations such as children on a playground or petty neighborhood disputes.

Again, these ideas can be put into a variety of forms (sketch, character monologue) or classically in the kind of journalism parody you find on websites such as *The Onion* or *Reductress*.

USEFUL DEFINITIONS: Satire and Parody

Satire is directing a personal point of view on something that is wrong in the world with the goal of promoting change. We show (perhaps through exaggeration but also through irony and other means) that a system or way of behaving is deeply flawed in a way that is damaging to the world or the people in it. Generally, satire provokes awareness of the systems and thinkings that are flawed rather than the mechanics of the system. We don't satirize the laws; we satirize the thoughts and intentions behind the laws. Some satire takes a position or argument to its furthest possible extreme to show the essential flaws or cracks in the argument.

In *parody*, we turn our point of view onto a form or genre in order to show the ridiculous elements of that genre. Most parody uses hyperbole and exaggeration to expose the inherent flaws of the form or genre.

Parody and satire are often confused in practice, perhaps because parody is a common tool of satire. *The Onion* is a parody of a newspaper (the form) in which the writers may express a satiric point of view about a topic (such as gun control). *The Colbert Report* was a parody of an *O'Reilly Factor*–style television news show, but it also contained satiric takes on the day's news, with a focus on conservative American politics.

13 CREATING COMEDIC NARRATIVES

Story and Narrative

At the most basic level, narrative and story are similar regardless of whether your story is dramatic or comedic. Before we start to talk about what makes comedic story unique, I want to take a moment to provide some general ways to think about story.

When I teach story to my students, I use a couple of very simple structures. The first, "Situation, Problem, Solution," breaks down as follows:[1]

- **Situation:** What do we need to know to understand the story? Who is the story about? What does normal look like in this particular world?
- **Problem:** Something happens that upsets the normal world and the people in it have to deal with this event or series of events. This is the bulk of the story.
- **Solution:** The problem is dealt with. It may not actually be solved; it might be that the characters come to terms with the fact that their situation has changed, but there is some sense of closure and moving on.

To tell a more solidly structured story, either a true personal story or a fictional one, all you really need to do is to fill out that simple template. Start by spending some quality time on the situation, setting up the exposition, and creating the sense of a world or a normal day and a character that will be affected. Next, introduce the issue or problem and explore and heighten that issue, until ideally you hit a moment of tension where it seems the problem is impossible, then you find some form of resolution. It's worth noting that the "problem" is carrying a lot of the weight of the story. Sometimes it is helpful to add to the structure to account for that.

So:

> Situation
> Problem
> Problem gets worse
> Solution

Or, if you are writing a sitcom with just one "A" plot,

> Situation
> Problem
> Problem gets worse
> Solution
> Solution creates a new problem
> New problem gets worse
> New solution is found that solves both the first and second problems

Another way to look at this simple sort of story structure is to use a format created at Pixar for their animated films:

> Once upon a time there was ______________________________.
> Every day, ______________________________.
> One day, ______________________________.
> Because of that, ______________________________.
> Because of that, ______________________________.
> Until finally, ______________________________.

In this structure, the situation is in the first two lines. This structure begins by introducing a main character of some sort and then sets up what normal is for that character. One day a problem of some sort arises. There are two lines in which you explore and heighten the problem and/or make it worse. The problem seems impossible to solve—until finally, a solution.

None of these structures are unique to comedy; even the traditional sitcom structure could technically be used to create a dramatic play or television show. Although comedic and dramatic narrative structures have strong underlying similarities, comedic and dramatic narrative are fundamentally different in many ways.

Comedic Narrative

Here are the common elements of a comedic narrative:

1. The audience has an awareness that the storyteller intends (or storytellers intend) to provoke laughter or amusement. Clues and details such as the presence of multiple comedy components reinforce that understanding. It's not unusual for there to be some sort of direct address to the audience that also confirms this—say, an opening musical number such as "Comedy Tonight" in the musical version of Plautus, *A Funny Thing Happened on the Way to the Forum*, which literally announces what the audience is there for.
2. Expectations are created clearly and early, establishing what constitutes normal in this world and for the central character. Then there is a departure of some sort from normal in a way that is unusual but makes sense logically (if not rationally). There is similarity here between comedy and the genres of horror and suspense. In these forms, as in comedy, there is a strong value on having the audience have roughly the same experience at the same time—a laugh in a comedy, a jump scare in horror.
3. The context of the world of the story creates or signals distance through the use of specific details. These details are often either highly unusual or out of proportion in some way.

The point of view from which the story is told may be also unusual, either from the perspective of an unlikely character or a third-person perspective that is especially close up or far away.

4. The painful elements are often surprising and exaggerated (a character gets hit in the face by a steel pipe), while their effects are minimized through incongruous detail (the steel pipe takes on the exact shape of the face).
5. The narrative is populated by comedic characters or characters that are revealing the comic aspects of themselves. Frequently a comic main character is put into a difficult situation and then attempts to use the only tools they have to solve their problems even though they are the wrong tools for the job.
6. There is reincorporation of story elements that create a feeling of pattern and repetition and the structure of the piece creates a sense of satisfaction in the viewer or reader. This is one of the primary sources of distance in comic narrative. An audience is aware that it is watching a comedy. They have psychological distance because they know that however complex or uncomfortable the events of the story may be, it will all end well. Comedies do not need to have a happy ending per se (think of Slim Pickens riding down to earth on an atomic bomb in *Dr. Strangelove*), but there is some kind of satisfying closure that brings pleasure.
7. Most comedic narratives tend to be much simpler conceptually than dramatic narratives and don't work well at length. It's telling that many of the classic comedic story types are quite short (essays, theatrical or television sketches) and often exist within a variety narrative of some kind (including old-school vaudeville-style revue as well as modern sketch, improv, and stand-up). Variety narrative could be said to be somewhat uniquely suited to comedy, and it has a structure of its own that we will look at later.

Now that we've established what comedic narrative is, we'll practice how to create it. The first step is to come up with a premise.

USEFUL DEFINITIONS: Farce

Farce is a type of comedy narrative in which initial misunderstandings rapidly snowball into improbable actions that are logical (based on available information) but not necessarily rational.

The action of a farce is driven by secrets and misunderstandings that are compounded by extravagant solutions or responses to the initial perceived problem. On stage and in films, farces frequently feature a great many doors—all the better to allow for missed connections and confusions of identity or for someone to accidentally overhear or mishear a conversation. Farces commonly employ a great deal of physical humor and slapstick. If you are watching someone run between two rooms pretending to be two different characters by switching between disguises, you are watching a farce. If the whole thing could be resolved if a couple of the characters just sat down and talked to each other but instead the solution is to hide the body under the exact couch where the police are going to choose to sit when they inevitably visit the house, it's a farce.

Comic Premise

Comic premise is the translation of a comic idea into a short thesis statement that provides a clear starting place and comic logic for a specific type of comic narrative. That statement will look different depending on the form. The premise for a comedic song is usually the title and is repeated in the chorus (as with Tom Lehrer's "The Vatican Rag"). The premise for an article on a news parody website like *The Onion* or *Reductress* is laid out in the headline. The premise for a sketch is going to provide information on who is in the scene and where it takes place but may also include things that are not made clear to the audience/viewer until later in the sketch, such as who or what is going to be affected by the events of the sketch. You can have a premise for a comedic television show like *Ted Lasso*—"American football coach is hired to coach a British football (a.k.a. soccer) team"—as well as premises for individual episodes of that show—"Ted's family comes to visit him." The premise for a section of a stand-up set is generally the distillation of a comic idea that the comedian will then explore and heighten.

A comic premise is bigger than a joke. It's the launching pad for multiple jokes. When we create premises, we are doing something fundamentally different from writing jokes. Jokes are a simple math problem. Premises are mini–alternate realities in which a lot of jokes (as well as characters, physical comedy, and point of view) can live and grow.

The transition between raw comedic idea and a comic premise that can be built on and explored isn't easy. As we have already established, forcing yourself to "come up with something funny" tends not to be a particularly helpful way of generating comedy. But even starting with an idea that you feel has potential for comedy isn't necessarily enough to get you writing or generating. A good premise makes the next step of creating the piece feel easy. It provides a springboard that launches you into the execution of your comedic idea. The process of translating a comic idea into a usable premise may feel mysterious, but it really just takes practice and the use of some particular tools.

As we did with jokes, you can start with the form of comedy you intend to create and then brainstorm elements that make sense within that form. Or you can start with a comic idea and explore it until you discover a strong premise that suggests a particular form.

Most jobs in comedy start with form. If you are writing on a late-night show, you are looking for certain kinds of jokes and premises for specific segments. If you are a writer/performer on a sketch show, you will be creating sketches of various types. Later in this chapter we're going to generate premise specifically for a sketch and sitcom. But understanding how to work both ways will allow you to more easily make comedy in multiple formats and make better use of your comedy ideas.

Starting with a Comic Idea

This is where a regular material generation practice can serve you. You may already have a list of ideas you want to work with, but if not, you can start with one of the lists or observation exercises that I detail in the generating material section earlier in the book. Once you have some good raw material, look it over and pay attention to what interests you or strikes you as having potential. For example, when I reread through my own lists from that earlier section, I was again struck by the presence of this weird barrel-shaped sewing table in my living room.

Sometimes the idea is already strong enough to immediately suggest a premise. More often, you need to play around and riff off of the idea to get it to the next step.

Here are some thoughts that were sparked for me by the sewing table: What are all the things in our homes (or in our parents' or grandparents' homes) that we don't see as strange because we associate them with familiar people and places? What might be hidden there? The context (like the little sewing table) is innocent, so we assume the contents will be too.

There are many little issues in our living spaces that we become oblivious to: a cracked floor tile that's been broken for decades, expired canned goods on the back of an upper shelf. I remember visiting my parents for a holiday, and the shower pressure was so bad that it was barely a trickle. It had slowly gotten worse over time, and my parents hadn't even noticed. You can get used to anything, even something really strange, if it happens incrementally.

My comedic intuition suggests that there is something to be played with in this initial line of thought. And practically, it's clear that some material here falls within the recognition/pain/distance triad. I can add pain and distance to these observations by thinking about unusual or strange things that a character might get used to.

Here are two comic ideas based on these thoughts: (1) What if there a black hole or a portal to a different dimension growing in my living room and I treat it the way my parents treated the shower pressure in the upstairs bathroom? (2) What if I looked closely at the embroidery held in that sewing table and discovered something dark and disturbing in the "handwork"?

The next step is to take these ideas and shape them so that they are more active and specific, turning them into an actual premise statement to support writing or improvising a first draft. Here two very rough possible premises based on the comic ideas I'm playing with:

1. A list of items found in the home of someone outwardly sweet or boring like a grandma that gets progressively weirder or more disturbing as it goes on.

2. A house that has a portal to a different dimension, but the people that live there treat it as if it if were a minor cosmetic defect that they haven't bothered to get fixed yet.

Now take your premise and decide on a form or filter you want to use. The second idea I have feels like it would lend itself to a sketch or story with multiple characters and events. I'm leaning toward using the first one as a short fiction piece, so let's build on that, since we're going to look at sketch later.

I've already started (somewhat unconsciously) tweaking my idea in the premise using the elements of recognition, pain, and distance. I've decided that the items are going to be disturbing or bizarre (pain), and I've added a character that provides some distance by being unusual or unlikely (a sweet grandmother). And I have the sense that this piece could be in the form of something written from the point of view of a character who could provide both recognition and distance. Maybe it's an uptight lawyer who is listing the items included in the will or a letter from a well-loved family member who has been cleaning out the house.

I'm going to go with the letter because I feel there's a fair amount of comedy to be mined from the incongruity of clueless family member and evil or disturbing details, plus there's opportunity for more recognition-based humor in little references or family in-jokes. And because it bolsters one final comedic element—the comedy logic of the piece.

For a comic premise to work well, it needs a clear and defined justification, an answer to the question "Why does this happen?" There's an OK comedy logic inherent in the idea of a lawyer choosing to list the contents of a house without commenting on their disturbing nature. It makes sense. But the best sorts of justifications are rooted in a point of view, a genuine observation about the way people perceive and function in the world. In this case, that logic is something I had already been thinking about when I began to play with this idea—that the strange becomes familiar over time or when it is presented in an atmosphere of everyday normality.

My new premise for this short comedic piece is a letter from Mom listing the items from Grandma's house for the family to divide up. That list includes details that indicate that Grandma was the Antichrist.

This premise gives me a comedic game to play, juxtaposing household items or cute family stories with things that evoke horror or the occult. It has a clear comedic logic: The person writing the letter associates the items with family and has missed or never questioned their possible larger significance.

The process for generating stand-up premise is very similar. Start with an observation or feeling about a topic and shape it as I did above. The difference is that the primary filter is going to be you, your persona, and your point of view. I could take my thoughts above and use them to write a series of jokes around going back to my parents' (or grandparents') house and seeing all the things I took for granted as a kid and realizing that they are much stranger or more disturbing than I realized at the time. There's also no reason I couldn't use the premise I just came up with in a stand-up set, but I'd probably need to frame it as a letter from "my" mom. Either way, the process I describe next works the same for writing stand-up from premise as it does for short fiction.

Writing a Short Comedy Piece

The next step for this kind of piece is to explore and heighten this premise using the game and the justification. You can just write it and make discoveries as you go, but for prose pieces like this it's often easier to brainstorm, making lists of as many beats, jokes, or examples as you can.

As you do so, you will likely make discoveries about the premise. For example, you may find that it's easier to come up with beats if Grandma is a vampire rather than the Antichrist. If you are brainstorming, feel free to explore that idea without having to go back and alter what you have already written. You may discover that a lot of your examples seem to be coming from a character with a slightly different comic perspective (maybe it's an uncle or cousin). Or it may be from a completely different perspective from the one I'm using. I'm creating this premise from my own cultural perspective of upper midwestern Irish Catholicism, but there are ways that this same premise might embrace a multitude of geographic, ethnic, and religious identities.

All of this is pretty common and part of the process. You're going to shift back and forth between generation brain and analysis brain multiple times before the piece reaches its final form. I find it is useful to separate those processes. While you are brainstorming, just let yourself brainstorm—let whatever ideas show up do so without shooting them down. And then move into analysis mode to make choices about what you like best and what you think works best. You don't have to be married to your first idea.

Once you have a good list, take the beats you like and put them into a rough outline order so that they build in intensity and absurdity. Then write your exposition. Exposition is an introduction that quickly provides your audience or reader with the information that they need to know to enjoy the rest of the piece. You are setting up their expectations and providing a clear sense of what "normal" is so that the audience can appreciate when and how things depart from normal.

For this premise, it's the opening of an email to the family from "Mom." It should establish who "Mom" is, perhaps referencing her book club or a family pet, and it should also establish her character and point of view: what she sees and doesn't see, her frame and filter. It should explain who the email is being sent to and its purpose.

At this point, you have everything you need to write a first draft. As I've indicated throughout this book, the key for this draft is to just get everything down on paper. The method you use isn't important; what's important at this point is to use the structure you've created and capture an initial complete version. So feel free to take on the persona of Mom in whatever way works for you and write longhand, on a computer, or improvise the email while you record it.

As you do so, you may discover more examples or possible directions for the piece. That's natural. Just make note of what you discover, but don't let those discoveries make you judge yourself or derail you from creating what you need to create. Force yourself to get through the whole thing you have outlined, even if you hate it as you go. Your approach to your first draft should be to just get things down on paper without evaluating. This is one reason I love using improvisation: The element of performance (even if it is only in front of a group of people you are creating with) forces you to make the thing rather than get stuck in all of the potential ways you could make the thing.

Once you have that first draft, you'll go back, edit, and revise again. I have some suggestions later in the book for how to do that.

Sketch

Let's say you want to make a specific kind of comedy—in this case, a sketch. You'll still want to start with a premise, but that premise will be shaped by what you know about the form of sketch comedy. A sketch contains most, if not all, of the components of comedy. There will be characters and jokes. The narrative will be short and fairly straightforward, and it will have some kind of point of view.

A good sketch premise generally contains (1) the characters in the scene, (2) their location, and (3) something that raises the stakes and makes this particular set of people in this particular environment interesting for an audience to watch. This sort of premise may set up the action, comic action, comic justification, or game of the scene, but it doesn't necessarily dictate those things—it just puts the pieces into play. It may suggest who or what is likely to be changed by the end of the sketch. Most sketches (unlike movies or plays) are about the change of just one person, one relationship, or one idea. A good premise should make you want to write or improvise it.

USEFUL DEFINITIONS: Parts of a Sketch

The *premise* is the beginning idea for a scene or sketch. It launches the action and usually indicates what that action will be, but does not dictate it.

Usually a premise indicates

1. Who is in the scene.
2. Where it takes place (at least initially).
3. Something that raises the stakes or indicates what makes this particular set of characters interesting in this moment for an audience to watch.
4. Who or what is likely to be changed by the end of the scene. Most sketches (unlike plays or films) are about the change of one person, one relationship, or one idea.

(continued)

The *action* is what happens—the events of the sketch. If you are improvising or writing a first draft, you are likely discovering the action as you create the sketch.

The *comic action* is the primary source of comedy in the scene. It might be the "game" of the scene (the first unusual thing that is explored and heightened). Most sketches have one primary comic action but could have several games that fall within that action. A good comedic premise will strongly set up the possibility for comic action.

The *point of view* is the primary truth or recognition in the scene. It is the main thing the sketch is saying to the audience. Most sketches have one primary point of view, one fairly simple observation. Point of view doesn't have to be satirical. The point of view of a sketch could be as simple as "It's really funny when we play dolphins on stage." That's a perfectly acceptable point of view, as long as it's actually true to the audience.

Creating premise for sketch comedy. Let's start by setting up a premise that would be fun to improvise or write. It's a different way of getting to a comic idea. I have found that if you start by creating a premise that contains aspects of recognition and pain and feels as if it would be fun to flesh out, you have a strong base that you can revise and make funnier.

What's a possible starting place for this premise we are creating? If we were improvising, we could ask our audience for a random suggestion such as a location where the sketch would take place. If you like, you could pull from your generation lists for a location. For now, let's use a park. What characters might be in the park? Two old friends. Now let's make it interesting. *Why* are these friends in this park?

- They could be former skateboarding rivals who want to settle a score.
- They could be spies who are meeting to exchange information.
- They could be teenagers who have snuck out of their homes to make out.

Raise the stakes just a bit more. These premises are fine, but they don't feel to me as if they are providing enough of a jump-start into a scene I want to write. Nor do they suggest much of a comedic game. What could we add to each of these premises to make them more fun to write or improvise?

- The former skateboarding rivals could be middle-aged parents of small children.
- The spies could be from middle school friend groups.
- The teenagers could be leaving for college the next day.

These all give us a little more to play with. My instinct (honed over years of writing and directing sketch comedy) is that we should keep going and raise the stakes even more. For example, the teenagers could be friends who made a pact to lose their virginity to each other so they weren't going off to college as virgins. For the second premise, we need to decide something about the issue between the middle school friend groups and make it important. As a rule, you should keep raising the stakes until you have something that gets you excited to start creating your sketch.

Once you have a premise you want to work with, it helps to restate it as clearly as you can before you start writing. Here are three restatements of the premises I just generated:

- **Premise 1:** Two middle-aged parents watching their children at a playground are former teenage skateboarding rivals.
- **Premise 2:** Two spies from warring middle school friend groups meet to negotiate terms for a coed birthday party.
- **Premise 3:** Two best friends meet at a park because they have made a pact to lose their virginity to each other so that they don't go off to college as virgins.

All three of these premises tell us the things we need to know: They give us a sense of who is in the scene (former skateboarders, middle school spies, virginal high schoolers), where they are (park), and something that raises the stakes (rivalry, need to negotiate, will they or won't they?), and they tell us something about what is going to change by the end of the scene (in the first two premises, someone is likely to win and someone to lose; in the third, the relationship is going to be altered in some way). There's a kind of implied comic justification in the second premise: The middle schoolers are acting like spies because friend groups of that age have a strong tendency toward behaving as if they are at war.

Writing the sketch. The next step is to "write" the sketch. I put the word *write* in scare quotes because writing in this situation is a fairly fluid concept that can be done alone or with a partner or partners. You can improvise a scene based on the premise. You can dive in and write it on paper or a computer. You can choose to outline the beats of the sketch before writing or improvising. You can do any of these alone or with a group in a writers' room.

Regardless of how you choose to do the writing, you want to start by clarifying any immediate questions for yourself and your collaborators. This is especially important if you are using improvisation. For the skateboarding sketch, two initial questions come to my mind: "Did the two know that their former rival would be at the park?" and "Is there a skateboard there?" You may have noticed that my initial premises did not include detailed characters, just relationships and some character attributes. You can choose to make some more specific decisions about those characters before you get started.

You could now start to create the scene based on this information. Because sketch is driven by human behavior, the *way* people say and do things and not just *what* they say and do, I find that it's less valuable to start by brainstorming beats as we did for the comic prose piece. Instead I recommend that you start without anything more than this and create a quick rough draft, making discoveries as you go. Those discoveries can lead you to create something funnier and more interesting than you might create if you make more decisions in advance.

But it can be hard to just jump in with only the premise, so it helps to begin by creating your exposition. For a first draft, exposition should define what normal looks like. This gives you more information to build from, and it's likely that your audience will better enjoy the shift you're making when you introduce the scenic issue, because they understand where you are shifting from.

Take your premise and see if you can establish normal in three sentences or less.

Here's an example from the first of my premises:

> TIM [*entering from right and shouting offstage*]: Isabella! No pushing on the play structure!
> CHRIS [*enters from left holding a skateboard*]: Yes, that's right, Noah, I'm going to hold on to this until you can prove you are responsible enough to have it back.
> TIM [*notices Chris and nods at him*]: Nice board.

We now know that they are dads. I made the decision as I wrote this exposition to make the two characters male because I wanted to play with the kind of status game that occurs between masculine characters. But it isn't required. It's an equally interesting dynamic if we change their gender identity. But it would be a different dynamic. We have a sense of how old they are and how old their kids are and their race, ethnicity, and class based on their names and their kids' names. Names are extremely useful as a way of identifying people and generations quickly which makes specificity in terms of naming valuable in shorter forms like sketch comedy. For some reason that makes me crazy, my students like to use "comedy" names instead—playing young adults out to dinner but calling everyone names like Shirley and Howard, which currently belong primarily to people in their eighties.

And I answered the question of whether there is a skateboard in the scene. There is.

Now we are ready to introduce the "scenic issue" from the premise: In this case, that they are former skateboarding rivals who have an old score to settle. Then we explore and heighten that issue. What was the source of their rivalry? How did it end? How long has it been since they last saw each other? How could they even the score now?

Or you could play with the "game of the scene," and use the first unusual thing that showed up in the exposition. The very first unusual thing in this scene is that at least one of these middle-aged dads is a skateboarder. Explore and heighten that. If the other dad is also a skateboarder (an obvious heightening), they can start to play a status game with each other. They can try to impress each other with their knowledge, they can reminisce about how good they were in the past, they can lie about their experiences.

I want to emphasize here that either of these two choices is fine. There are many other equally fine directions that could also be explored. I have no real knowledge of skateboarding or skateboarding culture, and someone who does might find something deeper or more interesting. The initial premise you create isn't set in stone. No one is going to be looking over your shoulder in judgment because you found something fun to explore in a potential premise you didn't see when you first created it. The comedic process is all about making discoveries. And if the new idea doesn't work out the way you thought it would, the old one is also there for you.

After you have explored and heightened the scenic issue or game for a bit, you will eventually find that something needs to shift. If the characters spend the first part of the scene making veiled threats toward each other, eventually they will need to stop threatening and start doing. If they spend the first part of scene boasting about their past glories, they will eventually discover that they know each other from the past. They might need to even old scores. An obvious way to do this is to have the characters begin to do skateboard tricks to prove they "still have it." That skateboard is onstage or onscreen, after all. But feel free to let that transformation happen in a nonobvious way too: Their kids are in the scene (albeit unseen), so perhaps the parents one-up each other by forcing their unseen children to compete. Perhaps their new field of competition isn't skateboarding at all but corporate in some way. What happens will also depend on what medium you are doing the sketch in. If it's on film or television, you could probably play with actual skateboarding tricks. If you are improvising, I'm taking that real skateboard away from you, right now, because somebody's going to get hurt. Regardless, you now have a new thing to explore and heighten.

Let's be clear: You don't have to have a transformation. If you have a strong and silly game, you can just explore and heighten it for a couple of beats and then end the scene once you've done so with a joke or reversal. It'll be a shorter scene and likely a little thinner comedy-wise, but that's fine.

I would personally like to advocate for the possibility of a scene with at least one transformation in it. The popularity of long-form improv has made modern-era improvisers and sketch writers—many of whom are former improvisers—a lot more comfortable with exploring and heightening, but less so with transformation. If you are improvising a long-form piece, the place you should edit a scene is just at the point where the scene is about to transform. As a result, a lot of writers and improvisers today don't have as much experience with playing or writing through the moment of transformation as they used to. Their instinct is to just end at the first editing point. This isn't necessarily wrong, but some of the best parts of my favorite sketches happen during and after moments of transformation. The sketch moves beyond the repetition and heightening of a single joke or game, there is more variety within the sketch, and it is ultimately (at least to me) more satisfying to watch.

A great example of this is a sketch I've already mentioned: Ashley Nicole Black's "Invisible Spy," from the first season of *A Black Lady Sketch Show*. We could happily just watch the first section about people not seeing her as a spy, but it's the second part, where she battles a foe who is herself "invisible," that fully pays off the concept and makes a larger point about how we devalue certain people's power. *And* it's really a cool fight.

Let's assume that your sketch has one or more transformations. Once a transformation occurs, you then explore and heighten the new version of the scenic issue you discovered (it's usually related to the first but heightened or more important in some fashion). Eventually this takes you to the climax of your scene, which is the point at which the question or issue raised at the top of the scene is going to have to be dealt with. In our skateboarding premise, it's likely to be "How will these two dads settle the score?" Or "Who will win this time?" Or "How is this interaction going to change the relationship between these two people?"

Once you reach that climax and the question is answered, there's not much left to write or improvise. You'll briefly play out any repercussions of what just happened if necessary. You might want to add a joke to button the sketch. This is often some kind of reversal. It could flip the entire scene (essentially making the full arc of the sketch into a setup for a final joke), or it could just provide a moment that reinforces whatever switch has happened over the course of the piece. Alternately, in a longer show, you could not even finish the sketch at all and instead transition at a good editing point into another, different piece. This is more common on television shows like *Mr. Show* or *Monty Python's Flying Circus.*

More Ways to Generate Sketch Premises

Start with another kind of suggestion. If you start with a relationship, the scene is likely to be more personal. Let's say we start with a classic, doctor/patient. Again, we play with raising the stakes. Where could they be that would be an unusual or important location for a doctor and a patient to meet?

An examining room. This is not particularly novel, but opting for the obvious choice isn't necessarily a bad thing. It isn't random. Important, interesting things can happen in an examining room. By the way, beware randomness—this is how middle schoolers generate comedy ideas. I know this from many years of Second City summer camps. Randomness gives you incongruity, which creates an initial laugh, but there's nothing to build on.

Someplace where a patient won't expect to run into their doctor, such as on a blind date, or at a restaurant or a protest march.

A location where their roles (and status) might be reversed: for example, at a garage where the patient is the mechanic and is diagnosing what is wrong with the doctor's car.

Regardless of the suggestion, I encourage you to raise the stakes (explore and heighten) until you have a premise that feels like it suggests action and/or a game.

Start with a personal story or an observation. When I was directing a show at Second City, one night we asked the audience for a list of things they loved as a kid. Someone suggested hide-and-seek. Backstage, one of the actors, Todd Stashwick, shared how when he was very young, he used to play hide-and-seek with mean neighborhood kids, and after he would hide, they would just leave. He would often stay hidden for quite some time before discovering that the game was over.

Here's how he and Nancy Walls turned that story into a premise. They set up a scene in which Todd played a version of himself as a kid—smart, obsessive, and a little bit obnoxious. Nancy played the mother of one of his friends and an adult version of herself as a kid—attractive, athletic, and effortlessly popular. He was at a birthday party at her house, the group played hide-and-seek, he hid, and the group didn't bother to look for him. He kept hiding. The scene started at midnight, as Nancy came downstairs to get a snack and Todd jumped out and surprised her.

Start with an existing character. I'll be honest—I find this to be the most difficult version of generating premise. I have spent hours in rehearsal looking for a premise to support a character and often ended up with a character demonstration rather than an actual scene. A character demonstration is a scene in which we know the "game" that the character does (accidentally insults people by sounding like they are coming on to them when they are just offering something to eat), and then we put the character in some place where they can demonstrate that particular game. This isn't a terrible way to come up with a premise. Where could we put that character? Make them the host of a party? Or a waiter at a restaurant? The game is then repeated several (likely three to five) times, heightening it along the way, and there is a final reversal to take the lights out or transition to another sketch. As I said, this isn't terrible, but it relies almost entirely on jokes and gets repetitive quickly.

Better, for my taste, is to think about how that character might affect someone else emotionally. Characters with a strong related game tend to be fairly rigid, so if we can connect them to other, less rigid characters who *can* change, we create potential for movement and variety within the sketch. Who might be most strongly affected by "Sex/Food Guy"? A couple on a date? We could raise the stakes a bit and we make our character a famous chef rather than a waiter. This adds pain elements because it will be harder for the couple to respond negatively. Maybe one member of the couple made the reservations for a special date night. They are hoping to impress their date, and they are deeply embarrassed by each inappropriate dish the chef serves.

If the initial character is less rigid and more dimensional, they can be the central character, the one who is changed or affected by the events. In this case, ask yourself: What is the worst thing that could happen to that particular character, or what would be the hardest experience for that character to deal with? You can work backward, too, as you might in a sitcom. What do we want to see happen to that character? What is the funniest thing that could happen to them, or the most interesting place they could end up? What can we set up in our premise that will eventually get them there?

TOOL: Game of the Scene

The "game" concept is important in comedy creation. Games contain recognition in the form of set rules that create expectations. They are frequently competitive and involve winning and losing (pain). They are played and thus have action. This action has consequences within the game, but it doesn't have major consequences beyond the game, which creates distance.

The heart of improvisation training (especially in the work of Viola Spolin and Augusto Boal) is learning through playing games. These are generally versions of cooperative children's games, ones that can be won or lost as a group. By playing the game by the appropriate rules, you gradually acquire the related skill. The term Viola Spolin uses for these "rules" in early editions of her book *Improvisation for the Theater* is *point of improvisation*, which I prefer to *focus*, which is used in later editions.

For example, the popular improv performance game "Freeze Tag" has its origins in an exercise that teaches performers the skill of creating and transforming imaginary actions and objects with clarity. In the classroom exercise, one player might be holding an imaginary rifle shooting at a bird. Another player (usually standing in a line behind the active players) calls "Freeze," takes the first player's exact physical position, and transforms the object to something new, like a telescope, by using it in a way that clearly demonstrates its transformation.

The performance version takes the basic structure (backline of performers, calling "freeze," transformation) and puts the point of concentration not on transforming the object but on transforming an entire scene. There's an automatic comic mechanism here that is reminiscent of joke structure. The audience is watching a brief scene that has created expectations and a sense of narrative. Through the replacement of one character, the physical position is reversed, and a completely new story is created. If improvisers play the game well, they are likely to generate laughter in their audience. If you go to see a performance at ComedySportz or another company that specializes in what is referred to as "short-form" improv, much of what you will be watching are similar adaptations of skill-building games in which the point of concentration has been altered to support a predictable comedic action.

I have strong feelings about equating short-form improvisation with game content and long-form improvisation with scenic content. Short pieces can be scenes, and long pieces can be games. But really, this is my own hill to die on and no one else much cares.

There are other reasons these sorts of games reliably generate comedy. The performers themselves are literally playing. It's a game; it has rules. It isn't real life, but they are doing something like real life. The element of play—doing a pretend, low-stakes version of something more serious—has its own place in humor theory. There is complicity with the audience. They have a sense of what the rules of the game are and play along with the performers. There's a high potential for failure (mistakes and misunderstandings), which creates the pain of tension. There's also the surprise of discovery happening simultaneously in both the performers and their audience.

Having a genuine game to play also brings a different quality to comedic acting when working with a script. Many of the Spolin games were originally designed to teach theatrical skills and were meant to be played while working with scripted material. For example, an exercise called "Touch to Talk" requires each player in a scene to create physical contact with their partner before they speak. They must maintain that contact for the entire time they are talking, and they must make new physical contact each time they speak (in other words, the game doesn't work the way it was meant to if the players just hold hands the whole time). When they play this game, players are required to generate a level of intimacy with their partner and thus between their characters. It raises the stakes of the interaction.

I have found that adding an actual game element during rehearsal of comedic scripts—a surreptitious game of tag during a large group scene or having a couple play "keep away" with an object while engaging in scripted romantic banter—can create comic tension and

(continued)

action that enlivens the performance. It can also provide discoveries of unusual elements of physical comedy. Playing these sorts of games in performance has an additional value of creating recognizable human behavior because the performers are actually doing something (playing the game) and not just pretending to interact with each other.

Playing games activates a comic performance for the audience. The audience is aware that there is some level of uncertainty, since the outcome depends on skill, strength, or luck. If we are playing a game, we are actually doing something—we are not pretending to do something. Yet we are also pretending to do a thing, and this paradox is also comedic.

Playing a game with the audience is a tried-and-true element of live sketch comedy. One of my personal favorite scenic games was in a student show I directed. The original sketch pitch was "Chipotle Anonymous." This is not my favorite sort of pitch. I've seen too many variations over the years (Knitters Anonymous, Supervillains Anonymous . . . You get the idea). They tend to be highly joke driven and repetitive. At the beginning of this version of the scene each character stood, introduced themselves, were welcomed, and then provided their Chipotle order.

When the sketch was first improvised in rehearsal, the thing that struck me and the rest of the ensemble was how much the exposition of the sketch made us want to share our own personal Chipotle order. This was likely heightened by the fact that there was (and still is, as of this writing) a Chipotle on the first floor of Piper's Alley Mall, where Second City is located. We all ate there frequently. After talking about it, we decided to take a risk and just play that initial game and include the audience. At the next performance, after the line of characters introduced themselves and their orders, Alan Giles, who pitched the sketch and played the moderator, gestured to a member of the audience. The game and pattern had been established. That first audience member instantly understood how to play and gave their own first name and their own distinctive order. That was it. Alan would just walk around the theater and point at people and get their standard order. I cannot tell you how much this simple game pleased the audience. They all knew how to play; they were all fascinated by the simple detail of learning minor private information about each other and drawing conclusions. They all wanted to share their own orders. Our stage manager Abby and I used to sit up in the light booth watching the scene every night and marvel at the delighted laughter. I swear we could have run that sketch for half an hour, and the entire audience would have been happy to just listen to everyone's order.

In addition to this more overt game, a common teaching in improvisation is to "find the game" organically within an improvised performance. This type of "game" consists of mutually discovered rules and can be based in the physical (no one gets closer to each other than six feet), narrative (every time the characters recover from terrible news, a new character enters with worse news), character (a character is continually set up to reveal their weaknesses), or point of view (performers take turns commenting on the content of the scenes they are engaged in).

Game is communal—it is something we create together with rules our audience can understand. The difference between comedy games and competitive sports is that in comedy the focus is not on whether we win but on how the rules of the game force us to make new discoveries and to skillfully justify and build on them.

Games can create subtext or conflict, as in romantic comedies where the main couple hides their attraction to each other with insults. The game is the text, but the subtext is their attraction. Games can provide a respite from the narrative, but in comedy they also flow in parallel with it. A comic character may be more or less invested in the narrative, but the game is the way they enjoy moving through the narrative. Game is one of the ways we know we are watching a comedy. It says, "This is happening, but it isn't too serious. We are doing a second thing as well, and it can't be too serious if we are all willing to do this second thing."

The term *game of the scene* was popularized by the Upright Citizens Brigade (UCB) but has been used in improvisation circles at least since the early 1960s. In the definition used directly by UCB, the game of the scene involves "identifying the first unusual thing in the scene" and then having players "repeatedly answer the question, if this unusual thing is true, then what else is true?"[2] In a sketch or improvisation that utilizes this tool, once the writer or improvisers have found the game, they explore and heighten it, creating a comedic pattern until it reaches a climax of some sort. In this version, the game is more likely to be focused on action and event than on behavior.

(continued)

As with all the other examples of "game" described here, "game of the scene" adds an element or metaphor of play to a comedic narrative. We are playing with the idea of story, taking a situation that creates an expectation and then toying with it—not necessarily reversing it, as we would in a joke, but instead embracing a new comedic reality. By treating this new reality logically, we can automatically generate aspects of recognition, pain, and distance. This makes game of the scene a highly useful tool for creating comedy.

For this type of comedy to work, it is important for the focus not to be on the fact that the thing is unusual (the pain element). Everyone has to abide by the altered reality the unusual thing creates, discover how it affects the characters, and watch them negotiate living within the new reality. This logical playing out of game provides recognition and distance. Additionally, playing a game in a narrative adds an element of misplaced focus: Everyone is doing the "wrong" thing. Like the Marx Brothers, who stop the forward action of the high stakes of a war to make a series of jokes or to produce magical things out of a trench coat, when we play a game onstage, we show that the true stakes of the situation are not *our* stakes in the situation.

This is not to say that the players or the characters themselves aren't aware they are in illogical territory. There is a saying about this at Second City: "You should play your character at the top of their intelligence." This doesn't mean that all the people you play are highly educated or use large words. It means that everything you and the audience see and perceive in a situation, your character also sees and perceives. Characters may still choose to behave in a way contrary to their best interests, but they aren't missing the obvious in a way the website TV Tropes refers to as "too dumb to live." One of my favorite improvisers, Neil Flynn (whom you might know from his role as the dad in the film *Mean Girls* or in the sitcoms *Scrubs* and *The Middle*), does this sort of call-out brilliantly. He will take in a situation and announce something along the lines of "I have a feeling this isn't going to end well for me and could conceivably cause me to find myself in Vegas wearing a barrel, but I'm curious so I'm going to do it." Comedically, this does two things: It adds a level of recognition, since it's funny to us that the character sees what we see; and it adds distance to the pain of whatever mayhem does occur, since the character is aware of the dangers and thus deserves whatever befalls them.

Scenic games can (and should) be heightened not just through action and event but also through the consequences and emotions they create. This is a particularly important note for those creating scenes using this tool as writers or improvisers. To extend the "if this is true" definition, it is not just "What else is true?" but also "What effect does this truth have on the characters within the scene?" as well as "How do the characters feel about the situation?" and "How does all of this change their behavior and relationships?"

Game of the scene vs. comedic driver. Another way to think of the game of the scene is what I refer to as "comic driver." There is an "uber"-game happening, and all the players in the scene are involved in driving that particular car comedically in the same direction. (BTW, I am not a pun person. The Uber reference was accidental, but I decided to leave it in.) When I direct sketch comedy, I find that each scene usually has a spine: one game, driver, or comic action. If the performers properly execute that comic action the sketch will work in performance. Again, this could be termed the game of the scene, but it doesn't necessarily fit the "if this is true, what else is true" model as neatly as it might. There is a more literal game being played between the performers or between the characters that makes the story make comedic sense. It has to be executed clearly and well; if it's not, the scene doesn't work.

Possibly my favorite sketch of all time was written by Sam Sterbenz, a student in the Comedy Studies program. It's called "Mustard."[3] The premise is that a man orders a cup of coffee at a coffee bar where (for reasons entirely unexplained) it is nearly impossible to pour a cup of coffee. Instead, what ends up in the cup is inevitably a squeeze bottle of mustard. It's an absurd game that heightens throughout the scene and makes me laugh every time I watch it. The point of view is a take on how once you have a thought in your head it can affect your actions, no matter how hard you try to make it go away. But the comic driver is that every character in the scene wants to get the customer that cup of coffee. They are really trying their hardest to make that cup of coffee happen. They simply can't help but put the mustard in the coffee cup. If you did the scene without that aspect, it would lose most of its absurdist joy.

Sketch Structure, Version 1

A sketch has five essential parts: exposition; introduction of the scenic issue; development or elaboration; climax; and resolution or button.

- **Exposition:** The situation. This is often the who, what, where of the scene, but it doesn't have to be. The most important part of exposition is that it provides the audience with what they need to know in order to enjoy the rest of the scene. It is useful to remember that what the writer/performers need to know and what the audience needs to know are different. We use the exposition to set up the audience expectations and understanding of what will happen next.
- **Introduction of scenic issue:** This is the problem, or the first unusual thing the scene will be exploring.
- **Development or elaboration:** This is where the scenic issue and the game of the scene are explored and heightened (generally a series of escalating examples of the comic action).
- **Climax:** This is where the scenic issue cannot be explored and heightened any further.
- **Resolution or button:** This is generally some form of minor reversal or joke that reframes the entire sketch.

Sketch Structure, Version 2

This is a modified version of the five-point scene structure taught at The Second City, which was created by the late great Mary Siewert Scruggs, an amazing human being, writer, and teacher and my best friend. In her version the introduction of the scenic issue and the climax are known as the first and second turning points of the scene.

The first three elements are the same as above: exposition; introduction of the scenic issue; and exploring and heightening. Then:

- **Midpoint:** There is a significant transformation of some sort; the initial scenic issue has been explored and heightened to the point that something is discovered or a new tactic is required on the part of the characters. Often the game of the scene transforms to a new game.

- **Exploring and heightening of the transformation**
- **Climax:** The issue or problem is brought to a head; something needs to be resolved.
- **Resolution:** The issue or problem is resolved; the repercussions of what happens at the climax are briefly explored, often followed by a reversal or final button.

Building Your Premise Muscles

One good way to get better at making premises for your own work is to look at comedy you admire and see if you can isolate the premise. Remember that premise isn't action, it isn't what happens—it is the pitch for what happens. See if you can do it in different mediums—say, the premise of a sketch versus the premise of an episode of a sitcom. Can you pick out the different premises within a longer stand-up set? I said earlier that the premise of a comedic song is usually its title or its chorus, but that type of premise also has an important element—the style of the song or the specific song or genre of song, if it's being parodied.

Earlier I presented two different premises, one of which makes more sense to me as a short prose piece (in the form of a letter) and another that's a sketch, and showed how I might adapt that same comic idea into a premise for observational stand-up. I encourage you to play around with adapting one comedic idea into different formats and pay attention to how premises need to change depending on the form.

Pitching premise. Being able to pitch a premise is a huge tool in collaborating on work with others. What constitutes a premise pitch generally depends on the format you're working in. For journalism parody, the traditional pitch is a headline for the article being pitched, and a song pitch is frequently the title or the chorus.

For a sketch you are going to improvise or write with someone else, I generally advise pitching just premise, not pitching any action. All three of the sketch premises I generated earlier in this chapter are a good example of this type of premise. If you are pitching a sketch you are planning to write by yourself (or have written already), you might pitch more; I recommend just the premise, action, comic action/game, and point of view.

If you have a writing group or are creating comic material for a sketch show with an ensemble, it's useful to work on pitching premises as a group. Pay attention to the kinds of questions your collaborators ask about your pitches and which pitches get the best responses. Pay attention to other people's premises. What elements in their premises make you feel as if you could get to work right away and easily create material? What premises feel like dead ends? Can you figure out why?

Be aware that a joke is not a premise. My experience as a sketch comedy director is that a high-concept idea based entirely on incongruity (like "Blind Cab Driver," a sketch I had to watch once in a class) is difficult to find a comic justification for and thus doesn't have legs—meaning it's going to be hard to explore and heighten or expand. Likewise, a good premise won't necessarily be laugh-out-loud funny when you first hear it. What you'll notice, instead, is that it creates lots of ideas, images, and interesting opportunities for different kinds of jokes, physical comedy, events, and characters. It's a springboard that launches you toward creating more comedy.

TOOL: Thinking About Structure

Your creation doesn't exist to serve the rules. The rules exist to serve your creation.

After you've broken things down into concepts and then put those concepts into practice, the success or failure of whatever you make doesn't come from how perfectly you followed some set of comedy blueprints. Outside of jokes, it's rare that starting with structure and plugging in variables will create good comedy. On the other hand, weak structure can really undermine great concepts and execution. A well-structured sketch, variety show, or screenplay supports an audience's innate understanding of what it means to be told a certain kind of story. It satisfies their expectations that events happen in a specific order, and it supports their sense of the story as comedic. Good structure provides and enhances the element of recognition.

So, how should we think about structure in a way that is useful to us as comedy creators and practitioners?

My preference when I think of comedic structure at the creation level is to keep it simple. Think of the structure as a rough map to follow as you explore your premise or idea. If I am writing a joke, I know I am setting up an expectation in a certain format and then reversing that expectation. As we did in the "how to write a joke" section, using that structure and plugging in certain elements can be a great way of generating a large number of jokes quickly. If I am writing a sketch, I know I can start with a premise, and this premise will suggest a comic action that can be explored and heightened until it ends or transforms in some way. I don't have to do anything more than that. When you are struggling to create your initial draft, simple structure makes the task more straightforward. There are so many possibilities that it's easy for our brains to get distracted. Thinking "All I need to do is 'this' and I will find my way to an end" can be helpful.

Structure isn't the interesting part, or the funny part. If you think of structure as a literal structure, it can be helpful. It's a shape. Your comedy is going to fit into that shape. But the shape doesn't have to be rigid or exact. Having a sense of shape assists in eliminating the unnecessary—it lets you know all the things you don't have do. However, what's interesting isn't the sequence of events. What's interesting is *how* the events happen and *who* they happen to.

It's not the map that interests us—it's the actual trip we take when we follow the map. The map is a good thing. I am pro-map. I am more pro-map than I am pro-GPS in this situation. You are better off as an artist by having a sense of the map in your head and then allowing yourself to follow the twists and turns and make discoveries along the way than in having something announce to you that a right turn is coming up in two point two miles. The point of comedic narrative, even more than dramatic narrative, is to enjoy the ride.

Focus on the creation part and let the map support it. Nowhere is this more true than when you are creating comedy in what I would term a "variety format," like a sketch show or a longer stand-up set. When you know that, for most of the live versions of these sorts of shows, you want your second to last section to be the funniest thing in your show, it can feel tempting to sit down to write "something really, really funny" to go in that slot. Which, as we have already established, is not the way to come up with comedy.

(continued)

If you are a stand-up, write your jokes and tell your stories. Don't worry about where they "belong" in a set until you have enough material to make a set. If you are writing a sketch show, write your rough drafts and then see where they fit into the running order of a larger show. Eventually, when you put things in order, you will get the sense that there is a hole somewhere—that you need more than a segue to bring some pieces of your act or show together. At this point, you might try to write something to fill that specific hole. But it's not unusual to find, when you try to figure out what belongs in that hole, that you have already created something you can move into that space.

Starting with theme can be tricky when creating variety-style shows. Each individual piece should have a point of view or thesis, but if they all share the same one, it will feel repetitive over the course of one or two acts. If possible, don't start with what the larger work is going to be "about"—write it, create the pieces, and then discover the larger thematic elements once you have the material in front of you.

Topic and theme are two different things. The sketch show I directed with students at my college during the pandemic had the topic of YA and children's literature, but the theme that emerged while we wrote it was identity. The power of these sorts of shows is that they aren't linear. Rather than "this happens and then this happens because of that," it's more of a puzzle. Each piece arrives (and with it the pleasure of novelty). If, by the end, there is a sense of coherence, it feels all the more powerful and interesting. Or not. A variety show can just be a series of interesting things. But there is intense pleasure for an audience when a series of seemingly unrelated interesting things comes together to form a larger more complete whole.

Sitcom

Many of the more complex aspects of story and narrative are, if not anathema to, then certainly hampered by comedy. The essential component of the joke (and almost all comedic narratives contain jokes) is the idea of setting up expectations and then reversing those expectations. That sort of trickery doesn't make it easy to sustain a long narrative or allow for suspension of disbelief. At a certain point the audience starts to assume disbelief and find it difficult to trust the narrative. The exception to this is farce, which so fully embraces this quality of rapid reversals that they become the actual driver of the narrative.

The two most classic comedic film structures are the parody, which borrows an existing dramatic structure, and anarchic films, which are based on the variety structures of vaudeville and stage revue with some thin and arbitrary plot placed on top to provide a through line of some kind.

The one longer narrative that is somewhat unique to comedy is the traditional sitcom, which started in radio and then moved to network television. In my comedy history classes, we discuss how the move from broadcast television to online and streaming platforms has altered the financial incentives that created sitcom so much that it's now nearly unrecognizable. However, it's still useful to look at how the elements of comedy function in longer narratives by looking at the relatively simple form of traditional sitcom.

Sitcom Characters

The backbone of sitcom is strong familiar characters. When you create a sitcom premise, you want to focus on putting those characters into a situation where they demonstrate their primary comic qualities. In my class, I assign my students to create a pitch for an original episode of *I Love Lucy*, *The Honeymooners*, or *The Dick Van Dyke Show*. We begin by watching episodes of the three shows that all have roughly the same core premise—one incredibly sexist to our modern sensibilities. Their premise: The wife goes to work and the husband has to take care of the home.[4] But the differences between the central characters of these sitcoms create versions of this premise that are quite different from each other.

In the *I Love Lucy* episode, Lucy, Ethel, Ricky, and Fred have an argument about whose job is harder and make a bet that for a week, the boys will take care of the home and the girls will get jobs. The result, as any comedy fan would know, ultimately ends up with Lucy and Ethel failing hilariously to wrap candy on an assembly line.

On *The Honeymooners*, Ralph Kramden is laid off from the bus company, and in order to pay their bills, Alice gets a job. And Ralph is eventually forced to pretend to be Alice's brother while her tall and handsome—from an early 1950s perspective—boss tries to finagle a date with her.

Dick Van Dyke's Rob Petrie is happy to have his wife Laura follow her dreams and take a temporary job as a dancer on *The Alan Brady Show.* But the results make him so personally unhappy that he agonizes over whether to tell her the job could become permanent.

Let's look at the main characters of each of these sitcoms and think about how the different versions of these premises are tailored to showcase the qualities of each character.

Lucy is childlike and playful and, most importantly, thinks she can do anything if she sets her mind to it, despite all evidence to the contrary. Additionally, Lucille Ball herself was a gifted technical physical comedian. This premise puts Lucy into action using the classic silent-film-style techniques of making the simple task of wrapping chocolates difficult.

Ralph Kramden is jealous and vain. Like Lucy, he is an adult child, but his problems come at him from the world or the emotional results of his own failings rather than from mechanical interactions with environment. We want to see Ralph explode or be humiliated—we want to watch his ego be crushed. So while there is some comedy to be mined from the role reversal of putting him into an apron—tied at just the right place to emphasize his bulk—and having him cook the supper for Alice when she gets home from work, the real joy of this episode is watching the slow burn as he has to suppress his anger and jealousy in front of Alice's boss when "Mr. Amico" shows up at the apartment to pick Alice up.

Rob Petrie is not a child. He wants to do the right thing and be a good guy in both his family and his job, but he does wrestle with childish feelings. Like Ricky Ricardo in *I Love Lucy* and to a lesser extent Ralph Kramden, he is not good at the work his wife does so competently, and like Ralph, he displays some jealousy. But the comedy here is in Rob's struggles both to hide his ineptitude and to make the decision about whether to share a potential long-term job offer with his wife, Laura.

You can see the how the comedy triad shows up here—we have recognizable characters with identifiable flaws who are being put into situations in which their flaws are most painful or obvious. The final piece is that they live within a simple structure whose predictability creates distance.

Sitcom Structure

For the purposes of the exercise of creating a pitch for an early television sitcom, I teach my students a simplified version of a traditional sitcom that has essentially one A plot. This is the standard for what you might see in early television and more recent sitcoms written for kids, the type you'll find on the Disney Channel or Nickelodeon. Most modern sitcoms have at least a B plot, but they may have additional C and D plots and an ongoing season-long story arc, as well as running jokes over multiple episodes.

This is a "two-act" structure. In television and theater, acts are longer chunks of narrative that end with some sort of break for the audience (in theater it's an intermission, and in television it's a break for commercials). It's not unusual to discuss films in terms of acts as well, but it's not quite the same thing, since there's less of an need to shape the story in such a way that the audience is more likely to come back after a break.

Here's a breakdown of the two-act sitcom structure:

TEASER: Sets up the world of the show, introduces the characters, and tells the audience everything they need to about these elements in order to enjoy the rest of the episode. It indicates what "normal" looks like. Depending on the show, the teaser may be a short scene before the opening credits (and a commercial break) or it may simply be an opening moment of act 1.

ACT 1: Introduces the act 1 issue or problem, explores and heightens the act 1 issue or problem, and then makes the problem worse. Then a solution presents itself: Is it going to work?

Commercial break

ACT 2: The solution to the act 1 problem creates a new (act 2) problem or issue. That new problem or issue is explored and heightened, and then made even worse. And then the problem gets resolved, usually in a way that resolves the act 1 problem as well as the act 2 problem.

TAG: The world resets itself, everything goes back to "normal." May happen briefly at the end of act 2 or after a commercial break and before the final credits.

Let's look at how this plays out in one of the sitcoms I have described earlier. I'll use the classic *I Love Lucy* episode "Job Switching," since it's the best-known of the three. You'll notice it's not an exact match to the structure I have provided. The comedy goal is as much "Lucy in the candy factory" silliness as possible, and that means breaking the structure a bit.

TEASER: Ricky is upset with Lucy because she bounced a check to her hairdresser. Fred and Ethel enter, and the four of them discuss how they handle money. This leads to a discussion of whether it is harder to stay home and do housework or go out to work

ACT I: The act 1 problem is "Whose job is harder?" They agree that the boys will quit their jobs for a week (welcome to the world of *I Love Lucy*, where logic takes second place to hijinks) and take care of the house, and the girls will get jobs.

Explore and Heighten Act 1 Problem: Can Ricky make breakfast? Can Lucy and Ethel even get a job? Ricky and Fred are clearly not doing great at housework, or cooking. Lucy and Ethel play games with the man at the employment office.

A Solution Presents Itself: Lucy and Ethel get a job in a candy factory, and Fred and Ricky decide to team up to make dinner together.

ACT 2: The act 2 problem is "Will Lucy and Ethel succeed at the candy factory? Will Fred and Ricky succeed with their dinner plan?"

Explore and Heighten Act 2 Problem: Lucy gets a job as a candy dipper, and it turns into a chocolate fight with her coworker. (Because we want more Lucy doing physical bits, this portion of act 2 starts a little bit early—before the commercial break). Fred and Ricky's dinner plans fully trash the Ricardos' kitchen (the pressure cooker explodes, rice boils over). Lucy and Ethel get a second shot at candy factory work, and we get the famous assembly line wrapping scene.

Make It Worse: Lucy and Ethel come home fired, exhausted, and stuffed with chocolate. Fred and Ricky have left a note telling them not to look in the kitchen. When the boys arrive back at the house, they apologize—they didn't know how hard it was to do the housework. Lucy and Ethel apologize too. (So the answer to the act 1 issue is that no one's job is harder, and the answer to the act 2 issue is that no one's plans will succeed.)

TAG: The world resets itself, Ricky and Fred present Lucy and Ethel with an apology gift—five-pound boxes of chocolates.

This is not in any way meant to be a complete guide or formula for writing sitcom. Rather, it's an opportunity to see how the comedy triad functions in a longer form using a simplified story and classic characters. If this type of comic storytelling interests you, I encourage you to try to map a more modern sitcom on top of this basic structure and see if you can find the places where they align and diverge. Even with multiple plotlines, running gags, and season-long story arcs, there is still a version of this basic structure underneath if you look for it.

If you are interested in doing the exercise of creating a full original pitch for an old-school sitcom, here are some suggestions for how to break the story for yourself. *Breaking story* is the term used in television for creating a narrative outline from a premise before writing the script. Television writers' rooms often "break story" as a group and then assign outlines to individual writers to actually write.

Creating a Premise and Breaking Story for an "A" Plot Sitcom

Remember that sitcom is essentially character driven. Your premise should come from thinking about what situations, actions, or experiences would be the most enjoyable to watch the sitcom's characters (especially the main character) do. Use lists to brainstorm and keep in mind the ways the characters function: What do we want to see Lucy do? How can we set Ralph up to fail? How do we put Rob Petrie or Laura in an impossible situation?

1. Most of the time, your first idea is just going to be a moment, an idea or an image—for example, "Lucy Gets a Vibrator" (this premise is mine; you don't get to use it). Once you have the idea, start to brainstorm off of it—make lists (this is where collaborating with others can be fun). What are a bunch of things that could happen with Lucy getting a vibrator?

    - She could not know what it is and bring it out in public.
    - She could get addicted to it. We could have her walk around literally vibrating.
    - She could have it with her and have it go off in her purse.

    Don't just expand these ideas linearly—expand them dimensionally. Use the game of the scene: "If this is true, then what else is true?" What is Ricky doing during all of this? Does Ethel also get a vibrator?
2. Make an even longer list than this, and then look through your list and pick the action or moment that feels like it's the best joke, the funniest thing that could happen to the character. This moment probably should be pretty close to the end of your act 2. In the *I Love Lucy* and *Dick Van Dyke* episodes, it is Lucy and Ethel (not) wrapping the chocolates on the conveyer belt, and Rob having to decide whether to tell Laura about the permanent job offer with the Alan Brady Show when she is talking about how much dancing in the show had meant to her. So figure out what that peak moment is.
3. Work backward to answer the question, "How did Lucy get to work in a chocolate factory?"

    - She went to an employment office.
    - Why did she go to an employment office?
    - She wanted a job.

> Why did she want a job?
> She needed to prove to Ricky that she could get a job.
> Why did she have that conversation with him?
> They got into a discussion about money because she bounced a check.

4. It won't initially be as clean as that—you might have a couple of ideas, for why something happened. Keep track of those ideas and then play with the ones that feel like they have the most potential: What can you most clearly visualize the characters doing? Don't feel like you have to use everything you come up with—it's always smart to start with more than you think you need.
5. Now take the sitcom outline and slot in what you have. Now is the time to ask, "What is the act 1 problem or issue? What is the new problem of act 2?" Clean it up, make it as crystal clear and simple as possible.
6. Now add fun stuff back in, go back to your initial lists. Are there jokes or bits you can use to fill out what you have?

Ta-da!—you have "broken the story." If you were going to write a script of this episode, you now have a complete outline to follow.

TOOL: Putting Characters into Comedic Stories

Characters live within narratives. Sometimes they are sharing their own story, as in a solo character monologue or a first-person story. Sometimes they are interacting with other characters within a sketch premise. There is an complex interrelation between character and narrative in comedy. You could say, as Steve Kaplan does in *The Hidden Tools of Comedy*, that we define a comic story by the presence of a comic character.

In a solo character monologue the entire narrative is in first person filtered through the character. These tend to be structured in two ways. Think of the first as a kind of extended joke. You are introducing the character, providing details that set up expectations—introducing

(continued)

their primary filter (either in or out of character), as in Cecily Strong's "Girl You Wish You Hadn't Started a Conversation With" or Lily Tomlin's Edith Ann, who nearly always begins her story by announcing her name and age (five years old). You then provide examples that either confirm those expectations or reverse them in some way that still feels congruent with those expectations. You can also have the character tell a first-person story of their own, often including some level of incongruity or irony, as Whoopi Goldberg does brilliantly when her junkie character Fontaine describes a visit to the Anne Frank house in Amsterdam.

Sitcoms are narratives designed specifically to showcase characters we come to know and understand. These sorts of characters are fairly static: They grow and change, but they don't grow very much, and we don't want them to fundamentally change. The joy of a sitcom character is in the kind of rigidity noted by Henri Bergson: Jack Benny is always miserly and vain; Lucy forever believes she can do anything; on *The Good Place*, Chidi Anagonye is so fixated on making the right decision that he can't make any decisions at all. Sitcom characters are defined by their strong and somewhat inflexible points of view, and it's easy to manifest that point of view as a comic game. They may be affected by the events of each individual episode, but their central comedic perspective remains the same regardless of what happens to them and doesn't change over time.

Sketch characters are usually defined by the requirements of the premise. Let's return to the series of sketch premises I created earlier. If we wanted to create characters for the middle school spy sketch, we might start by thinking about the types of kids who inhabit a middle school—the ones on the sports teams, the popular ones, the theater kids, etc. They are going to have a single clear comic perspective defined by their school group and the role they hold in that group. In fact, for the purposes of this sketch we need two things: We need the group, and then we need the person in that group most likely to be the "spy" chosen to scope out the opposing group. We want a character who is likely to be the best choice to play the game of the scene.

As I mentioned earlier, finding a sketch to feature a character you have already created requires looking at that character and then asking, "What's the most incongruous place for this person to be?" (Generally, this is called a "fish out of water" premise.) Or, "What's the worst thing that could happen to this character?" It's tempting in this format to place a character in a situation where they will clearly demonstrate these traits or games as in a sitcom, but until we know the character and who they are, that's not particularly interesting for the audience. A character-driven premise needs more than simply a place for them to do what they do, it requires some level of stakes either for the character or for the people they are interacting with.

On the other hand, when you are working with an ensemble of character-focused performers, it can be quite effective to take a good premise and cast it with characters that already exist in the group's repertoire. You might need to change surface character details (occupation, marital status) to fit the new scenario, but the right fit with fully developed characters can add richness and dimension to a simple premise.

Persona-type characters exist in both sketch and sitcom as the audience's representative. Their job is to respond to the larger and less realistic characters and allow us to accept the presence of those characters in a semirealistic world. You can think of a persona character in some ways as a traditional "straight man"—their job is to be the audience representative. They connect to the audience to provide direction on how to feel about the larger character. Since the more extreme comedic characters tend to be somewhat rigid, the persona character can take on the task of giving the scene a clear arc by being affected and changed by the events occurring in the scene.

Longer narratives like films or novels put their primary comedic characters into a situation that requires genuine change over the course of the narrative. These characters have a strong point of view and narrow skill set. A longer narrative puts the comedic lead in a situation where they are unable to do the thing they need to do. The results of that struggle create lasting change for the character in question. This is why it can be difficult to create good sequels to comedic movies using the same protagonist: The events of the initial film create such profound change in the protagonist that a second similar journey feels false or forced.

14 VARIETY NARRATIVES

We're now going to dig into what I call variety narratives. In a variety narrative, a set of disparate elements (sketches, songs, jokes, skilled clowning) are put together in such a way that the audience has the feeling of being told a story. There may or may not be specific connections between the pieces, such as recurring characters or a theme, but there is a kind of underlying pattern in the way the pieces change in energy and tone or build in intensity and skill that takes the audience on a journey.

Historically, a lot of comedy took place as part of a larger performance that contained elements designed to delight, awe, fascinate, or otherwise grab the attention of an audience. Variety entertainment in the form of circuses, vaudeville, burlesque, or cabaret was the dominant form of entertainment in the West during the nineteenth and early twentieth centuries. Classic television variety shows like *The Ed Sullivan Show* or *The Carol Burnett Show* are less dominant than they once were. But while these traditional forms have waned, variety is still at the core of comedy in performance, and there is a significant amount of overlap between old-school variety structures and modern sketch revue, and improv.

But before we go too far into that world, let's revisit the world of jokes and the variety form of the stand-up set.

How to Write a Simple Stand-up Set

You have probably already noticed that I don't give a lot of examples from my own work in stand-up in this book. There's a reason for that—I haven't done a lot of stand-up. I first started working in comedy during the 1980s, which was the time of an enormous boom in club-style comedy of the sort that was 100 percent not my taste. It was also an incredibly misogynistic culture that I had really no desire to be a part of. (To be honest, the improv world in the 1980s wasn't a whole lot better . . . but it was a little better.) Later, I found the alternative comedy scene much more welcoming and interesting, but by that time I was fairly entrenched in the worlds of improvisation and sketch.

Then I began teaching comedy history in a college program, and my course included a segment on the development of American stand-up comedy and an assignment for students to write and perform their own five-minute stand-up set. I did a lot of research, and I discovered not only that I enjoy stand-up but also that a lot of what I already understood about other types of comedy was directly useful in this form. So, with the caveat that I am not an experienced stand-up, I want to take a moment to pull together that information for those who are interested in creating in this specific kind of solo performance.

Step 1: Write some jokes. If you have gotten this far, it will come as no surprise that the first thing you need to do is write a lot of jokes. An incredibly large number of jokes. Probably ten times as many as will end up in your final set (and because stand-up sets evolve as you build them in front of an audience, it will likely be even more than that).

To recap from the earlier section on jokes, here are some ways to approach this:

- Start with basic joke structure. Create a setup and then brainstorm multiple punch lines for that setup.
- Start with a general topic area, and brainstorm ideas around that topic area, then turn those ideas into jokes.
- Create a premise and brainstorm jokes within that premise, as we discussed earlier in the section on creating premise.

The above is basically a recap of the information already presented in the sections on joke writing and creating premise. I encourage you to go there to get more detailed information.

Step 2: Revise those jokes. Sort through your jokes and pick the ones that feel promising and revise them.

Step 3: Sort the jokes into groups. A good way to start is to put your jokes into some form where you can look at them individually. You can use index cards or Post-It notes or a computer program. Just get the jokes in a form where you can see them separately and move them around easily.

What kind of groups you sort them into depends on what kind of jokes you write. If you work from premise, they may already be sorted by topic or comic idea. Some jokes might feel like they belong in multiple places. I encourage you to make a list of these jokes in your notebook or add a code to the index card they're on. They can be useful for transitions and filling holes in your set.

Step 4: Find themes and premises. Look at each of the groups. Look for the jokes within a group that feel as if they belong together. Is there a theme, a unifying premise, or a common point of view? Is there a subcategory within the group? You may have twenty jokes about turtles—Why turtles? Don't ask me, they're your jokes—but out of those twenty, there might be ten really good ones about having a childhood turtle pet that all fit together nicely. Then set the jokes about Galapagos tortoises aside for the time being.

Step 5: Create beats for your set. Take the chunks that already have some kind of coherence and/or contain your funniest material and feel like they work well and turn them into "beats."

Roughly arrange the jokes from each group so that they get progressively funnier. Read them aloud to yourself in that order. That may be all you need to do, but you might find you want to revise the individual jokes for a better flow or create transitions that better connect them to each other. They might all fit within a larger story, and if so, you'll do a bit more writing to flesh that out.

Step 6: Turn the beats into a quick-and-dirty five-minute set. Generally, a five-minute set equals two to four beats plus a minute or so of introduction. Pay close attention to that introduction. Just as with the opening of any variety-style show, this is where you are teaching your audience how to watch you. For the most part, your choice of material for this set is going to define what is important to put into the introduction, but this is also where you want to think a little bit about your stage persona. If you are a small blond human who likes to dress as if you are two minutes away from going clubbing and your material is about your love of domestic chores like baking, you will want to reconcile (or at least call out the incongruity of) those two things in the intro material.

For now, your funniest beat should go last. Your second-funniest beat should go first. If you have more than two beats, plan to have your least funny beat go before your last beat (this way, if you are running out of time, you can just skip to the end).

Read or perform the beats in order. Keep your funniest beat last. You may need to play around a bit with the rest of the order for logic or flow reasons. You might want to write some extra material (or pull material you've already written) to transition between beats. How you do it really depends on the kind of comedy you create, but generally you don't need as much transition between beats as you might think. We change subjects all the time without transitions in conversation and stand-up is really a conversation with an audience.

Sketch Running Order

We're about to get heavily into the weeds of my area of expertise. If there is one thing I know well, it is how to make a running order for a live sketch revue. For our purposes here, I am defining "running order" as the intentional choice and ordering of the various elements (scenes, improvisation, songs, skill-based acts) in a variety performance. In other words, it is the narrative of a variety performance. Even if you don't work in sketch, this kind of structure is at the heart of many longer comedy forms.

A good running order does a number of important things:

- It teaches the audience how to watch the show. It should explain or indicate who is in the show, what kind of show the audience can expect to see, and how and whether the different pieces of the performance are connected to each other.

- It creates flow, energy, and rhythm for the show as a whole. It may alternate different types of scenes or acts to create a variety experience. It allows the audience to see the cast in a variety of combinations and relationships. The elements of the show can build in difficulty of execution or get progressively funnier.
- It creates context for the audience to watch certain scenes or performers. Introducing a performer playing close to themselves early in the show makes the audience more aware of their level of skill when they play a more extreme character later in the performance. A scene may call back information from a previous scene or foreshadow a moment that will happen later. Scenes with more challenging styles or content can happen later in the show once the audience trusts the performers and writers. Weaker or more delicate material can be protected by being placed in slots where the audience might be more forgiving or in what my colleague Norm Holly refers to as the "amnesia slot," one followed by a particularly strong or memorable piece.
- It serves the needs of its medium. A theater running order is looking to have the audience return after intermission and for the show to finish strongly. A television sketch show is looking to get viewer's attention, thus they might put some of their strongest material at the beginning of the show. In vaudeville, they wanted to clear the house quickly at the end of the performance so that a new crowd could enter the theater, and to encourage the audience to leave, they put a deliberately terrible act in the last slot (this was known as "playing to the haircuts").

A good running order can make mediocre or serviceable material look better than it is. A bad running order can hide or lessen the appeal of quality material. Remember that I am referring to both the selection of material as well as the order in which it is presented. As we've established all along, the goal is to create more than you need, to work from abundance. When you're working in a variety format and your goal is to create a performance experience that has some level of thematic or structural unity, you're not just going to be able to write *x* number of pieces and arrange them into a coherent whole. It has been my experience that to create a strong forty-five-minute sketch revue, you generally need to create three times as much rough draft material as will end up in the final product. This doesn't mean you will only create forty-five minutes of good material; there will likely be more than forty-five minutes of material you enjoy and want to use, but there will be good pieces that are just too similar to better pieces, or strong material that doesn't flow with or feel of a piece with the rest. And that's not even taking into account casting and balance issues.

When I look at a running order, I start with what I refer to as the "tentpoles." These are the pieces you need to have in place first—the parts of the show that hold up the rest.

The first thing I am looking for is a strong *runout* scene. This is roughly the second to last piece or slot in the show. I say "slot" because a runout doesn't have to be a single piece—it can be several pieces that function together as a set. Even when I have a single strong scene to use in the runout, I will often build on the energy it creates by immediately following it with two or three quick blackouts. In a traditional vaudeville running order, this slot was where the headliner played. Your runout should be your best scene. It may or may not be the funniest scene, but it should be the scene you want your audience going home remembering.

The next most important slot is the *opener*. This sets the tone for the entire show, teaching the audience what sort of show they can expect to watch. Like a good joke, it sets up expectations that are either fulfilled or subverted as the performance progresses. All other things being equal, you want to see all of the central players in the ensemble during this opening slot if not in the opening piece. It should create some energy going into the show, pique the audience's interest for what is to come.

In a live two-act show, I am also looking for a strong *first-act closer*. In vaudeville, this was the next most important slot to that of the headliner, and this is roughly true for all sketch. The most important thing to remember about your first-act closer is that it should send your audience out into the lobby for intermission excited to come back for more in act 2.

One of my personal favorite first-act closers in a Second City show is a scene titled "Orchestra." The premise is that a student orchestra no longer has the budget for instruments and has to "improvise" in order to play. The bulk of the cast is in the house, and they divide the audience roughly into sections that are directed to use their bodies and items they already have on them to make music (clapping, jingling keys, etc.). The cast improvises with each other and the people in their section; the audience gets to actively participate in two "numbers," ending with a full audience and cast performance of "Twist and Shout." The audience leaves the theater for intermission with something to talk about with their friends, buzzing with a tiny bit of performance adrenaline. And they all want to come back and see the performers they had so much fun playing with.

Of course, if you are doing one act or a show in another medium, you don't have the need for one scene that will make the audience excited to come back after intermission. On commercial television, you might build in miniversions of this sort of act closer before the ad breaks. If your TV show is on HBO or streaming, then you won't need to do so. In that case or in a live show in one act, you might still choose to put a particularly funny or energetic scene in the middle of the show to provide a bump of energy.

The show *closer* is a much less important slot than you might assume it to be. If the director and the cast have done their job, the audience won't need much to finish out the performance. They will want to be prepared for the show to end. They will likely be interested in seeing the members of the ensemble whose work they have enjoyed one last time before the curtain call. In musical theater, the closing number is usually a reprise from a song earlier in the show, not a number that is new to the audience. There are a lot of commonalities between classic musical theater show structure and sketch comedy running order. That's not surprising when you understand that traditional American musical theater has its roots in variety revue. A musical number that isn't particularly challenging in terms of style or format works well for sketch material here too. A piece reincorporating characters or elements that have already appeared in the show will provide a sense of closure and of having been told a story for the audience. At the highest level of difficulty, your closer can do all those things while simultaneously providing a new insight or angle that reframes the show as a whole and allows the audience to discover something new about what they have just experienced. This isn't required, by the way, and it doesn't need to be particularly complex, nor should it be. It's a reprise of sorts to remind the audience of what they have watched rather than begin something fresh. The idea is to demonstrate some unity among the variety of pieces in the show in a way that feels organic and not forced or obvious.

Once I have those tentpoles in place, my next choices are driven by how I want to showcase or protect the other material my cast and I have created. But there are some additional things to take into consideration.

Act 1, scene 1 (or just scene 1 if you are doing a one-act show) comes after the opener and is a good place to slow the show down and to help the audience start to get to know the ensemble. At Second City, this is frequently a two- or three-person scene focusing on the characters' relationships with each other. At this point in the show, the audience is generally comfortable with something well performed and structured that includes comedic recognition in terms of characters and situation but is not necessarily hugely laugh heavy. There's an opportunity for the audience to settle in, get their bearings (maybe get their drinks from a server) but still be entertained and reassured that they are in capable hands. It's relatively easy for writer/performers to create these types of scenes (and to enjoy playing them), and this is the ideal space in a show for that sort of relationship-focused scene.

There are a couple of spots in a running order that are naturally more forgiving of delicate or "in process" material (or, let's be honest, material that just isn't as good as the rest but that you need to include for casting balance or other practical reasons). Act 2, scene 2 is probably the safest and most protected slot in any running order. The audience has returned after intermission, and they're fully invested in the show at this point, so they're willing to be patient with something slower or different from the rest of the performance. This is also a somewhat forgettable point in the show: If the piece placed here isn't particularly strong, the audience isn't likely to pay much attention or remember. Conversely, in a very strong show, this can turn out to be an audience favorite. Almost anything "works" here, and if it's very good it will work even better. There is a roughly equivalent slot about two-thirds of the way through act 1 (or two-thirds of the way through a one-act show). It isn't quite as protected as act 2, scene 2 but can serve a similar purpose of "hiding" a weaker piece or supporting a more delicate piece.

Another forgiving slot is right before the runout at the end of the show. I've listed it on the outlines as the "goofy" slot. This slot is not so much "protected" as it is earned. If you have done your job in the rest of the show and the audience feels warmly toward your ensemble, you have an opportunity here to showcase something the cast really enjoys doing or just makes them laugh, like the "Magical Ponies" scene I mentioned in the section on thick and thin comedy. At this point, everyone is playing together and the audience feels as if they have been let in on a secret handshake of some sort, they feel indulgent and they enjoy just seeing the people they have come to know and enjoy have a good time together.

Giant Running Order Disclaimer

Creating a good running order is not an exact science. You can't just follow the structure and get a good show. (Remember, your creation doesn't exist to follow the rules—the rules are there to support your creation.) You can break all the so-called rules and still have an amazing show. There are Second City directors who have made a point of building running orders that deliberately break certain rules—and then announce proudly at regular intervals thereafter, "There are no rules!"

This is not to say that structure isn't fundamental to a good sketch or variety show. The arc of the audience's experience and the way they interact with the process of the performance has a direct effect on the show as a whole. There's an underlying logic you still need to wrestle with to make a show work for an average audience. Often, if you look closely at the structure of these "rule-breaking" shows, you'll notice that the essential elements of the structure have been maintained—they've just been moved around a bit to accommodate the big change, or something special has been inserted somewhere to shore up the structure of the show that brings things back into balance.

For example, the iconic Second City revue *Piñata Full of Bees* started with a shocking opener. It was the worst nightmare of every audience member who comes to a left-wing comedy club. The show began with loud discordant rock music, then lights came up on the cast wearing gas masks with one member in the center of the stage on a microphone intoning rhetoric through a rubber Ronald Reagan mask. An unfortunate member of the audience was pulled up onstage and dressed in an Uncle Sam costume to represent America and tried for sins against humanity. Things began to seem as if they would truly get out of hand as the cast actually grabbed the audience member as he tried to escape back to his seat. Then, suddenly, the music changed to "Eye of the Tiger," the "victim" turned out to be cast member Jon Glaser, and the entire cast participated a ridiculous high-energy stage fight ending with Glaser triumphantly (and ironically) shouting out victory for American exceptionalism.

This initial opening scene broke a lot of the "rules" I generally espouse for an opener—it was very challenging both in form and content, and it introduced none of the cast playing themselves. What it did do brilliantly was teach the audience that this show was going to be dramatically different from other Second City shows they had experienced and that they should expect a level of discomfort and in-your-face satire. It also demonstrated that the audience was in good hands—that the discomfort would be balanced with highly skilled performances, savvy stagecraft, and a sophisticated point of view.

So far, so good. But I'd like to point out that this opening piece was not the total of the "opening slot." It was followed by a traditionally structured classroom scene in which all of the performers played versions of themselves, and which commented on the ironic perspective of the opener. And that was followed by a traditionally structured and very funny two-person scene containing a lot of strong jokes. These two scenes provided the audience with the necessary elements of a good running order—familiarity with the cast, a sense of being in the presence of skilled writer/performers—and allowed the show to teach the audience some new conventions that would be used throughout the performance.

Metanarrative

As humans we make meaning—it's a thing we do. Put two unconnected pieces of information next to each other and our brains will generate a story that connects them (this is story coherence bias). In the same way, when we watch a sketch show or other variety-style format, we'll start to make meaning out of random interactions between characters or repeated patterns of relationships between performers. For example, it isn't unusual that casting and balance concerns will cause certain actors to appear more frequently together in scenes than others. An audience might infer that those actors like each other better than other cast members or that there is some sort of feud going on between two performers who don't often appear together (and sometimes the audience is right).

Part of the pleasure of watching sketch shows with an ensemble cast is the sense of "getting to know" the ensemble. In addition to watching the events of each individual scene the audience is discovering multiple aspects of each performer's skill and persona. They are getting a sense of the group point of view, what the ensemble cares about and enjoys playing, and what they do not (this happens even when you have a show without any strong theme or focus on social or political satire). It's why audiences enjoyed seeing Horatio Sanz on *SNL* or Harvey Korman on *The Carol Burnett Show* break character and laugh at the antics of another cast member. We feel like we are getting an insight into the dynamic among the players.

It's important that a director or head writer pay attention to these aspects of metanarrative as they put together a running order. At the simplest level, if we introduce a performer early in the show playing some version of themselves, it will seem much more exciting and skillful when they return later in the show playing a more extreme character. Callbacks and runners reward the audience for paying attention and create a feeling of story and narrative through reincorporation. A piece where a strong political point of view or content is placed early in the show will often create a frame or filter for the audience that makes later material feel more politically slanted than it would without that context. Or a set of scenes that create a consistent dynamic between two players can create tension or a sense of narrative in the audience that feels more fulfilling if it is recognized and pays off in some way.

In a Second City touring company I directed, there was a series of sketches featuring Adam McKay and Brian Stack. As performers, they enjoyed playing a dynamic in which Adam was high status and Brian was low status, and the scenes they created together often included an absurdist setup in which Adam's character tricked Brian's character in some way or presented a bizarre situation that Brian's character tried desperately to understand and justify. One day, Brian brought in a short blackout in which he reversed these roles. He looked over at Adam and asked him to turn his head one way and then the other as if Adam had dirt or paint on his face. Brian then nodded and said simply, "That's what I thought. You're an asshole."

The blackout wasn't particularly funny on its own and wouldn't necessarily have worked well with two other members of the ensemble playing the same parts, but it got big laughs when we put it near the end of our show, because it reversed the dynamic that had been created in the previous scenes. By giving Brian a moment of control, it corrected an imbalance the audience had perceived, albeit perhaps unconsciously.

Both Adam and Brian are cisgender straight white men, and even without that blackout, the little bit of audience discomfort their character dynamic created didn't strongly alter the audience's experience of the show. But it is especially important that a director or writer pay attention to elements that inadvertently create this sort of metanarrative in regard to cast members who represent marginalized communities of any kind. It's helpful to look at the arc of the show and think of each performer and ask, "What story is being told about this person?" or "What would I believe about them after watching this performance?"

This is not just important to think about in terms of individual cast members. Audiences can infer theme where none was intended. So also ask, "What is the journey we are taking the audience on? What might they take away from the performance?" Some sketch shows have an explicit theme or point of view, but it's not necessary. It is, however, valuable to be aware that there will always be some sort of story that shows up and to make adjustments if it isn't the story we meant to tell.

Running Order Outlines

The two outlines in this section are based on the two-act running order that Norm Holly contributed to *The Second City Almanac of Improvisation*. Over the years I have changed or moved around elements as I have created my own shows and taught running order structure to my students in the comedy major and the Second City directing program. There are a lot of similarities between these two structures, but it's useful to look at them both and see where the differences are.

As with any narrative structure, I find these outlines most useful as a diagnostic. When a running order doesn't seem to be working the way I thought it should, I'll compare what I have to the outlines to help figure out where the issues are in what I've created.

Outline of a Two-Act Running Order for Sketch

Act 1

- **Opening slot / introduction:** Should introduce the cast playing roles close to their own personas. The material in this slot should not be too challenging in terms of content or form. It may introduce the theme of the show in a nonovert manner, but should clue the audience in to the type of show they can expect to see.
- **Act 1, scene 1:** Usually this is a relationship or behavior scene with two or three performers. This is the point in the show where the audience is most receptive to a slower scene and is likely looking to see the show reflect the kinds of people and situations they recognize. Use this slot to introduce the performers as skilled actors playing characters but still close to their own personas. If the opening slot is scenic, or if the skill slot is an improvised game with an introduction, this may be flipped with the act 1 skill slot.
- **Act 1 skill slot:** This can be a solo song or duet, an improvised game or style scene. It demonstrates the abilities of the ensemble in realms beyond acting. Traditionally, in a Second City touring company "best of" show, this is a full-cast improvised game.
- **Act 1 group slot:** This is often a more heavily character-based piece, generally high energy, and showcases how the ensemble plays together. Now that the ensemble's personas have been established, here we can demonstrate their versatility and start to challenge audience assumptions a bit.

- **Act 1, scene 2:** This is a slower-paced relationship or behavior scene; it might build on themes set up in scene 1. This extends the performers' credibility as actors. It may also more obviously state the theme of the revue. This is a good slot to introduce a scene with a strong satiric point of view.
- **Act 1 runout:** This speeds the first act to its conclusion. This slot may echo the skill slot, calling back the idea of very skilled performers.
- **Act 1 closer:** This is usually the funniest scene in the show—not the best scene, but the funniest. Although it is preferable to make this a full-cast scene, that is not as important as making this scene the most laugh heavy. The act 1 closing slot is one of the most important slots in the revue. It is what may or may not inspire the audience to return after intermission.

Act 2

- **Act 2 opener:** Along with act 2, scene 1, this is one of the most forgiving spots in a two-act running order. It is important for the audience to again see all of the members of the ensemble within the first few scenes of act 2, so a full-cast scene is a good fit here, especially if the first-act closer was not a cast scene. A piece in this slot can be more challenging in form or content than anything in act 1. This is a great place to put a piece that has a strong satiric point or is somewhat intellectually or stylistically challenging. Depending on how this scene begins, it may be a good idea to begin act 2 with a blackout or throwaway song to regain the audience's attention after intermission and then follow with the longer scene.
- **Act 2, scene 1:** This is the sweet spot of the two-act sketch running order. If you did your job in act 1, the audience will be willing to watch almost anything here. At Second City this was traditionally a long two-person relationship scene. This scene can be more challenging in terms of content than anything in act 1. If the act 2 opener is slow and scenic, you may need to insert a couple of blackouts or short scenes before this piece to

keep the energy up. A longer and more scenic act 2 opener can take the place of this slot entirely. This is also a good slot to protect something that's delicate or might be difficult for the audience, or a piece that's less well developed but necessary for balance or cast morale. It's also the first place I might try out a new scene being developed for a new show.

- **Act 2 skill slot:** This is a reminder to the audience that they are watching skilled performers and allows those performers to execute an unexpected skill. If it is a song or an improvisation, its degree of difficulty should surpass that seen in act 1.
- **Act 2, scene 2:** This slot serves to balance the act and show in terms of casting, content, and style. Ideally, this scene builds on the themes set up previously in the show and reinforces the audience's awareness that this is a group of skilled comic actors with a strong point of view, but much of what happens in this slot depends on the choices made for the first two slots of act 2 and the act 2 runout.
- **Goofy slot:** Ideally, by this point the show has earned the audience's trust and respect, and they are interested in seeing you (or allowing you to) play around a little bit. This is where you put the pet scene that makes the cast laugh—your Magical Ponies, Space Pirates, etc. This is also where you can put your dirty or very dark material. By this point, the audience should know they are watching skilled dramatic and comic performers and should understand the theme of the show. What they are not expecting is for everything set up thus far to be thrown out the window. That can happen here.
- **Runout:** In a traditional vaudeville running order, this is where the headliner plays. This is where your best scene goes—not necessarily your funniest scene, but your best scene. This is the scene you want the audience to walk out of the theater remembering. I often choose to follow this scene with two or three blackouts. It is clear to the audience that the show is about to end.
- **Closer:** Doesn't need to be long, but ideally pulls through any thematic threads of the show and provides the audience with a clear sense of finish. It's often a song.

Outline of a One-Act Running Order for Sketch

- **Opening slot / introduction:** Should introduce the cast playing close to their own personas, should not be too challenging in terms of content or form (could simply be a string of three blackouts), possibly introduces the theme of the show.
- **Scene 1:** Usually this is a relationship or behavior scene with two or three performers. This is the point in the show where the audience is most receptive to a somewhat slower scene but is looking to see the show reflect the kinds of people and situations they recognize. Introduces the performers as skilled actors playing characters close to their own personas.
- **Skill slot:** Often a solo song or a duet, an improvised game, or a style scene; it demonstrates the abilities of the ensemble in realms beyond acting.
- **Group slot:** Often a more heavily character-based piece, generally high energy, and showcases how the ensemble plays together. Now that the ensemble's personas have been established, here we can demonstrate their versatility and start to challenge audience assumptions a bit.
- **Scene 2:** Again a slower-paced relationship or behavior scene, ideally one that builds on the themes set up in scene 1 and extends the performers' credibility as actors.
- **Skill Slot 2 / Smart Slot:** Often a satirical piece or a genre scene. Depending on the slots around it, could also be a song.
- **Goofy Slot:** Ideally you have earned the audience's trust and respect and they are interested in seeing you (or allowing you to) play around a little bit. This is where you put the pet scene that makes the cast laugh—your Magical Ponies, Space Pirates etc. This is also where you can put your dirty stuff or a piece that might offend the audience if you place it earlier in the show.
- **Runout:** This is where your best/funniest scene goes. The show is building energy to the end. I often follow this with two blackouts before we get to the closer.
- **Closer:** Doesn't need to be long, but ideally pulls through any thematic threads of the show and gives the audience a clear sense of finish. It's often a song.

Quick-and-Dirty Running Order

Do you have some comedic material you want to put up in front of an audience to see if it works? Use the suggestions below as a quick way to create some useful structure.

- Figure out what your best scene is and put it at or near the end.
- Make sure you see everyone in the ensemble within the first slot of the show (roughly the first ten minutes). I'm assuming here that you are doing a show with an ensemble. If it's true variety with a number of different acts then this part doesn't matter. If it's a variety show with a star, this is less of a concern.
- Alternate between large group and smaller scenes.
- Don't put any scenes next to each other that the audience might assume are connected such as two scenes with similar casting, content, or style. The last person to speak in one scene probably shouldn't be the first to speak in the next.
- A pretty good rule of thumb for estimating length is to think of each sketch as being five minutes without any interstitial stuff (blackouts, introductions, transitions between scenes) adding to the time. You may find that the material you create generally runs shorter or longer, and if so you can adjust accordingly.

This is also a pretty good rough outline for creating a running order of improv games. Generally, you should also vary the types and styles of games and the roles of the ensemble (playing vs. hosting).

Running Order Hierarchy of Needs

Running order hierarchy of needs is my way of thinking about how to put together material depending on where it is at in the process of creation. When we put material up in front of an audience to get feedback, it needs to be complete in some way, and the running order is part of that completion. At this point you need to set up a structure that doesn't get in the way of understanding how and whether the material works. As you move toward a finished product, you can think about the more advanced elements that provide polish and the sense of seeing a larger whole.

Casting

- **Basic:** Have we introduced the audience to the cast in the first few scenes of the show? Do we see the cast throughout the show so that we remain familiar with who they are? Have we accounted for any situations in which the audience might be confused and think the same actor is playing the same character in two different scenes? Have we accounted for practical things like costume changes or time for a cast member to get to a certain place in the theater to enter from the house?
- **Advanced:** Do we feel like we are gradually getting to know the cast over the course of the show? Do they establish their personas and abilities for us and then surprise us with new skills or ways of displaying those personas? Do we need to establish a certain player's credibility with the audience in order for them to play a difficult character later in the show? Do we feel like we discover their relationships to each other or how their individual points of view meld into an ensemble perspective?

Variety

- **Basic:** Does the show alternate between scenes of different cast sizes, energies, styles, and content?
- **Advanced:** Does the show surprise the audience with its variety? Does a sketch or moment fulfill the need for variety in a manner that is unusual or novel? For example, the Second City Mainstage revue *Southside of Heaven* had a false start in which it appeared that there was a short electrical outage and while the musical director and stage manager pretended to be resetting some computer issues cast members came out and chatted with the audience pretending to vamp for time. Audience answers were recorded during this talk, and when the show started "officially," those recordings were used to explain to the audience that they had been tricked. The variety here was outside what's normally used in sketch comedy. But it did many of the things a normal "opener" does (for

example, introducing the cast) and allowed for a quieter, more intimate two-person song to happen in what would normally be the opening slot. Could you create connected suites of material with similar content or tone that builds in complexity and understanding so that they function together in some interesting way? There will still need to be some underlying variety here in terms of energy or casting.

Shape

- **Basic:** There are three basic tentpole scenes/sets of scenes that help give the show a strong shape. The opener sets the tone of the show for the audience and introduces the cast. Your peak scene is the one the audience will remember most clearly after they leave the performance. Your closer provides some feeling of finish to the experience. In a two-act show, you are looking at two "peak scenes"—your first-act closer and your second act runout (the scene or set of scenes immediately before your closer). Think of the path through this two-act show from the audience's perspective:

  Opener: "I understand what sort of show this is and how to watch it. I'm excited and interested to see what happens next."

  The audience now watches a variety of scenes that to some extent or another play out the promise of the opener.

  Peak scene #1 (likely at the end of the first act): "Wow, that was great! The show is good and I really liked that scene. I'm excited to come back after intermission and see the rest of the show."

  For first part of the second act, the audience is very forgiving and happy to watch almost anything, they trust that the show will continue to be as good as it has been so far.

  Peak scene #2: "Wow, that was really great! And it left me feeling something or thinking something. I really liked this show!"

Closer: "The show is ending and the great feelings created by the peak scenes are coalescing into my appreciation for the performers/writers."

- **Advanced:** You can get very advanced in terms of shape. You can set up characters or stories in the first part of the show and bring them back in the second part of the show. You can play with scaring or tricking your audience early on in the show and then win them back by skillfully making their initial discomfort worth their while. Your closer can reframe the journey of the show and suggest a new way to understand what has been viewed.

Content

- **Basic:** Is there anything that is going to be challenging to the audience in terms of form or content? It should go later in the show. Are there runners or callbacks? Generally, the first two parts of a runner should be separated from each other by no more than three scenes, and then you can put the third part wherever you like (often near the end of the show—this reincorporation creates the feeling of having been told a story).
- **Advanced:** If there is challenging content later in the show, introduce the possibility that this type of content will happen in the show in a less overt or challenging manner earlier on. A theme for the show should be introduced lightly early on and then built throughout.

Ultimately, in an original show, content dictates form. You may need to break all sorts of running order "rules" to make your content make sense as larger whole.

PART 3

MAKING IT FUNNIER AND BETTER

Congratulations!—you made a comedy thing.

It might be a single joke or short stand-up set, a sketch, a story, or a silent pantomime. Now you get to do the fun part: You get to make it better. Or at least, I think it's the fun part, and my sense is that a lot of other comedians do as well. We push through the terrible first draft of our comedy thing to get to the next part, where we get to make it funnier. If you used any of the creation exercises in this book, you used at least one of the aspects of recognition, pain, and distance to generate a piece of comedy, but even (or especially if) you didn't, now is where the three elements of comedy really become useful.

I want to remind you that you don't have to revise everything you create, nor should you. If you've gotten this far, I'm sure you already understand the lesson of working from abundance. This is where it really becomes important. *Only revise the things that feel good to you, the ones that already "work."* In my long experience, the stuff that feels like it "should" work often just doesn't. So read through what you've created or put up on its feet in some simple way and then only move forward with the good stuff.

You don't have to trash the other work you've done. You can. If you never want to look at that hospital sketch or the chocolate chip pancakes joke again, feel free to delete it or otherwise erase its existence from the world. You can also opt to put it in a file on your computer or in a physical paper file and revisit it later. If you are keeping it, there is probably something you like about it. I encourage you to find a way to make a note of that thing you like. Stick a real or virtual Post-It note on the file so you know why you kept what you kept in case you decide to revisit it. But otherwise, don't bother. Just take the things that are already good and make them better.

15 MAKING IT FUNNIER

Once you have a sense of what material you want to keep working on, the next step is to get it up in front of an audience of some kind. This might begin with a family member or your roommate, but eventually it's valuable to have an audience beyond your immediate circle. If you are a beginner, I recommend that you find a group of similarly interested people and meet regularly to try out your jokes or sketches on each other. If you write sketch or other longer forms like plays or sitcoms, it's very helpful to have other people read your work aloud so you can hear how it sounds.

If you're at a more developed part of your career, this is where you bring your material into a writers' room or present it in front of an audience by putting newer material into an existing set. At Second City we are deeply lucky to have the improv set that happens after the regular show where we can improvise a scene from premise in front of an audience or reimprovise it after we've worked on the initial version in rehearsal and get real-time audience feedback.

Before you put your material up in front of a test audience it does need to be complete—not done, not perfect or completely finished, but finished enough that it doesn't require explanation from you before or after you present it. You want to get responses to the thing you made, not the potential thing you might make.

Before you present, you should also do a quick edit of the kind I recommend in the section titled "How to Rewrite a Joke." Read over what you have written or review what you are planning to do. It's particularly helpful at this stage to do so out loud. Do some basic proofreading. Look for anything that might be confusing to your audience. Clean up any dialogue or language that's particularly messy. Check the basic structure elements: For example, if it's a joke, is the punch line at the end of the line? Before you present your material, you should have a sense of what you want to learn or get from the audience (beyond uproarious laughter, general acclaim, and acknowledgment of your genius). This doesn't have to be complex: Does it make sense? What parts did they like? What parts did they want more of?

If you are a stand-up going to an open mic of some kind, it is especially important to keep your expectations low. Other comedians who don't know you are unlikely to be a good audience. They may or may not laugh at your jokes and if they do, they might not laugh in the way you want them to. If possible, have a friend record your performance so you can watch it later. Or do a voice recording on your phone. Many of my students report after doing a stand-up set that they have zero memory of what they said or how they said it. And my experience as a sketch director is that it's quite common for the performers to have a completely different experience of the show than I did from the audience.

Working with Expectations

Let's say you walk into the living room of your family home and your parents are watching a show on the television. It's a police procedural. You know almost immediately. How do you know?

The music and underscoring has a certain driving bass line; the dialogue is quick and concise and delivered in measured but slightly intense tones of voice. The colors onscreen tend to be grays, blues, tans, and khakis. There are windows with slatted blinds. If you watch a little bit along with your parents, you are going to see a certain set of characters—police detectives, district attorneys, blue-collar suspects, tough-talking witnesses. Seeing even a few of these elements in combination will immediately give you an idea of the type of show. More than that, if you are familiar with the genre you will have expectations beyond these things. You'll assume types of storylines: detectives solving a case, but also likely detectives having issues in their personal lives that get in the way of their solving the case; murders that mirror stories about murders you've heard about on the news; lawyers getting surprising admissions from clients on the stand.

But you probably won't actively think through any of this. You'll process the idea that it's a police procedural very quickly, probably within seconds of your entering the room and seeing the TV. As we have discussed earlier, our fast brain is hardwired to make assumptions and jump to conclusions based on our previous knowledge. Just a snatch of theme music is likely to trigger associations. Or maybe not. My own expectation here is that the bulk of my readers are Western television watchers who are familiar with American television programming, and that your parents (if they are alive and you are able to visit them in a "family home") watch Western commercial television as opposed to a K drama or a Bollywood musical. Expectations are cultural and relative.

So, let's back the scenario up a bit. You are walking into a living room in a house. You already have an expectation as you read that sentence of what that room will look like based on *your* previous life experience (houses you've been in before, living rooms you've seen most recently, the types of living rooms you associate with the area and type of home you have entered). As humans we are always predicting—we always have an expectation based on our previous experiences. As I noted in the chapter on humor theory, it has been suggested that the initial mechanism for humor and laughter may have evolved as a way to make it valuable and enjoyable for humans to double-check this tendency to automate our experience of the world by jumping to expectations.

Expectation is a form of recognition. We expect because we recognize, and that recognition leads to a whole slew of assumptions. A great deal of comedy relies on either creating an expectation and reversing it (as in a joke) or creating an expectation and confirming it (as in a physical gag like slipping on a banana peel).

When you are revising your comedy, regardless of the form, one of the first things you should look at is how you are setting up the expectations of your audience. The single biggest note I give to students or comedians I am working with is to "introduce yourself" or "tell me what normal looks like." At the improv school UCB, this is termed "establishing a base reality," and they suggest that it needs to happen before you can find the game of the scene. I'm not sure why so many novice comedians shy away from intentionally setting up expectations. Perhaps it's the fear of appearing too obvious. More likely it's the assumption that an audience already knows the thing the comedian knows and is excited to get to the interesting bit the comedian enjoys. Regardless, it never hurts to start with clarity and then ease back on it.

In stand-up and solo performance, the comedian's persona creates an expectation of the sort of comedy we will experience when we watch them. The initial few jokes of their stand-up set will acknowledge the expectation the audience already has, based on the comedian's appearance and the venue they are performing in, as well as set up expectations for the comedy to come.

I encourage you to think of audience expectations as a puzzle to be solved. What do you want your audience to assume is going to happen? What are all the ways you can create that assumption? What do they have to know to enjoy or understand what you're about to do? There isn't anything wrong with simply stating those things immediately and succinctly. During the pandemic, I directed a student television sketch show around the theme of kid and YA literature. In one of the sketches, we parodied the American Girl book series by portraying the experience of the 2020 historical American Girl doll—Kayleighhh. The opening of the sketch literally began with a girl announcing, "Wow, the new historical American Girl doll!" and then opening a box with the doll inside along with her tiny accessories (a little mask, a laptop computer that had her Zoom class inside). There were good jokes in it, but more importantly it created strong audience expectation and clarity for the sketch to come, in terms of the parody as well as some social satire about the events of the pandemic year.

Traditional sitcoms set up expectations at the most obvious of snail's paces—here are the characters, here is what you need to know about them, here's what else you need to know about the setting of the show. Very old-school sitcoms like *The Brady Bunch* or *Gilligan's Island* have theme songs that lay out the entire back story of the show and introduce us visually and descriptively to the primary characters and the roles they play, often followed by a short teaser that does much of the same thing again! More recent sitcoms do this less and much less overtly (especially now, when the assumption is that you aren't just coming upon any given episode of a sitcom cold but rather have elected to stream it from the beginning with the pilot). But there are still moments of clear expectation setting with more subtle introductions to the primary players or the premise of the show.

You should have a very good idea that a film is a comedy within the first few minutes of watching it. The choice of music, colors, the presence of a performer whom we know to be a comedian who is playing some version of their recognizable comedic persona (Will Ferrell, pompous idiot; Jackie Chan, nerdy action hero). All of these elements don't just create expectation that the film is a comedy; their very presence provides distance on events (it's a comedy, therefore I shouldn't worry about whether the humans in this car crash are OK). But again, it's important to remind ourselves that for the audience, this expectation is rarely conscious—it happens automatically. Our brain will create an expectation based on whatever is available to it, intentional or not. So here's my advice to those of you who want to be funnier: Make it intentional.

TOOL: Risk and Failure

It's a truism in comedy that you need to get used to failure. As Stephen Colbert has said, "You gotta learn to love the bomb." You can make an educated guess as to what your audience finds recognizable, painful, and has distance on, but that educated guess is surprisingly easy to get wrong. And because the best, most resonant comedy tends to involve extremes or unique aspects of the first two elements, it is all too easy to misjudge—to provide too little distance or include elements that confuse or threaten your audience. Every audience is different, especially when you are working out new material. Material that worked brilliantly for one group gets no response from another. Or worse.

I used to advise my students to value failure. But that's silly—no one really values failure. Failure sucks. What we need to value is the

(continued)

thing that put us into the position to fail in the first place: taking a risk. When we risk, we tempt failure, and any comedian worth their salt will do this time and again. We also need to recognize that failure is a natural result of valuing risk. And regardless of how "safe" you may play it in comedy, there will still be times that you fail, possibly spectacularly.

If that's the case, there's no reason to play it safe. Take risks. Try things. See what happens if you do something you think no one would be interested in. See what happens if you remove all the traditional setup and punch line jokes from your act. See what happens if you reveal something onstage that is genuinely recognizable and painful for you but you would swear no one else would get or understand. Risk on its own is a useful pain for comedy. An audience can sense a genuine risk on the part of a performer, and it gives the whole thing a kind of high-wire-act tension that is likely to be released in laughter. It's thrilling to be in the room when something is genuinely being risked and the outcome is uncertain. This is part of the appeal of improvisation as comedy—the audience is aware that what they are watching might fail at any moment, and this awareness generates tension that heightens the audience response.

By the way, choosing to be offensive for offensivenesss's sake isn't a genuine risk. The performer whose goal is to make their audience as uncomfortable as possible isn't risking much (except maybe eventually their career). In the moment, the tormentor has all the power. Yelling at the audience isn't a risk if it isn't leading somewhere—unless you consider that your audience has cell phones with cameras and can record your tirade and share it with the planet. On the other hand, seeing how long an audience will put up with the tension of being yelled at and seeing how you can create distance for them that will allow them to laugh at that discomfort *is* a risk. It may or may not be the kind of comedy that is to my taste, but that's a different question. I personally feel strongly that if you are going to work in this way, you have a responsibility to your audience.

Can you, like Tig Notaro did in her famous set at Largo, reveal something deeply uncomfortable and personal to an audience—telling them, for example, "I have cancer"? And have it be true but also find the way to make it a moment of shared recognition (real truth in this instance) and pain and create laughter through bravery and honesty? It was a big risk, but the payoff was enormous.

But also, you don't have to do that. Valuing risk and understanding and accepting failure as a natural outgrowth of that risk also requires having a good sense of what you need to take care of yourself in any given moment. You don't have to risk your mental health or safety to make comedy. You just don't.

Know why you are taking any given risk. You have an instinct or a prediction that an audience is going to respond in a certain way, and you want to test it. If it works, you know something, but if it doesn't work, you also know something. That failure should be valuable to you. Your prediction was off in some crucial way, and you can learn from that. It may be that what you created needs more distance or more recognition, and you can adjust your material appropriately. Or maybe this was simply the wrong audience or environment for what you wanted to do and it requires a different context to be successful. Presenting your work in a different context is a useful way of adjusting recognition and distance. Or maybe your instinct was just wrong, and you can learn from that too. That's the reason to learn to love the bomb.

Next Steps of Revising

A lot of your first-revision questions are going to rely on adjusting elements of recognition. What did the audience know already, and what do you need to provide that they might not know? Are those elements in the work, where the audience can see and hear them, or are they just in your head? You will also be adjusting larger elements of pain and distance through looking at comic action, logic, and point of view.

If you've completed a strong first draft—and by "draft," I mean an early version; it doesn't have to be on paper, you can create a physical performance piece "in draft"—you should be able to answer the questions below. These might be provisional answers that will change as you revise, but you'll save a lot of time by analyzing and identifying these elements first before making any big changes.

1. What's the premise now? It's not uncommon to start with one premise for a piece and discover at some point during the initial drafts that the premise has shifted or changed. See if you can describe the current premise in one simple clear sentence. If you find you're using the words *and then* more than once, you don't have a clear premise. You'll need to have that before you do anything else.
2. What expectations have been set up and how? What does the audience need to know in order to enjoy the piece? How and where did you provide that information? If there are characters in the piece, is it clear who the characters are, where they are and what they are doing? If the answers to these questions are (in order) "I don't know, I don't know. I don't know, and no," you know what your next step is: Revise the exposition or the initial beats of the piece. These questions represent the most frequent feedback I give when I direct a sketch show or note a stand-up set. It's the first and easiest fix you can make.
3. What's the game or comic driver of the piece or beat? What thing is being explored and heightened? If you haven't done so already, it's useful to name it for yourself. What's the primary comic action in what you created? My experience is that for sketches, short comedic pieces, and each beat of a stand-up set, there is one primary comic action or source of jokes. It's not that there aren't additional or tangential moments that generate laughter, but identifying that comedic core will make your rewrite easier. Most of the hard laughs in your piece will stem from your ability to better execute that core in some way. Remember: The comic driver may not be in the words. It can also be in the physical interplay between the performers while they speak the dialogue. It might be connected to character or point of view. It might be a performance or timing issue.
4. What's the comic logic? What's the justification for why the game or comic issue occurs or is allowed to occur? This is the second most frequent note I give on student work, and it's another space where we are using the element of recognition. The audience has to understand the rules of the world and accept them in order to enjoy the results. This logic doesn't have to be complex or convoluted, it just has to be introduced and

accepted. Why does one character allow another to behave in a certain way? Why doesn't everyone onstage announce "This is wrong and weird" and then walk out of the scene? In a stand-up set, how do you bring the audience into your personal reality so that they know the rules of your world and know how to play along with you? The comedian Tim Robinson in his sketch show *I Think You Should Leave* is the master of finding simple permission structures that allow his characters to go completely and utterly out of control. Good comic logic is a gift you give to your audience. It means that they aren't confused, they feel safe and in good hands, they can just sit back and enjoy the comedy—even if it's as extreme as Robinson's work can get.

If the comic logic is good and works, can you develop or extend it in some way? Can you make the specific details (names, places, character behavior) more closely aligned with the world your comic justification creates?

5. What's the point of view? What are you showing or saying that reflects what you see that is true in the world? Is the piece saying or showing that thing? Could it be implying the opposite of what you intended? That's a common issue for comedy especially when we use elements like irony. You may not have thought about the underlying meaning or message of the piece when you first created it, but now is the time to ask yourself, "Why do I want to show this to an audience?"

   I want to remind you that a perfectly good answer to this question is "It's funny." In other words, there's a combination of recognition, pain, and distance that you can't quite tease apart or explain, but you believe an audience will connect with it. Having said that, it's still useful at this point to dig into this "why" just a little bit if you can, for two important reasons. First, the next time you get it up in front of people you'll want to have a sense of what you think their response will be. More importantly, you don't want to be the guy who thought he was doing a joke about trees and accidentally made his audience think that he was promoting a return to Nazi-style fascism. And yes, I chose the masculine "guy" here on purpose, but this phenomenon isn't exclusive to men. We all will make this kind of mistake at some point or another, but better to avoid it if possible.

Now we get into the deeper work. What you made is good, but you're looking to make it even better. Or what you've made "works," but there's something that just isn't hitting right when you get it up in front of an audience. At this stage, you aren't going to use all the suggestions below. Use them selectively depending on the situation. Some of these suggestions are focused on diagnosing problems and some are about improving what you already have.

Digging Into the Comedy Triad

Recognition. If something isn't hitting the way you expect it to, it's often a recognition problem. What do you assume that an audience knows or understands that they may not? Do they get the references you are making? This is always an interesting question when our companies play in front of foreign audiences for whom English is a second language. Do people in Germany know what a raccoon is? Raccoons aren't native to Europe. Germans might know the word, but it's not particularly salient. Is there another animal that works just as well? If not, can we find a place to bring up raccoons earlier in the set or the show in a nonobvious way so that it's more available to the brains of the audience later when we make the raccoon joke?

The other recognition piece that is useful diagnostically is logic, comedic and otherwise. A lot of revising of jokes is making the logic function better. Is the comedy math of the joke as clean as it can be? You may need to make subtle changes to both the setup and the punch line. Then there is the internal logic of the whole piece. What is true about the world you have created, and how does it function? Do you play by those logical rules throughout the piece or do the rules change? If they do, how are you handling that change? There's no shame in just calling it out Monty Python style, but if you don't do something, that change in scenic logic can get in the way of the laughs.

Even if events make logical sense they sometimes don't "feel" true to your audience. This is usually a comic justification problem. You haven't figured out a compelling enough reason for them to buy the behavior being presented. This is why farce is such a hard form to do well. You don't just have to make the logic work—all that outrageous behavior has to also feel possible.

Finally, what sorts of recognition can you add or adjust to make the piece funnier? Can you make the names more specific and appropriate to the characters? What recognizable details can you add? Can you make each character's behavior more specific to them? Are the references current or a little outdated? There's a comedy superpower involved in being just a little bit ahead of your audience in terms of topical references, mentioning things or using turns of phrase they have heard about but don't yet expect anyone else to know. There is a similar superpower in using an obscure reference from the past that everyone knows but may have forgotten. This is such a common part of social media humor that it's now hard to find a good reference that hasn't already been shared somewhere, but if you can, it's gold.

Pain. Another primary diagnostic question is to look at where the pain is in the piece. You can get a lot of mileage from the sort of novelty and surprise that comes from recognizable detail. But that's just one kind of pain. Look closely at the types of pain you are using and when you use them. This is where the humor theories can be helpful. Are you using incongruity, tension and release, or superiority? Where and how?

If you are using tension, do you know when and how you are releasing it? Can you create a delay of some sort to hold that tension just a little bit longer in order to get a better laugh?

Another way to use the pain element to improve your comedy is to raise the stakes. Is the situation important for you, your audience, for your characters? Can you make it worse or heighten it in some way? Exaggeration of characters or situation can often simultaneously add distance.

Distance. This is where you double-check on the effect the pain elements of your work have on your audience.

One useful question to ask yourself is "Who or what is the object of the joke?" and then follow that with "Do they deserve it?" Are you making fun of someone based on traits they have no control over? Or are their problems the result of their own choices? The second is always going to be funnier. Have you communicated this clearly to your audience?

If you are using pain elements that are particularly likely to be seen as taboo or offensive, pay attention to how you use them. Have you created enough distance on these elements for your chosen audience? How have you done so? You can't predict what might upset any individual audience member, but you can be thoughtful about providing space for your audience to process anything that is particularly painful or might be traumatic for an individual. That can be as simple as not ending a scene with a joke about a dark or painful topic or providing distance by having a character acknowledge that something difficult or complex has been raised.

Looking at Structure

Revision is where an understanding of the various comedy structures really becomes useful to me. I find that taking what you've written or created and then mapping it against the traditional structure for the form you're working in can reveal problems or issues. If it's a joke, can you diagram the setup and the punch line within it? Try mapping your sketch to one of the two structures presented in the section on writing sketch and see what you discover.

For longer pieces like sketches, sitcoms, or stand-up sets, it can be particularly helpful to literally create a visual of the structure. Draw the structure on a piece of paper or white board and fill in the events. Try using index cards or Post-It notes so you can move beats and jokes around.

You can apply structures interchangeably—many of them overlap in some way. You could map a play or a film onto a running order structure and see what that tells you about what your longer narrative needs. Dan Harmon uses a structure based on Joseph Campbell's hero's journey when he writes sitcoms like *Community*, and although that doesn't work well for me, it works for him and for writers who have been in his writers' rooms.

Paying Attention to the Five Comedy Components

It can be easy during revision to focus on the components of narrative and joke, but if you don't keep physical comedy, character, and point of view in mind as you revise, you are missing out on some useful elements of your revision. Balance the painful elements of a joke by giving it to a safer or more absurd character (or performer) to provide distance. Conversely, bringing up particularly dark or painful subject matter in service of a stand-up beat whose point of view is shallow might initially get laughs but also might drag down responses to later parts of your set because you've lost the trust of some of your audience.

As a performer, pay attention to how the rhythm of your delivery and your timing needs to be adjusted. What words does your audience need to hear that you might not be emphasizing? How does your persona frame your comedy to make it feel more or less painful? Can you adjust what you wear or how you move to set up different expectations? What about adding elements of visual comedy like slides or video or drawings like Demetri Martin does?

TOOL: Taking a Comedy Class

An easy way for a beginner to get an early audience is to take a class offered at a local comedy club or improv institution. If there isn't one near you, there are many good classes available online at The Second City and elsewhere. In person is better if at all possible. You miss some very important aspects of feedback like laughter if you are taking a class virtually.

I'm a comedy teacher. I've run large comedy programs both at the college and community level. I'm very pro-comedy class. Classes provide a structure, assignments, and deadlines. They are a great place to meet and work with other people who are interested in comedy in the same way you are. Watching how other comedians work—observing their process, seeing their failures in addition to their successes—can be as useful to your growth as creating your own work. Classes also give you an opportunity to get immediate feedback on early drafts of whatever kind of comedy you want to make.

Approach your comedy classes with an open mind—don't judge the assignments you are given or look for your instructor or classmates to revise your comedy for you. You should treat feedback from your instructor and classmates the same way you would treat the response of an audience: *with curiosity*. Did they understand what you were trying to do? Why or why not? If they give you suggestions for revising your work, don't argue with it. Listen and write it down, and

(continued)

ask questions if you are confused. And then make the revisions that make sense to you. You are ultimately the expert on what you want your comedy to be. If there's something that isn't working in what you have made, you don't have to fix it the way someone else would. Listening to those suggestions can be useful to help you understand the problem, but you own the solution.

Any good comedy class should give you lots of opportunities to make comedy and to share it with your classmates. It should recognize that comedy is relative, that different comedians approach comedy differently, and that different audiences have different tastes. Speaking of taste, pay attention to the fact that your instructor, the institution you are taking class with, and your classmates will also have certain tastes in comedy. It can be helpful early on in your development if those tastes are a closer match to what you like to create. One way of getting a sense of this is to go to performances offered by the theater or club where you are thinking of taking the class or watch student work from the school you want to attend.

As a more advanced creator, it can be helpful to take a class somewhere that challenges you to create something different or stretches your skills in some way. Regardless, be very wary of instructors or programs who suggest that there is one and only one way to make comedy or that if you work with them and only them, you will become famous or immediately get professional work. Trust your gut, and if an environment feels uncomfortable to you, pay attention to that feeling.

Don't waste your time following gurus, and definitely don't put up with bullying from classmates or abuse of any kind from a teacher. If a mentor does get you a job or an opportunity, you should absolutely thank them, but don't feel like you owe them or like they own you in some way. There's a lot of potential for bad behavior in the comedy field, and one way abusive people will try to get power over you is by giving you a chance that feels too good to be true. Be suspicious of those situations. I'm not saying you shouldn't accept the job or part—just be careful. If you deserved a chance, it's because of your talent and hard work. Don't let someone else take credit for your original work or make you feel like you owe them something you aren't comfortable giving.

Finally, the Obvious

Here are some suggestions that should be obvious but are often forgotten in the revision process.

Start with what does work. What consistently gets laughs or responses? What pleases the audience most when you test your material? Can you center the elements that do work and build up to them in some way?

Sometimes you just need to edit. Look at how much you can cut out and still keep the piece working. What doesn't need to be there? Extra words, extra characters, extra stuff? Know yourself. I am almost always holding on to one good but unnecessary sketch in my show, and everything is better after I cut it.

Sometimes the comedy equation is good but the actual format or medium is standing in your way. Is a sketch premise really a joke or a blackout? (See above about cutting everything that doesn't work.) Is it a joke that should be a cartoon because it's better with a picture? Does your stand-up beat make more sense if you add characters or turn it into a longer story? Maybe the idea requires the reality of video to make it come alive, or, vice versa, it needs the conventions you can only play with in live performance.

Or to go back to what I started with in this section, maybe it's not working and you need to put it away and work on something else. Why are you revising it? Is it good and working, or does it feel as if it "should" work? How would you feel if you put it away and came back to it? Or never looked at it again? Don't keep banging your head against a wall for one joke or sketch. Life's too short, and you'll always be able to write more.

16 MAKING IT BETTER

The last class of the yearlong Comedy Survey course that I teach to first-year comedy majors is devoted to a discussion of gray areas of comedy creation under the umbrella term of "comedy ethics." It makes sense to me to do the same here.

It's really two different discussions. The first is focused on what I call good comedy hygiene; setting up comedy practices for your own protection and so you can be a good collaborator and member of the comedy community. The second is more complex. How do you as a comedian choose to handle the potential of comedy to cause harm? What lines do you personally draw in terms of what you will or won't present to an audience?

I leave it for the end because I believe that you won't be able to answer these questions fully until you've practiced a bit and have a better understanding of how you make comedy and what kind of comedy you want to make. But I've been working in comedy for a long time and I have some thoughts to share to guide that process.

Good Comedy Hygiene for Collaboration and Originality

Collaboration. A great deal of comedy work is done in collaboration with other comedians, whether in writers' rooms, creating through improvisation (as we do at Second City) or directors who work with and shape the material of solo performers. In many ways this kind of collaboration is vital in comedy; just as with taking a comedy class, collaboration with others provides a level of early audience feedback and laughter.

If you are creating jokes or sketches in collaboration with a group, I strongly encourage you to set aside a bit of time before you start collaborating to set up some simple group rules and norms in terms of how you will work together and ownership of the ideas generated during the process. But don't create too many rules. If you have created more than ten or twelve, that's likely more rules than the group will follow.

Ideally, there are clear and natural consequences for breaking those rules or norms. For example, when I work with sketch groups, one of my rules is that we start on time, and if someone is late, we don't stop rehearsal to go back and fill them in. When I work with a nonprofessional group that has an ongoing regular performance, I make a rule that anyone who misses the rehearsal before the show will not be in that week's show.

The writers create the comedy, the performers bring their talents and skills to bring the material to life, the director shapes and edits the material and performances and is responsible for the final overall look and feel of the piece. It's not unusual in comedy groups for everyone to take on these roles at different times. I encourage having a director or project leader who is not also creating while leading (this position can rotate). At the very least, it is helpful to be clear about who is in which role at any point in the process. When you are performing, it can be tempting to rewrite a sketch that isn't working instead of finding a character or acting choice that supports what already exists.

Here's my personal recommendation: Stick with the assumption that everything created within a particular collaboration belongs to the group and is not going to be used elsewhere without explicit permission from the other members. It's very hard to remember who exactly contributed what and when. It's bad for the creative process to spend time keeping track of who contributed what in the moment of generation or revising.

If you are a solo performer working with a director (or vice versa), it is especially important to decide in advance who is the primary writer of the piece and how you will handle issues of authorship and credit if the director contributes original writing.

I also recommend that if you are in a collaborative process and you come up with something you think is brilliant, don't attempt to "save" it for another more "important" situation. Stopping and evaluating every idea you have is a waste of time and ultimately bad for your own creative process. In my experience, the more ideas you have, the more ideas you will come up with, and doing this kind of picking and choosing can have a constipating effect and slow the flow of ideas.

Originality. There are very few completely new or original ideas in comedy. An idea is just an idea, and any single idea can be executed in a million ways. I believe it's counterproductive in the comedy generation phase to worry about whether or not any given idea has already "been done." Develop the idea and see where it takes you. Your version of a joke about how dads like to give advice or how hard it is to get up in the morning is going to be filtered through your life experience and point of view. It may end up being drastically different from what someone else has done with the same initial inspiration. Note the very different ways that the three sitcoms I mentioned in the chapter on longer narratives played out the exact same initial premise.

On the other hand, I once had a class I was teaching and a company I was directing come up with nearly identical sketches on the exact same day. Both sketches had the exact same premise: a take on the US Supreme Court's focus on originalism in which the Founding Fathers attempt to write the US Constitution with an eye to allowing for every possible eventuality (like predicting the internet and social media). Neither group's iteration of the idea was very successful, but I'm also certain there are other versions of this same idea out there in the world, and they may have worked better.

I also worked with a company that created a terrific original sketch that worked brilliantly. We were incredibly proud of it, only to discover that it was nearly beat for beat identical to one that had been on HBO's *Mr. Show.* This was odd in that the sketch was really a group creation with multiple iterations that I had a strong hand in shaping, and I know for certain that I had not previously seen the sketch in question (although I probably should have). It genuinely sucks to discover you have created something so similar to something that already exists. My sincere belief, though, is that the best thing to do in this situation is exactly what my class and I did: We stopped doing the sketch. I encourage you to do the same if you discover that a joke in your act or a premise you have developed is dramatically similar to one that someone else has written. If you came up with a good joke or a good premise, you'll come up with another one. Let it go.

Thinking About Comedy Ethics

If comedy uses the elements of recognition, pain, and distance in order to generate humor or laughter in a given audience then by this definition comedy itself is essentially amoral. Comedy doesn't care about ethics. It doesn't judge the difference between a laugh at the expense of a marginalized group from a laugh that embraces the unity of all beings.

People who do horrific things laugh. It's entirely possible to make comedy for people who do horrific things. You could even consider that kind of comedy "good" in that it is well crafted and elicits the intended laughter from its audience.

One of my favorite quotes from the stand-up comedian George Carlin begins, "I like to push people's buttons, find out where they draw the line, deliberately step across it."[1]

Being aware of offense and taboo in your work is in many ways an extension of the revision process. Just because comedy is amoral doesn't mean that it needs to be unkind. You are making comedy for other human beings with lives and beliefs and trauma and sadness, and it's useful to your comedy to be thoughtful about what audiences might perceive as too painful. As the essayist and creator of the television series *Shrill*, Lindy West, says, "A comedian who doesn't censor himself is just a dude yelling."

The elements that are most likely to be perceived of as offensive or taboo include

- **"Low" or vulgar humor.** This is often comedy of bodily functions, nudity, sex, or profanity. This is sometimes known as "blue" humor. Insult humor and slapstick is also included in this category. I currently find that audiences have a much higher tolerance for profanity and comedy about bodily functions than they did when I first started out working in comedy.

- **Travesty,** or mockery or easy jokes at the expense of something sacred or deeply serious. Specifically, the term *travesty* describes parody or mockery of religious rituals such as the Catholic mass. In my experience, sketches mocking religion are the most likely to provoke complaints or strong negative responses from an audience. As are sketches that reference Hitler or Nazis. Coincidentally, Hitler and Nazis are also one of the most popular sketch topics for middle school students who take the Second City summer camps.
- **Sick or macabre comedy,** which makes fun of topics seen as too tragic or deeply painful to joke about. A subset of this kind of comedy is known as gallows humor in which people who are in a tragic or near death/death adjacent situation make light of their circumstances (for example, those about to be executed, soldiers at the front lines, surgeons in an operating room).
- **Comedy about innocent victims** or about personal attributes or disabilities that are out of someone's control.
- **Comedy based in race, ethnicity, sexuality, or other identities.**
- **Comedy that takes pleasure in the misfortunes of others** or practical jokes in which the victims are set up to look stupid and fail.

I'm not advocating that you strive to avoid every area where it is possible to give offense. Some of the best comedy, some of my favorite comedy, falls into one (or more) of these categories. These categories are all related to specific types of pain or cultural taboos. If you are going to use them in your comedy, you want to be particularly vigilant in thinking about how and whether you provide enough distance or whether the recognition aspect of the joke includes a deeper insight or point of view that balances out the discomfort. I've seen people use the George Carlin quote from earlier as a motto for their own comedy, but for me the second half of the quote is far more important:

> I like to push people's buttons, find out where they draw the line, deliberately step across it, *take them with me, and make them glad they came.* (italics mine)

Making Your Comedy More Ethical

My initial theory of comedy contained the word *truth* instead of *recognition*. But even though we may be mining our own personal truth when we create comedy, the laughter of an audience does not require or even imply truth. It implies recognition. That recognition can be very far from the truth. It can just as easily be a lie or a grotesque exaggeration of a stereotype. What our audience "recognizes" could be the repetition of a slur or slander. They will still laugh, and an audience that laughs together can be reinforced in feeling that their recognition is, in fact, truth.

When we make comedy, we are intentionally choosing to manipulate elements of pain, and as a result the intention to never at any time offend anyone or make anyone uncomfortable ever at any time is not sustainable for comedy creation. We cannot control for all conditions of others' feelings, experiences, and preferences. It's not possible to know all the details of the lived experience of every member of every audience.

It is hard to tease out whether offense has happened at the speaker's mouth or the listener's ear. One meaning of the word *offensive* is "causing someone to be deeply hurt, upset or angry," and a second is "being actively aggressive, making an attack." It is entirely possible to offend without knowing and unintentionally cause hurt by trespassing on a sensitive subject. Your audience may assume you are attacking them when you discuss a topic that is offensive to them personally.

And of course, you can choose to make comedy that is intentionally offensive to certain audience members. You can do this with righteous intent to attack hypocrisy and dangerous belief systems to affect change. But you can also do it simply because your comedy and its related elements of recognition, pain, and distance aren't geared toward everyone in the audience in front of you. And from your perspective the audience should be aware of what they are getting themselves into by coming to watch you perform.

What humans find offensive and wrong is as relative as what we find funny. What we perceive as offensive or inappropriate is influenced by our beliefs about the world, the culture and values that were instilled in us as we were growing up, the culture(s) we currently inhabit, and the values we currently hold. Taboos are what is forbidden to be practiced or spoken of. If I believe that a balloon is sacred, that it represents something important in my value system, then a gag that involves popping a balloon, or a standup bit about making balloon animals, could be deeply offensive to me.

Offense is a very specific sort of pain for any individual or group. It evokes a pain that, for a multitude of reasons, they don't have the ability or the desire to have distance on. The essence of being offended is the belief that the speaker should have known (or did know) that this particular topic is sacred or off-limits.

We also cannot predict how society and culture will shift over time: which elements will suddenly increase in their perceived pain, which elements will be more or less recognizable, what taboos will no longer be in place, and what new things will become taboo. The jokes about heterosexual men being uncomfortable with the fluidity of sexuality that felt self-aware, edgy, and even downright progressive on the sitcom *Friends* in the 1990s now feel homophobic and retrograde to many of us during a rewatch in the 2020s.

Behaviors or language that felt benign to a general population at one point in time feel dramatically less so as circumstances change or new information becomes available. It's important to point out that what the general population assumes to be benign is not necessarily benign to every member of that society—often quite the contrary. We make comedy with what we have and what we know right now based on our own experience. It's impossible to control for what will happen later. We have to assume that the comedy we make may one day be less funny as the world and audiences change.

I have a lot of conversations with my students about what it means to be "ethical" as a comedian. How do we make choices as we manipulate the elements of recognition, pain, and distance so that we make something that fits our personal criteria of what is good and acceptable?

A comedy value system based on "If they laugh, it's good" is, to me, not an ethical system. People laugh for all sorts of reasons. They may laugh because they are uncomfortable, they may laugh because they are shocked or surprised. And they may laugh because they agree with a thing that is recognizable and is also wrong, insensitive, or downright evil.

To truly be ethical, we have to move beyond the feedback of audience laughter that provides us with an understanding of whether they "got" it. But how can we tell what comedy makes our audience feel connected to each other in a way that is powerful and, on some level, "good," as opposed to comedy that reinforces a negative or harmful belief structure?

There are some truisms in the comedy world around this topic. "Don't punch down" is often repeated as a way of making comedy more ethical. In the "Don't punch down" ethos, you can only make fun of those who have more power than you, not less. I think that's a good start. But it can be hard to determine where the real power and power dynamics are. Is it fair game to make fun of something your manager (who has more power than you) is deeply sensitive about, like a speech impediment? Technically this is punching up, but is it really? If you are making fun of a speech impediment and you don't have one, then are you, in actuality, punching down?

I struggle too because there is such a rich tradition of laughing at characters who are the embodiment of a certain kind of universal human flaw or mistake, who see the world through a distorted perspective. We are punching down here, but really at our own errors and biases. We laugh at the foibles and flaws we see in ourselves when they are exaggerated and confined in a single character who possesses these flaws without our individual complexities. Yet how do I reconcile the pleasure I find in recognizing myself in some of these characters with the fact that there are humans who also display pronounced versions of this behavior because of neurologic or psychologic conditions beyond their control?

As someone who came of age in comedy in the 1990s, I often discover that something I used to find quite funny now feels wrong or off in some essential way. But it isn't just a matter of not performing or watching work from the past. The composition of the audience and the experience of an individual can also alter the pain/distance balance at any given performance.

I recently had a long conversation with a student who was deeply upset by the use of a stereotypical depiction of a member of their minority group in a sketch show. The sketch in question was created by someone who was a member of that minority group, and the sketch had a turn that pointedly reversed the stereotype and celebrated the character in question. What sticks with me, though, was my student's sadness and anger at the feeling of being a nonwhite person alone in a primarily white audience who were laughing at the stereotypes at the top of the sketch. This student felt that the audience was likely to remember the stereotype as much or more than the later sophisticated reveal. Does that mean the sketch should not have been included in the performance? I don't have a great answer to that question.

I'm now going to share something personal that might make the readers of this book uncomfortable—not for the sake of comedy but to explain how my own response as a creator and audience member has changed.

In my introduction I wrote that I have three offices, but I wrote much of the first draft of this book sitting in a room at Lurie Children's Hospital while my teenage daughter Nora was undergoing treatment for stage 4 liver cancer. She died of that cancer shortly after her seventeenth birthday. There are things connected to that traumatic experience that are so deeply painful to me that I'm never going to have enough distance on them to laugh. I find that I'm not personally offended or upset by jokes about cancer, but when cancer is used as a kind of generic "worst thing that could happen," I feel resentful at being reminded of my personal pain in service of something not particularly thoughtful or artful. I know many women who feel equally strongly about the use of rape jokes in comedy, especially when employed by male comedians.

I want the comedy I create to allow audiences to share the things they recognize, recognize what they share, and maybe ask themselves why they have never thought about those shared assumptions. I want to use comedy to point out not just obvious incongruities but also the incongruities that I and my audience have missed because it never occurred to us to see them. That's hard to do well but also valuable. I might choose to cause individual audience members to be uncomfortable for a bit in order to get to that value. I don't want my audiences to be comfortable all the time—I want them to be a little bit off balance and to be surprised by the work I create. I know from experience that they'll be more likely to laugh.

I don't want the comedy I create to intentionally hurt anyone, but I also value the ability of comedy to "afflict the comfortable and comfort the afflicted."[2] While the element that comedy manipulates is recognition, there is opportunity to strive for something deeper than recognition. I strive to use comedy to share with my audiences some aspect of our shared truth.

Not everything I create in comedy will be fully truthful, but I can look for the elements that resonate, that create laughter that has value to the audience members who experience it. And I can choose to continually question myself and my comedic community as I do so because while comedy itself is amoral, I am not. This is my personal comedy ethos. It may not be yours. If not, I encourage you to take some time and think about what yours might be. It won't just make your comedy funnier, it will make it better, too.

APPENDIX

COMEDY TO WATCH AND LISTEN TO

Below I've presented a few highly incomplete and personal lists of things to watch if you are interested in having more experience with the comedy referenced throughout *Funnier*.

As I am writing this, we're at a weird juncture for those who are interested in specific examples of comedy in performance. On the one hand, through streaming services, libraries, pay-per-view services like Amazon, and sites like YouTube, we can access more comedy content, old and new, than in any previous era of history. At the same time, it's not always possible to access that content consistently, because it is randomly removed for a variety of reasons (some justified, such as copyright infringement). Every semester I need to go through all of the links on the learning management system for my comedy classes to make sure everything I want my students to watch outside class is still available. In fact, for in-class viewing I've gone back to using DVDs so that I know I have access to the content I want to share when I need to share it.

Also, if possible, you should go see comedy films in a theater with audiences. It is an entirely different experience to see comedies in the format they were created for with a live audience.

That being said, the following lists offer a place to start.

General Comedy Documentary

- There are excellent clips in *Make 'Em Laugh*, a 2009 PBS documentary series (produced by, among others, Jerry Seinfeld) if you ignore the embarrassing "comedic" intros by Billy Crystal and you are prepared for the occasional use of the *n*-word—occasionally thoughtfully, as when Dick Gregory recounts how he approached charged moments in his early stand-up career, but also casual use in interviews with comedians like George Carlin, a strong reminder of how mores and the sense of what's acceptable change over time.
- I also recommend CNN's *History of Comedy*. I don't love the way it is organized, but it has strong clips and interviews and also includes an uncredited "blink and you'll miss it" moment of me teaching improv in a black turtleneck sometime in the early 2000s just after the section on the Groundlings and before Rachel Bloom talks about taking classes at the Upright Citizens Brigade.
- *Vaudeville*, American Masters. I show this documentary in my Comedy History class, and I always stay in the room to watch the guy at the beginning who squeezes the duck's butt so that it sings "*Ma!*"

Silent Film

- A good episode from the 1980s British documentary series *Hollywood* called "Comedy: A Serious Business," narrated by James Mason, with interviews with directors and performers who worked in the industry, is frequently available on YouTube.
- Charlie Chaplin, *Modern Times*
- Buster Keaton, *Sherlock, Jr.*
- Fatty Arbuckle and Buster Keaton, *The Bellboys*
- Harold Lloyd, *Safety Last*
- Mabel Normand, *Mabel at the Wheel*. It's directed by Normand and has a very young Charlie Chaplin before he settled into his "Little Tramp" character.

Early Sound Film

- Mae West. *No Man of Her Own* is a good example, but even better, look for clip compilations on YouTube. Mae West was as much a one-liner writer as she was an actress.
- WC Fields, *The Man on the Flying Trapeze*. Also look for clips on YouTube.
- Laurel and Hardy, *The Music Box*
- The Marx Brothers, *Duck Soup*. Their first six films are their best—the five they produced for Paramount and their first at MGM, *A Night at the Opera*.
- *The Thin Man* is a brilliant "what if the screwball comedy couple got married and then solved mysteries" with William Powell and Myrna Loy. I named my kids Nick and Nora.
- *His Girl Friday* is a brilliantly funny comedy from this era with Cary Grant and Rosalind Russell.

Radio

- George Burns and Gracie Allen. You can find lots of examples from their radio show on YouTube; I especially recommend the pilot episode of their TV show, which is also frequently available on YouTube.
- Jack Benny, any of his early radio work. Search for "Your Money or Your Life Jack Benny." He and Carole Lombard are both brilliant in one of my favorite Ernst Lubitsch films (speaking of great early film comedy directors), *To Be or Not to Be*.
- *The Goon Show*, with Peter Sellars, Spike Milligan, and Harry Secombe, is the British radio predecessor to *Monty Python's Flying Circus*. It's like a children's adventure story on LSD. Most of my students are lukewarm, but the ones who love it *love* it.

TV Sitcom

- *I Love Lucy*, "Job Switching"
- *The Dick Van Dyke Show*, "To Tell or Not to Tell"
- *The Honeymooners*, "Brother Ralph"

Sketch

- *Big Train*, "Big Train"
- *A Black Lady Sketch Show*, "Invisible Spy." I mention this one several times throughout the book, and I show it to my students as an example.
- *The Carol Burnett Show*, "Went with the Wind"
- *Caesar's Writers*. This is a filmed panel discussion with some of the biggest and most influential comedy writers of the latter half of the twentieth century (including Carl Reiner, Mel Brooks, and Neil Simon). It also provides a good sense of the comedy-writing process.
- *Mr. Show with Bob and Dave*, "The Audition"
- *Ten from Your Show of Shows*
- Ernie Kovacs. I encourage you to search "Blackouts" on YouTube to get a sense of his work and point of view.
- The "Mustard" sketch is currently available on YouTube. Search for "Mustard sketch."
- Nichols and May, "Teenagers"
- Tim Robinson, *I Think You Should Leave*. My personal favorites are "Don't Know How to Drive" and the iconic meme-generating "Hot Dog Car," both of which provide good examples of how he sets up permission structures for his characters to go crazy.
- It's not sketch, but I encourage you to watch Hugh Laurie's brilliantly stupid and twitchy Wooster opposite Stephen Fry's Jeeves in the BBC adaptation of Wodehouse's stories.

Stand-Up

- George Carlin, "Ten Words You Can Never Say on Television"
- Phyllis Diller. She's really a one-liner comedian, so it's less important to see a routine, but you do have to *see* her; so much of what she did in her stand-up was in her over-the-top persona. If it's available, I like the set she did on *The Carol Burnett Show*.
- Hannah Gadsby, *Nanette*

- Dick Gregory. Look on YouTube for some of his early stand-up. He also has later clips where he is funny, but primarily in his other guise as an activist.
- Mitch Hedberg, "Three Easy Payments," *Mitch All Together*
- Tom Lehrer, "The Vatican Rag." By the way, in 2022 Tom Lehrer released the copyright to all of his songs. Currently they are all at www.tomlehrersongs.com.
- John Mulaney, "Quicksand" and "Special Victims and Ice T," *New in Town*
- Bob Newhart, "Driving Instructor." As with almost any comedy done by men in this era, there's a level of misogyny (women don't know how to drive?!), but this is a good example of the way he does what is really solo sketch comedy, responding to an invisible and unheard partner.
- Tig Notaro, *Live*, "Hello, I Have Cancer"
- Richard Pryor, "Live in Concert"
- Joan Rivers. Look for some of the early sets she did on *The Tonight Show*.
- Mort Sahl. Sahl did his "political explainer" on multiple talk shows over the years, and it showcases his snarky grad student persona. There are generally clips available—search for "Sahl and politics."
- Jerry Seinfeld, "Airports"
- Henny Youngman, "Take My Wife, Please"
- Improvisation. *Inventing Improv* is a PBS documentary about the work of Viola Spolin with improv examples. (Full disclosure: I assisted on the documentary demonstrating exercises and I'm interviewed.)

TV News Jokes

- If you are looking for examples of news jokes, check out "Weekend Update" on *SNL* and *Late Night with Seth Meyers*—especially the "Closer Look" and "Jokes Seth Can't Tell with Jenny Hagel and Amber Ruffin" segments.

Other Media

- The *Good One* podcast hosted by Jesse David Fox is an ongoing wealth of good examples of stand-up and sketch comedy (and while it is billed as a "podcast about jokes," there's a lot of useful content about the other comedy components) especially recommended Kristen Schaal, Naomi Ekperigin, and Tig Notaro.
- Ziwe. Check out her YouTube series *Baited*. A personal favorite is the one with Aparna Nancherla, who refuses to be.

ACKNOWLEDGMENTS

I started working on this book in the summer of 2016, and I have been noodling over these ideas for even longer, so there are many people to thank:

My supportive editor, Megan Stielstra, who helped me with the structure and forced me to put all my comedy footnotes in the text, saying calmly, “May I introduce you to the em-dash?”

I owe an enormous debt to the people who spent hours hashing these ideas out with me over the past eight years and who read and gave feedback on multiple drafts: my friend, road warrior, and traffic anger translator, Jen Ellison; my sister, Julie Liss; my husband and partner in all things, Kelly Leonard.

My colleagues at Columbia College Chicago (especially my partners in the Comedy Writing and Performing Major, Grace Overbeke and Ric Walker), and a special thanks to my Comedy Studies faculty ensembles, past and present, including the late great Mary Scruggs, whose sharp understanding of comedic sketch writing shows up in a thousand small ways all over this book.

My research assistant, Clara Dossetter, without whom these pages would contain multiple examples from the same three comedians.

My mentor and teacher, Sheldon Patinkin, who taught me about running order, hired me to teach improv at Columbia College, and left me all his comedy books filled with salty marginalia (“If this guy compares Chaplin to God one more time, I’m going to puke”).

All my students past and present, at The Second City, Columbia College, and Northwestern University: You are the reason this book exists.

The comedians and improvisers I have been lucky enough to direct at The Second City (giving me multiple examples to use from our work together). It's a true privilege to be in a room making work with some of the greatest comedians of our time. A special shout-out to my current, one and only Redco, who indulge me when I say things like "Do a scene with that dance teacher character" and then they show up to rehearsal not just with the scene but with fully executed choreography (that they later have to teach to all the understudies).

My kids: Nick, who watched all the old movies with me on "classic movie night" and is now a terrific comic actor and writer in his own right, although now he mostly applies his skills to professional Shakespeare (BTW, he plays the customer in the "Mustard" sketch in the version online). And Nora, the funniest of us all. She was a baby when I wrote my first book and was cracking up the nurses from her hospital bed at Lurie while I wrote the first draft of this one. #TeamNoraForever.

NOTES

Introduction

1. E. B. and Katherine S. White, *A Subtreasury of American Humor* (Coward-McCann, 1941), xvii.

Part 1: Thinking About Comedy

1. Fang Tian et al., "Getting the Joke: Insight During Humor Comprehension—Evidence from an fMRI Study," *Frontiers in Psychology* 8, no. 1835 (2017), https://pubmed.ncbi.nlm.nih.gov/29093693/.

2. Mary Beard, *Laughter in Ancient Rome: On Joking, Tickling, and Cracking Up* (University of California Press, 2014).

Chapter 1

1. Leonard Probst, *Off Camera* (Stein and Day, 1978), 125.

2. It's all about diameter and square inches—one twelve-inch pizza has roughly the same area in square inches as 2.3 eight-inch pizzas. Quoctrung Bui, "74,476 Reasons You Should Always Get the Bigger Pizza," *Planet Money*, February 26, 2014, https://www.npr.org/sections/money/2014/02/26/282132576/74-476-reasons-you-should-always-get-the-bigger-pizza.

3. Beard, *Laughter in Ancient Rome*, 15.

4. *The George Burns and Gracie Allen Show*, pilot 1950.

5. The quote is generally attributed to Horace Walpole.

6. This saying is likely older than this, but the first instance in print appears to be Steve Allen, who included it in "Allen's Almanac," *Cosmopolitan*, February 1957.

Chapter 3

1. *The Onion*, January 22, 1997.

2. Two ducks were sitting in a pond. One said "Quack." The other duck said, "I was going to say that." Richard Wiseman, "The Truth About Lying and Laughter," *The Guardian*, April 2007.

3. Sid Caesar, *Caeser's Hour.*

4. Viola Spolin, *Improvisation for the Theatre* (Northwestern University Press, 1972). In later editions, this term has been changed to *focus*, but I personally prefer the term *point of concentration*—I find it more specifically useful.

5. Matt Besser, Ian Roberts, and Matt Walsh, *The Upright Citizens Brigade Comedy Improvisation Manual* (Comedy Council of Nicea, 2023), 64.

6. John Cleese, "How to Write the Perfect Farce," *The Guardian*, February 2017, https://www.theguardian.com/stage/2017/feb/17/john-cleese-farce-bang-bang-fawlty-towers-rat-manuel-feydeau.

7. Steve Kaplan, *The Hidden Tools of Comedy* (Michael Wiese Productions, 2013), 26 (Kindle).

8. Gerald Nachman, *Seriously Funny: The Rebel Comedians of the 1950s and1960s* (Watson Guptill, 2004).

9. John Wright, *Why Is That So Funny? A Practical Exploration of Physical Comedy* (Limelight, 2007), 75.

Chapter 4

1. Scott Weems, *Ha! The Science of When We Laugh and Why* (Basic Books, 2014), 45 (Kindle).

2. Christopher Hitchens, "Why Women Aren't Funny," *Vanity Fair*, January 1, 2007.

Chapter 5

1. Roger Rosenblatt, "The Age of Irony Comes to an End," *Time*, September 24, 2001.

2. Plato, *Philebus*, in *The Philosophy of Laughter and Humor*, ed. John Morreall (SUNY Press, 1987).

3. John Morreall, *Comic Relief: A Comprehensive Philosophy of Humor* (Wiley-Blackwell, 2011), 7 (Kindle).

4. Beard, *Laughter in Ancient Rome.* Interestingly, he also goes on to say it should also involve "no pain or harm"—thus including distance.

5. Morreall, *The Philosophy of Laughter and Humor.*

6. Order of St. Benedict, 4:54.

7. This joke may or may not be attributable to Phyllis Diller, but it was found in the enormous file of fifty-three thousand jokes she donated to the Smithsonian. See "Phyllis Diller's File of 53,000 Jokes," *Weekend Edition*, March 11, 2017, www.npr.org/2017/03/11/519807672/phyllis-diller-s-file-of-53-000-jokes.

8. This is a reference to a *New Yorker* cartoon drawn by Will McPhail. The tagline is "Sorry I'm late, I hit every traffic light coming home."

9. *The Pink Panther* (STX Entertainment, 2006).

10. Sigmund Freud, *Wit And Its Relation to the Unconscious* (Moffat, Yard, and Company, 1917).

11. Morreall, *Comic Relief*, 18 (Kindle).

12. Steve Martin, *Born Standing Up* (Simon and Schuster, 2007), 110.

13. Dave Itzkoff, "Eric Andre Isn't a Prankster, He's a 'Benevolent Attacker,'" *New York Times*, June 18, 2020, https://www.nytimes.com/2020/06/18/movies/eric-andre-netflix.html.

14. A. P. McGraw and C. Warren, "Benign Violations: Making Immoral Behavior Funny," *Psychological Science* 21 (2010): 1141–49.

15. Or terms like "relief," "release," or "resolution" used in other humor theories.

16. Written by Soren McCarthy for a student show I directed.

17. J. A. R. A. M. van Hooff, "A Comparative Approach to the Phylogeny of Laughter and Smiling," *Nonverbal Communication* (1972): 215, https://www.researchgate.net/profile/Kathy-Sylva-2/publication/328486788_Play_its_role_in_development_and_evolution/links/5bd0755592851cabf26467aa/Play-its-role-in-development-and-evolution.pdf#page=209.

18. There is also research that other animals, including dogs, will display behaviors like sneezing and curling their lips to indicate that they are playing and not fighting.

19. Matthew M. Hurley, Daniel C. Dennett, and Reginald B. Adams Jr., *Inside Jokes: Using Humor to Reverse Engineer the Mind* (MIT Press, 2011).

20. http://phd.meghan-smith.com/wp-content/uploads/2015/09/Laughter-with-others-and-ESM.pdf; Laura E. Kurtz and Sara B. Algoe, "Putting Laughter in Context: Shared Laughter as Behavioral Indicator of Relationship Well-Being," *Personal Relationships* 22, no. 4 (2015): 573–90, https://doi.org/10.1111/pere.12095.

Chapter 6

1. Daniel Kahneman, *Thinking, Fast and Slow* (Farrar, Straus and Giroux, 2011).

2. This is the comedy mechanism posited in *Inside Jokes*.

3. Lee Chambers quoted in Megan Slack, "You Should Never Paint Your Living Room This Color, According to a Psychologist," *Homes and Gardens*, August 23, 2021, https://www.homesandgardens.com/news/the-color-you-should-never-paint-your-living-room#:~:text='While%20red%20as%20a%20color,heart%20rate%2C'%20he%20says.

4. *Vaudeville*, American Masters, written and directed by Greg Palmer, produced by Rosemary Garner (1997), PBS.

Chapter 7

1. Actually, he didn't say it exactly like that. The exact quote is "Try not. Do. Or do not. There is no try." Spoken by Yoda, played by Frank Oz, from the film *Star Wars Episode V: The Empire Strikes Back*, directed by Irvin Kershner (1980).

2. *2 Joke Queens: Amber Ruffin and Jenny Hagel* (SXSW Live Studio Interview), March 19, 2019, YouTube, 21:17, https://www.youtube.com/watch?v=eZ6KNCxeg9U.

3. I learned this prompt from Second City and Annoyance director and teacher Mick Napier.

4. This is a version of an exercise I learned from my colleague Norm Holly.

5. Stephen Levitan (executive producer / cocreator of *Modern Family*), "A Modern Farewell," season 11, episode 199, of *Modern Family*.

Chapter 8

1. Tina Fey, *SNL*, November 2000.

2. *Jimmy Kimmel Live*, June 2024.

3. *The Late Late Show with James Cordon*, September 2017.

4. *The Late Show with Stephen Colbert*, May 2017.

5. *Late Night with Seth Meyers*, March 2023.

6. You can look it up on the *New Yorker* website. It's caption contest #754 drawn by Drew Dernavich.

7. I make no claims to this as a great (or even original) cartoon. Just an example. It's possible and even likely that someone has done something like this before. Again, what we are doing here is just practice. If, when you practice, you accidentally create something similar to something someone else has done, good for you! It shows that you get how this works and that you have been paying attention.

8. Written by Alison Tolman for a student show I directed.

9. Written by Jeff Gandy, who went on to be the first head of the Second City Training Center's kids program.

Chapter 9

1. Examples are from a scene titled "Shower" created for The Second City Toronto by Tim Sims.

2. *Make 'Em Laugh*, PBS.

3. David Wooley interview.

Chapter 11

1. Louis C.K., *Shameless*, 2007.

2. "Questions for Stephen Colbert: Funny About the News," *New York Times Magazine*, September 25, 2005, https://www.nytimes.com/2005/09/25/magazine/funny-about-the-news.html.

3. *Make 'Em Laugh* interview.

Chapter 12

1. Nicholas Epley, *Mindwise: How We Understand What Others Think, Believe, Feel, and Want* (Knopf, 2014).

2. I learned this exercise from my Second City colleague Norm Holly.

3. My colleague Lillie Frances here, who a number of years ago while working on the Second City Training Center curricula pushed for including Raves in that exercise. Playing with positives creates a different dynamic.

4. This sketch was cowritten by my students Blythe Inana and Zelda Sidener.

5. This is the subject of a very funny sketch that comedian Brendan Jennings created for a student show I directed.

Chapter 13

1. I learned this version of structure from my colleague Lillie Frances.

2. Matt Besser, Ian Roberts, and Matt Walsh, *The Upright Citizens Brigade Comedy Improvisation Manual* (Comedy Council of Nicea, 2023), 64.

3. As of this writing, the "Mustard" sketch is still available on YouTube.

4. The iconic "Job Switching" episode of *I Love Lucy*; "Brother Ralph," *The Honeymooners*; and "To Tell or Not to Tell," *The Dick Van Dyke Show.* All three of these are generally available on a streaming service if you are interested in doing this exercise yourself.

Chapter 16

1. *Make 'Em Laugh*, PBS.

2. Attributed to Chicago humorist Finley Peter Dunne from a syndicated newspaper column.